METACOGNITION IN LEARNING AND INSTRUCTION

NEUROPSYCHOLOGY AND COGNITION

VOLUME 19

The purpose of the Neuropsychology and Cognition series is to bring out volumes that promote understanding in topics relating brain and behavior. It is intended for use by both clinicians and research scientists in the fields of neuropsychology, cognitive psychology, psycholinguistics, speech and hearing, as well as education. Examples of topics to be covered in the series would relate to memory, language acquisition and breakdown, reading, attention, developing and aging brain. By addressing the theoretical, empirical, and applied aspects of brain-behavior relationships, this series will try to present the information in the fields of neuropsychology and cognition in a coherent manner.

The titles published in this series are listed at the end of this volume.

METACOGNITION IN LEARNING AND INSTRUCTION

Theory, Research and Practice

Edited by

HOPE J. HARTMAN

Department of Education,
The City College of the City University of New York,
New York, NY, U.S.A.

KLUWER ACADEMIC PUBLISHERS

DORDRECHT / BOSTON / LONDON

Library of Congress Cataloging-in-Publication Data.

ISBN 0-7923-6838-X

Published by Kluwer Academic Publishers,
P.O. Box 17, 3300 AA Dordrecht, The Netherlands.

Sold and distributed in North, Central and South America
by Kluwer Academic Publishers,
101 Philip Drive, Norwell, MA 02061, U.S.A.

In all other countries, sold and distributed
by Kluwer Academic Publishers,
P.O. Box 322, 3300 AH Dordrecht, The Netherlands.

This printing is a digital duplication of the original edition.

Printed on acid-free paper

Second Printing 2002

Printed in the United States of America

DEDICATION

This book is dedicated to my wonderful husband, Michael J. Holub, and to organ and tissue donors everywhere, one of whom recently saved Michael's life by donating her liver after she tragically died. I hope that this dedication has a metacognitive benefit for readers who have not made arrangements to become organ and tissue donors, by telling their families of their wishes. Readers' metacognitive awareness of themselves as potential organ/tissue donors can enable readers to take control of their desires and destinies so they can help others either before or after they are gone. Perhaps increased public awareness of the tremendous need for organ and tissue donations could have saved the life of my dear friend and accomplished educational sociologist, Jann Azumi, who died seven years ago without having a potentially life saving bone marrow transplant.

CONTENTS

CONTRIBUTORS

Eleanor Armour-Thomas, Professor of Education, Queens College of City University of New York, Flushing, NY, U.S.A.

Alice Artzt, Professor of Education, Queens College of City University of New York, Flushing, NY, U.S.A.

Patricia Carrell, Professor of Applied Linguistics, Special Assistant to the Provost, Georgia State University; Atlanta, GA, U. S. A.

Dorothy Ellis, Professor of Humanities, La Guardia Community College, U.S.A.

Howard Everson, Vice President of the Teaching and Learning Division, Chief Research Scientist, The College Board, New York, NY, U.S.A.

Linda Gajdusek, Georgia State University, Atlanta, GA, U. S. A.

Annette Gourgey, City University of New York, NY, U.S.A.

Hope J. Hartman, Professor of Education, City College of New York, Professor of Educational Psychology, City University of New York Graduate School and University Center, New York, NY, U.S.A.

Richard E. Mayer, Professor of Psychology, University of California, Santa Barbara , U.S.A.

Paul R. Pintrich, Professor of Education and Psychology, University of Michigan, Ann Arbor, U.S.A.

Gregory Schraw, Professor Educational Psychology, University of Nebraska-Lincoln, U.S.A.

Robert J. Sternberg, IBM Professor of Psychology, Yale University, New Haven, CT, U.S.A.

Sigmund Tobias, Distinguished Scholar, Professor of Educational Psychology, Fordham University, New York, NY, U.S.A.

Teresa Wise, Georgia State University, Atlanta, GA, U. S. A.

Christopher A. Wolters, Professor of Educational Psychology, University of Houston, Houston, TX, USA

Barry J. Zimmerman, Professor of Educational Psychology, City University of New York Graduate School and University Center, New York, NY, USA

PREFACE

The term metacognition, coined by Flavell almost a quarter of a century ago, has become one of the more prominent constructs in cognitive and educational psychology. It is generally defined as cognition about cognition or thinking about one's own thinking, including both the processes and the products. My own interest in metacognition began in 1974 with my doctoral dissertation research, which focused on comprehension monitoring and clarification (Hartman-Haas, 1981). Metacognition is especially important because it affects acquisition, comprehension, retention and application of what is learned, in addition to affecting learning efficiency, critical thinking, and problem solving. Metacognitive awareness enables control or self-regulation over thinking and learning processes and products. Sternberg's (1985) triarchic theory of intellectual performance, and extensive research on metacognition in reading (e.g. Garner, 1987), mathematics (e.g. Schoenfeld, 1989) and other areas, show the importance of metacognition for academic success.

This book is intended for a broad spectrum of people interested in thinking, teaching and learning. It has relevance for researchers, teachers and students at all levels of schooling, and it has implications for thinking, teaching and learning in nonacademic contexts, such as at work and at home. Information about metacognition, while not exhaustive, spans theory, research and practice, summarizing where the field is now, presenting some innovative theory, research and applications to metacognitive development and instruction, and suggesting directions for the future. In this collection we try to highlight some current issues and approaches as seen by some of the most active contributors to the field.

As reflected in the title, chapters in this volume span the areas of theory, research and practice. Chapters emphasizing theoretical contributions include a framework for metacognition in mathematics teaching and the role of metaskill and will in problem solving. Chapters emphasizing research include a study of relationships between subject area learning, motivation and self-regulation and research on monitoring of standard English speech acquisition. Chapters emphasizing practice include domain-general applications of metacognitive strategies as well as domain-specific applications.

THE BOOK'S ORGANIZATION

Although all chapters in this collection focus on metacognition, each contributor approaches the topic from a slightly different perspective. These different perspectives on metacognition have been organized around the BACEIS Model of Improving Thinking (Hartman & Sternberg, 1993) because reflective thinking is the essence of metacognition. This theory is briefly summarized here in the preface and in more detail in Chapter 3. The BACEIS model is a theory of factors which affect intellectual performance. The BACEIS acronym stands for the following: **B** =behavior, **A**=affect, **C**=cognition, **E**=environment, **I**=interacting, **S**=systems (See Chapter 3, Figures 1 & 2 for the structural model and an illustration, respectively). This systems model suggests that internal factors of the student's cognition and affect are related to each other and are also related to interacting external factors from student's academic and nonacademic environments. The combination of these factors and all of their reciprocal influences has implications for a student's intellectual performance in and out of school. In several chapters throughout this edited collection the reader will find applications of the BACEIS model to instructional design, to guide research, and to critique existing approaches to teaching for and with metacognition.

Many current programs and approaches to improving thinking skills, such as metacognition, tend to be overly narrow, often ignoring the affective domain and features of the environmental context. The BACEIS model is a comprehensive theory of internal and external factors affecting the development, retention, and transfer of thinking and learning skills. To improve a student's metacognition in particular or intellectual performance in general, one may intervene at any point in this complex array. The first two parts of this collection concentrate on aspects of metacognition which emphasize the student's internal supersystem: cognitive and affective components respectively; the next two parts address aspects of metacognition that are related to the student's external supersystem, comprised respectively of the academic environment and the nonacademic environment. Teacher thinking in the academic environment is the theme of Part III of the book, while cultural influences from the nonacademic environment are considered in Part IV. The final part is a concluding chapter by Robert J. Sternberg, discussing several chapters in this collection and his own view of metacognition as a subset of expertise.

The BACEIS model is compatible with Gruber (1985)'s description of the evolving-systems approach to creative work, which views the creative person as a system of loosely-coupled subsystems (knowledge, purpose, and affect). Each component system has a partially independent organization, different rules, and different relevant time scales. These components are in constant interaction. The "loose coupling" idea is important to contrast with a "tightly meshed set of gears," because it suggests that each system can exhibit some independent evolution (pp. 175-176).

Metacognition, conceptualized as the highest level of thinking in the cognitive component of the BACEIS model, can have a wide and varied impact on students' affect and intellectual performance in and out of school as well as on teachers' successes with their students. Teachers have at least two roles with regard to metacognition: to develop their students' metacognitive knowledge and skills, and to apply metacognition to their own instruction, curriculum and assessment. Both roles are addressed in this collection.

Hartman and Sternberg (1993) hypothesized that the full implementation of the BACEIS model would enable students to develop a differentiated, refined, elaborated, and interrelated structure of knowledge, skills, and affect in all of their academic subjects. Consequently students will learn, retain, and transfer what they learn more effectively than when compared to implementing a discrete skills approach. The basic concepts underlying the approach are: *differentiated*, meaning that major types of knowledge, skills, affect, and characteristics of the environments involved in thinking and learning are recognized and explicitly attended to; *refined*, meaning that existing knowledge, skills, and affect are enhanced; *elaborated*, meaning that new knowledge, skills, and affect, and new dimensions of existing knowledge, skills, and affect are developed; and *interrelated*, meaning that knowledge, skills and affect are developed in conjunction with: (a) each other; (b) subject-specific content; (c) content across subjects; and (d) everyday life experience.

The goal of this book is to stimulate people in many different fields (e.g., psychology, education, cognitive science), and in many different types of positions (including instructors, researchers, counselors, administrators, tutors, curriculum developers, staff developers, evaluators, instructional planners, editors, and software developers) to think about how to maximize the effective use of metacognitive knowledge and skills in order to enhance thinking, teaching and learning. The remainder of the preface describes the chapters in this book on metacognition in relationship to the collection's theory-based organization.

Part I: Students' Metacognition and Cognition

The cognitive component of the BACEIS model is in the internal supersystem in its own subsystem, separate from the subsystem of the student's affect The cognitive component includes metacognition, cognition, and learning strategies, which are viewed as having three major applications: critical thinking, creative thinking and learning strategies. The metacognitive dimension includes metacognitive knowledge and skills, some of which are domain-general and some which are domain-specific.

The chapters in this section of the book emphasize the characteristics and development of students' metacognitive skills and knowledge through explicit efforts of their teachers. The first three chapters stress applications of research on metacognition to the development of students' metacognitive knowledge and skills, while the last chapter in Part 1 is an empirical study of students' knowledge monitoring processes.

Chapter 1, by Schraw, gives a preview of several chapters in this collection in addition to presenting some of his own work in the field, which highlights general aspects of metacognitive awareness. His main thesis is that metacognitive knowledge is multidimensional, domain-general in nature, and teachable. He describes two aspects of metacognition (knowledge of cognition and regulation of cognition) and how they are related, and he describes four instructional strategies for constructing and acquiring metacognitive awareness.

Chapter 2, Gourgey's chapter, discusses metacognitive instruction in college-level, basic reading and mathematical problem solving skills through an introductory course in thinking skills for students who did not meet the college's proficiency standards. Her description of students' reactions to learning to think metacognitively elucidates problems and potentials for teaching metacognition.

The third chapter is one that I wrote to summarize some of the recent literature on metacognition in learning to stimulate thinking about how teachers can develop students' metacognitive knowledge and skills to improve their learning across subject areas. Included are methods I have used for over a decade with ethnically diverse students and teachers at virtually all grade and school levels and in essentially all subject areas. Techniques are described for constructing and using graphic organizers, self-questioning, and for other metacognitive strategies which transcend the content domain.

Everson and Tobias's research, in Chapter 4, focuses on a method of objectively and efficiently measuring one aspect of metacognition - students' knowledge monitoring ability - and examines the predictive validity of this assessment procedure for students' performance in college, as measured by grade point average.

Part II: Students' Metacognition and Motivation

Affect is the second component of the BACEIS model's internal supersystem. The affective subsystem includes a student's motivation, attitudes and affective self-regulation. The two chapters in this section of the book both focus on relationships between metacognition and motivation.

Mayer's Chapter 5 emphasizes motivational, cognitive and metacognitive aspects of problem solving and addresses the critical issue of transfer. He explores metacognitive strategy training in reading, writing and mathematics, and argues that successful problem solving depends upon three components: will, skill, and metaskill. The role of will in problem solving is treated in depth.

In Chapter 6 Wolters and Pintrich report their research on contextual or domain-specific differences in seventh and eighth grade students' self-regulated learning and their motivation in mathematics, English, and social studies classrooms. Their research suggests that while there are some subject area differences in cognitive and motivational components of self-regulated classroom learning, they may be less pervasive than similarities across contexts.

Part III: Metacognition and Teaching

The external supersystem of the BACEIS model consists of the academic environment and the nonacademic environment. Part III of the book focuses on the academic environment, which includes teacher characteristics, subject area content, the school and classroom environment and instructional techniques. There are three chapters in this section, all of which address the teacher's use of metacognition for instruction. The first, by Artzt and Armour-Thomas, provides a theoretical framework for metacognition in teaching which is similar to that described for metacognition in learning in Chapters 1 and 3 by Schraw and Hartman, respectively.

Artzt and Armour-Thomas's chapter is an exploratory study of teachers' metacognition. They developed an innovative metacognitive framework using a "teaching as problem solving" perspective to analyze instructional practices of beginning and experienced high school mathematics teachers by examining their thoughts before, during and after conducting lessons.

"Teaching Metacognitively" is a chapter I wrote on the use of metacognition in teaching. This chapter explains what is meant by teaching metacognitively, why teaching metacognitively is important and describes metacognitive techniques I have used in my own teaching and methods I've used to enhance other teachers' metacognition about their instruction.

Research on science teaching and learning emphasizes the importance of active, meaningful learning, with metacognitive processing by both teachers and learners. This chapter describes some of my research on metacognition in science learning and instructional methods for strengthening science professors' metacognition about their teaching and for developing students' metacognition about their science learning.

Part IV: Students' Metacognition and Culture

The fourth component of the BACEIS model is the nonacademic environment of the external supersystem. The nonacademic environment includes socio-economic status, family background and cultural forces. Students' language, and the extent to which it matches that of the classroom, can be an extremely important factor affecting academic performance. It is dependent upon the student's family backgrounds and cultures. This section of the book has two chapters focusing on cultural-linguistic issues and metacognition. The chapter by Ellis and Zimmerman is an empirical study of students whose cultural background emphasizes nonstandard English as the dominant language, while the dominant culture emphasizes standard English. Their research focuses on self-regulation of standard English speech. The chapter by Carrell and her associates concentrates on reading metacognition of students whose cultural background has languages other than English and who are in a (standard) English dominant academic environment (sometimes called English as a Second Language students).

Chapter 10 is Ellis and Zimmerman's innovative research on self-regulation while learning standard English speech. Their research, based on a social-cognitive view of self-regulation, compares the traditional laboratory approach to improving standard spoken English with an approach that emphasizes self-monitoring and self-regulation.

Carrell, Gajdusek and Wise's Chapter 11 on metacognitive strategies in second language reading summarizes recent research and describes their own study in progress in which college English as a second language students receive training in four reading strategies. This chapter emphasizes the importance of complete teacher explanations in strategy training, including instruction in declarative, conditional and procedural knowledge about the reading strategies.

Part V: Conclusion

Several chapters in this collection were included in a special issue of *Instructional Science* on metacognition. This book concludes with Chapter 12 by Sternberg, the invited discussant for the special journal issue, who highlights the contributions and convergences, and thoughtfully critiques each paper included in that issue. In addition, he presents an insightful case for metacognition as a subset of expertise, with an emphasis on the expert student. His basic thesis is that metacognition converges with other abilities linked to school success in the construct of developing expertise. Because Schraw's and Sternberg's chapters predated those written by Ellis and Zimmerman and by me, our four chapters are not discussed in them.

REFERENCES

Flavell, J. H. (1976). Metacognitive aspects of problem solving. In L. Resnick, d., *The Nature of Intelligence.* Hillsdale, NJ: Lawrence Erlbaum Associates.

Garner, R. (1987) *Metacognition and Reading Comprehension.* Norwood, NJ: Ablex Publishing Co.

Gruber, H. (1985). From epistemic subject to unique creative person at work. *Archives de Psychologie*, 53, 167-185.

Hartman-Haas, H. J. (1981). Story clarification: Comprehension-directed problem solving. *Dissertation Abstracts International* 41 (10).

Hartman, H. J. & Sternberg, R. J. (1993). A broad BACEIS for improving thinking. *Instructional Science.* 21 (5): 401-425

Schoenfeld, A. (1989). Teaching mathematical thinking and problem solving. In L. B. Resnick & L. E. Klopfer Eds. *Toward a thinking curriculum: Current cognitive research.* Alexandria, VA: Association for Supervision and Curriculum Development.

Sternberg, R. J. (1985) *Beyond IQ: A triarchic theory of human intelligence.* New York: Cambridge University Press

ACKNOWLEDGMENTS

Many of the contributors to this book are widely recognized as outstanding theorists, researchers, and practitioners in the area of metacognition. I am deeply grateful to them, especially Robert Sternberg, for contributing their insights and efforts. The authors exceeded my already high expectations by producing chapters which offer many important new insights into theory, research and practice in metacognition. Gregory Schraw and Sigmund Tobias also served as manuscript reviewers, so I thank them doubly. Annette Gourgey is a contributor, she reviewed all three of my chapters, as well as other chapters; I tremendously appreciate all of her thoughtful and incisive comments and suggestions. I am also grateful to the other people who reviewed earlier versions of the chapters: Alice Corkill, Cathy Fosnot, Annie Koshi, Nancy Lay, Rayne Sperling, and Claire Ellen Weinstein. Patricia Alexander was very instrumental in helping me develop the special issue of *Instructional Science* on metacognition which inspired this book so I am very thankful for her assistance and support.

The anonymous reviewers of an earlier version of this manuscript made significant contributions to this collection and I am indebted to them for their thoughtful analyses and constructive feedback.

Almost a decade of support from the Aaron Diamond Foundation for the City College of New York Tutoring and Cooperative Learning Program facilitated my work on theory, research and practice regarding metacognition in learning and instruction. I greatly appreciate their support.

I am also deeply indebted to the wonderful people at Kluwer: Christiane Roll, for her patience and understanding about the delays in communication and in completing the manuscript and her persistence in obtaining the reviews, Sue Vorstenbosch for her assistance with preparation of the manuscript and maintaining communication, and Peter Goodyear and Dorien Francissen for helping get the book off the ground.

Heidi Dannucci was enormously helpful in preparing the manuscript; she scanned numerous chapters to disk, and cleaned up the numerous scanning errors with impressive accuracy and efficiency. As the finish line approached, Heidi reformatted the manuscript so that it could be done professionally and on time.

My husband, Michael Holub, was endlessly patient and supportive throughout the process of developing this book. His persistent optimism helped sustain my efforts and I will be eternally grateful for his love and understanding. Michael, my mother and father, Lillian and Philbert Hartman, and my daughter and her husband, Alicia and Jeffery Volkheimer, are forever sources of inspiration.

Hope J. Hartman   June, 2000

METACOGNITION IN LEARNING
and INSTRUCTION

PART I: STUDENTS' METACOGNITION AND COGNITION

The chapters in this section of the book focus on the cognitive component of the BACEIS model of improving thinking, which consists of metacognition, cognition and learning stratgies. They emphasize the development of students' metacognitive skills and knowledge through the explicit efforts of their teachers. While the first three chapters stress applications of research on metacognition to the development of students' metacognitive knowledge and skills, the last chapter is an empirical study of students' knowledge monitoring processes.

In Chapter 1, Schraw gives a preview of several other chapters in this collection and presents some of his own work on general metacognitive awareness He makes three important points: that metacognitive knowledge is multidimensional, it is domain-general in nature, and amenable to instructional intervention.. He describes two aspects of metacognition (knowledge of cognition and regulation of cognition) and how they are related, and he describes four instructional strategies for constructing and acquiring metacognitive awareness. Schraw's argument about the domain-general nature of metacognition is supported to some extent by some of Wolters and Pintrich's research (Chapter 6) and is consistent with my applications in Chapter 3, while it conflicts with some of the domain-specific approaches found in other chapters which focus on the use of metacognition in specific subjects, such as mathematics and science. Schraw's chapter was written for a special issue of *Instructional Science* on metacognition which included several of the chapters of this book, and preceded the chapter by Ellis and Zimmerman and my three chapters, which is why they are not discussed in his chapter.

Gourgey's Chapter 2 describes her rich experience with metacognitive instruction in college-level basic skills courses, with an emphasis on basic reading and mathematical problem solving skills. Her innovative approaches and enlightening description of students' reactions to learning to think metacognitively highlights some of the problems and potentials for teaching metacognition.

Chapter 3 was intended to introduce teachers to metacognition and its role in intellectual performance, and to stimulate their thinking about effective ways to promote the development of metacognitive knowledge and skills in their students. It reviews some of the recent literature on metacognition and includes methods I have used for over a decade with students at virtually all grade and school levels and in essentially all subject areas, such as graphic organizers and self-questioning.

The final chapter in this section provides an important contribution to understanding issues involved in measuring students' metacognition. Everson and Tobias's research involves development of an objective and efficient method of measuring one particular aspect of metacognition, students' knowledge monitoring ability. It examines the predictive validity of their assessment procedure for students' performance in college, as measured by grade point average.

CHAPTER 1

PROMOTING GENERAL METACOGNITIVE AWARENESS

GREGORY SCHRAW

ABSTRACT. I describe two aspects of metacognition, knowledge of cognition and regulation of cognition, and how they are related to domain-specific knowledge and cognitive abilities. I argue that metacognitive knowledge is multidimensional, domain-general in nature, and teachable. Four instructional strategies are described for promoting the construction and acquisition of metacognitive awareness. These include promoting general awareness, improving self-knowledge and regulatory skills, and promoting learning environments that are conducive to the construction and use of metacognition.

This paper makes three proposals: (a) metacognition is a multidimensional phenomenon, (b) it is domain-general in nature, and (c) metacognitive knowledge and regulation can be improved using a variety of instructional strategies. Let me acknowledge at the beginning that each of these proposals is somewhat speculative. While there is a limited amount of research that supports them, more research is needed to clarify them. Each one of these proposals is addressed in a separate section of the paper. The first makes a distinction between knowledge of cognition and regulation of cognition. The second summarizes some of the recent research examining the relationship of metacognition to expertise and cognitive abilities. The third section describes four general instructional strategies for improving metacognition. These include fostering construction of new knowledge, explicating conditional knowledge, automatizing a monitoring heuristic, and creating a supportive motivational environment in the classroom. I conclude with a few thoughts about general cognitive skills instruction.

A FRAMEWORK FOR UNDERSTANDING METACOGNITION

Researchers have been studying metacognition for over twenty years. Most agree that cognition and metacognition differ in that cognitive skills are necessary to perform a task, while metacognition is necessary to understand how the task was performed (Garner, 1987). Most researchers also make a distinction between two components of metacognition, *knowledge of cognition* and *regulation of cognition* (although see Flavell, 1987, for a alternative view). Knowledge of cognition refers

3

H.J. Hartman (ed.), Metacognition in Learning and Instruction, 3–16.
© 2001 *Kluwer Academic Publishers. Printed in the Netherlands.*

to what individuals know about their own cognition or about cognition in general. It includes at least three different kinds of metacognitive awareness: declarative, procedural, and conditional knowledge (Brown, 1987; Jacobs & Paris, 1987; Schraw & Moshman, 1995). Declarative knowledge refers to knowing "about" things. Procedural knowledge refers to knowing "how" to do things. Conditional knowledge refers to knowing the "why" and "when" aspects of cognition.

Declarative knowledge includes knowledge about oneself as a learner and about what factors influence one's performance. For example, research examining what learners know about their own memory indicates that adults have more knowledge than children about the cognitive processes associated with memory (Baker, 1989). Similarly, good learners appear to have more knowledge about different aspects of memory such as capacity limitations, rehearsal, and distributed learning (Garner, 1987; Schneider & Pressley, 1989).

Procedural knowledge refers to knowledge about doing things. Much of this knowledge is represented as heuristics and strategies. Individuals with a high degree of procedural knowledge perform tasks more automatically, are more likely to possess a larger repertoire of strategies, to sequence strategies effectively (Pressley, Borkowski, & Schneider, 1987), and use qualitatively different strategies to solve problems (Glaser & Chi, 1988). Typical examples include how to chunk and categorize new information.

Conditional knowledge refers to knowing when and why to use declarative and procedural knowledge (Garner, 1990). For example, effective learners know when and what information to rehearse. Conditional knowledge is important because it helps students selectively allocate their resources and use strategies more effectively (Reynolds, 1992). Conditional knowledge also enables students to adjust to the changing situational demands of each learning task.

Regulation of cognition refers to a set of activities that help students control their learning. Research supports the assumption that metacognitive regulation improves performance in a number of ways, including better use of attentional resources, better use of existing strategies, and a greater awareness of comprehension breakdowns. A number of studies report significant improvement in learning when regulatory skills and an understanding of how to use these skills are included as part of classroom instruction (Cross & Paris, 1988; Brown & Palincsar, 1989). These studies are important because they suggest that even younger students can acquire metacognitive skills via instruction. Although further research is needed, it is likely that improving one aspect of regulation (e.g., planning) may improve others (e.g., monitoring).

Although a number of regulatory skills has been described in the literature (see Schraw & Dennison (1994) for a description), three essential skills are included in all accounts: planning, monitoring, and evaluating (Jacobs & Paris, 1987). Planning involves the selection of appropriate strategies and the allocation of resources that affect performance. Examples include making predictions before reading, strategy sequencing, and allocating time or attention selectively before beginning a task. For example, studies of skilled writers reveal that the ability to plan develops throughout childhood and adolescence, improving dramatically between the ages of 10 and 14 (Berieter & Scardamalia, 1987). Older, more experienced writers engage in more global as opposed to local planning. In addition, more experienced writers are better able to plan effectively regardless of text "content", whereas poor writers are unable to do so.

Monitoring refers to one's on-line awareness of comprehension and task performance. The ability to engage in periodic self-testing while learning is a good example. Research indicates that monitoring ability develops slowly and is quite poor in children and even adults (Pressley & Ghatala, 1990). However, several recent studies have found a link between metacognitive knowledge and monitoring accuracy (Schraw, 1994; Schraw, Dunkle, Bendixen, & Roedel, 1995). Studies also suggest that monitoring ability improves with training and practice (Delclos & Harrington, 1991).

Evaluating refers to appraising the products and efficiency of one's learning. Typical examples include re-evaluating one's goals and conclusions. A number of studies indicate that metacognitive knowledge and regulatory skills such as planning are related to evaluation (see Baker, 1989). With respect to text revisions, Bereiter and Scardamalia (1987) found that poor writers were less able than good writers to adopt the reader's perspective and had more difficulty "diagnosing" text problems and correcting them.

There are two main points I would like to emphasize about knowledge of cognition and regulation of cognition. The first is that the two are related to one another. For example, Swanson (1990) found that declarative knowledge of cognition facilitated regulation of problem solving among fifth and sixth-grade students. Schraw (1994) reported that college students' judgments of their ability to monitor their reading comprehension were significantly related to their observed monitoring accuracy and test performance. Pintrich and colleagues (Pintrich & DeGroot, 1990; Wolters & Pintrich, this volume) found that knowledge of strategies was related to self-reported strategy use. Schraw, Horn, Thorndike-Christ, and Bruning (1995) reported a similar finding.

The second is that both components appear to span a wide variety of subject areas and domains--that is, they are domain general in nature. Gourgey (this volume) reported anecdotally that metacognition in mathematics is the same as in reading. She also reviewed four general strategies (i.e., identifying main goals, self-monitoring, self-questioning, and self-assessment) that have been shown to improve learning in all domains. Schraw et al. (1995) provided empirical evidence to support the conclusion that adult learners possess a general monitoring skill. Wolters and Pintrich (this volume) reported that strategy use and self-regulation were correlated highly in three separate domains.

In summary, metacognition consists of knowledge and regulatory skills that are used to control one's cognition. While metacognition is used in a general sense to subsume a number of individual components, all of these components are intercorrelated (Schraw & Dennison, 1994), and yield two general components corresponding to knowledge about cognition and regulation of cognition. Preliminary evidence suggests these two components are intercorrelated somewhere in the $r = .50$ range.

ISSUES OF GENERALITY

Two questions come to mind when one asserts that metacognition is a domain-general phenomenon. The first is how domain-general metacognitive knowledge is related to domain specific (i.e., encapsulated) knowledge. Despite two decades of research, those interested in the study of expertise typically do not draw a clear distinction between cognitive and metacognitive skills (Glaser & Chi, 1988; Ericsson & Smith, 1991). Most researchers appear to assume to that both types of knowledge are encapsulated within rigid domain boundaries (Siegler & Jenkins, 1989). My own view is that cognitive skills tend to be encapsulated within domains or subject areas, whereas metacognitive skills span multiple domains, even when those domains have little in common. Evidence supporting this view has been provided by Schraw et al. (1995) and Wolters and Pintrich (this volume). A detailed discussion of the generalization process is provided by Karmiloff-Smith (1992).

A second question is how metacognition is related to cognitive abilities. There is growing consensus that the acquisition of metacognition does not depend strongly on IQ, at least as it correlates with group-administered, paper-and-pencil tests. In a recent comprehensive review, Alexander, Carr, and Schwanenflugel (1995) reported that content-specific knowledge was modestly related to IQ, and that strategies and comprehension monitoring were not related at all. These findings are consistent with the main conclusion from the skill acquisition literature that IQ is of greatest importance in the early stages of skill acquisition, but is unrelated to skilled performance during latter stages of learning (Ackerman, 1987). Indeed, Alexander et al. (1995) have referred to traditional measures of IQ as a threshold variable that constrains knowledge acquisition initially, but becomes far less important as other skills such as task-specific strategies and general metacognitive knowledge come into play. Well organized instruction or the use of effective learning strategies may in large part compensate for differences in IQ. In many cases, sustained practice and teacher modeling leads to the acquisition of relevant task-specific knowledge as well as general metacognitive knowledge that is either independent or moderately correlated with traditional IQ scores (Ericsson, Krampe, & Tesch-Romer, 1993).

In general, one can expect metacognitive knowledge and regulation to improve as expertise within a particular domain improves. Though there is substantial debate on this point, many researchers believe that metacognitive knowledge is domain- or task-specific initially. As students acquire more metacognitive knowledge in a number of domains, they may construct general metacognitive knowledge (e.g., understanding limitations on memory) and regulatory skills (e.g., selecting appropriate learning strategies) that cut across all academic domains (see Schraw & Moshman, 1995). Older students in particular may construct general metacognitive skills that cut across a wide variety of tasks. This suggests that as students advance, they not only acquire more metacognitive knowledge, but use this knowledge in a more flexible manner, particularly in new areas of learning.

Metacognitive knowledge may also compensate for low ability or lack of relevant prior knowledge. One especially compelling case in point was provided by Swanson (1990), who found that metacognitive knowledge compensated for IQ when comparing fifth and sixth-grader students' problem solving. High-metacognition students reported using fewer strategies, but solved problems more effectively than low-metacognition students, regardless of measured ability level. This study suggested two important findings. One was that metacognitive knowledge is not strongly correlated with ability, although there does appear to be a modest, positive relationship between the two (Alexander et al., 1995). Second, metacognitive knowledge contributes to successful problem solving over and above the contribution of IQ and task-relevant strategies. These findings suggest that one may have average ability as measured by paper-and-pencil tests, yet possess a high degree of regulatory knowledge.

In summary, there is reason to believe that metacognitive knowledge and regulation are qualitatively different from other cognitive skills (Karmiloff-Smith, 1992; Schraw & Moshman, 1995). Metacognition appears to be more durable and general than domain encapsulated cognitive skills. While high levels of domain specific knowledge may facilitate the acquisition and use of metacognition, domain knowledge does not guarantee higher levels of metacognition. Moreover, individuals high on the metacognitive awareness dimension may use this knowledge to compensate for domain-specific knowledge, although this point requires further research.

PROMOTING METACOGNITIVE AWARENESS

Thus far, I have argued that metacognition differs from cognition, is multidimensional, and domain-general in nature. The gist of my argument has been that metacognition fills a unique niche in the self-regulatory phylum, by providing domain general knowledge and regulatory skills that enable individuals to control cognition in multiple domains. Metacognition is flexible and indispensable in my view. How then might one go about improving these skills?

There are four general ways to increase metacognition in classroom settings (Hartman & Sternberg, 1993). These include promoting general awareness of the importance of metacognition, improving knowledge of cognition, improving regulation of cognition, and fostering environments that promote metacognitive awareness. I examine each of these separately, then make several summary comments about the utility of general skills instruction.

Promoting General Awareness

Students need to understand the distinction between cognition and metacognition to become self-regulated. Teachers, other students, and reflection each play an important role in this process. Teachers model both cognitive and metacognitive skills for their students. The more explicit this modeling, the more likely it is that students will develop cognitive and metacognitive skills (Butler & Winne, 1995). Other students provide effective models as well, and in many situations, are better models than teachers (Schunk, 1989). Frequently, students are better able to model cognitive and metacognitive skills, and provide a powerful rationale for these skills within the student's zone of proximal development, compared to teachers.

Extended practice and reflection play crucial roles in the construction of metacognitive knowledge and regulatory skills. This is especially true when students are given regular opportunities to reflect on one's successes and failures (Kuhn, Schauble, & Garcia-Mila, 1992; Siegler & Jenkins, 1989). Studies examining the construction of theories of mind also suggest that reflection, both as a solitary and group endeavor, contributes to the breadth and sophistication of such theories (Astington, 1993; Montgomery, 1992).

In teaching my own classes at the university, and when observing skilled teachers in their classrooms, several instructional principles emerge regarding the promotion of metacognitive awareness. The first is for teachers to take the time to discuss the importance of metacognitive knowledge and regulation, including the unique role it plays in self-regulated learning (Schon, 1987). Second, teachers should make a concerted effort to model their own metacognition for their students. Too often teachers discuss and model their cognition (i.e., how to perform a task) without modeling metacognition (i.e., how they think about and monitor their performance). For example, as a former math major, I have seen hundreds of mathematical proofs performed in college classrooms, but I cannot ever remember any of my instructors describing their thought processes (i.e., a metacognitive analysis of their proof) as they performed the proof. Third, teachers should allot time for group discussion and reflection, despite the many pressures from jam-packed curricula and district performance demands (Rogoff, 1990).

Improving knowledge of cognition

Earlier, I made a distinction between knowledge of cognition and regulation of cognition. The former included three subcomponents; declarative, procedural, and conditional knowledge. I have used an instructional aid for a number of years to improve knowledge of cognition. Many of my former students who are public school teachers have adopted this aid as well, which I refer to as a *strategy evaluation matrix* (SEM). A sample of a SEM is shown in Figure 1. Many anecdotal reports suggest it is an effective way to increase metacognitive knowledge. In addition, empirical studies also suggest that using summary matrices like the SEM may significantly improve learning (Jonassen, Beissner, & Yacci, 1993).

Figure 1 includes information about how to use several strategies, the conditions under which these strategy are most useful, and a brief rationale for why one might wish to use them. The purpose of each row of the SEM is to promote explicit declarative (column 1), procedural (column 2), and conditional (columns 3 and 4) knowledge about each strategy. Of course, comparing strategies across rows adds an even more sophisticated level of conditional knowledge about one's strategy repertoire.

There are a variety of ways that a teacher could use a SEM in the classroom. The basic idea is to ask students, either individually or in a group, to complete each row of the matrix over the course of the school year. As an illustration, imagine a fourth-grade teacher who introduces the SEM during the first week of school. He informs students that they will focus on one new strategy each month, and should practice four additional strategies throughout the year that can be included in the SEM. Students are given time each week to reflect individually and as a small group about strategy use. Reflection time might include exchanging thoughts with other students about when and where to use a strategy. Extra credit can be earned by

Promoting Metacognition

Figure 1

A Strategy Evaluation Matrix

Strategy	How to Use	When to Use	Why to Use
Skim	Search for headings, highlighted words, previews, summaries	Prior to reading an extended text	Provides conceptual overview, helps to focus one's attention
Slow Down	Stop, read, and think about information	When information seems especially important	Enhances focus of one's attention
Activate Prior Knowledge	Pause and think about what you already know. Ask what you don't know	Prior to reading or an unfamiliar task	Makes new information easier to learn and remember
Mental Integration	Relate main ideas. Use these to construct a theme or conclusion.	When learning complex information or a deeper understanding is needed.	Reduces memory load. Promotes deeper level of understanding.
Diagrams	Identify main ideas, connect them, list supporting details under main ideas, connect supporting details	When there is a lot of interrelated factual info	Helps identify main ideas, organize them into categories. Reduces memory load.

interviewing other students in the same grade, or older students, about their strategy use. Students are expected to revise their SEMs as if a mini-portfolio.

Teachers I know who use SEMs find them very useful. One strength of SEMs is that they promote strategy use (i.e., a cognitive skill), which is known to significantly improve performance. A second strength is that SEMs promote explicit metacognitive awareness, even among younger students (i.e., K-6). A third strength is that SEMs encourage students to actively construct knowledge about how, when, and where to use strategies.

Improving Regulation of Cognition

SEMs presumably are effective at improving knowledge of cognition, but may not impact regulation. One approach that I have used is a regulatory checklist (RC). The purpose of the RC is to provide an overarching heuristic that facilitates the regulation of cognition. Figure 2 provides an example of an RC modeled after the problem solving prompt card used by King (1991). Figure 2 shows three main categories, including planning, monitoring, and evaluation. The RC enables novice learners to implement a systematic regulatory sequence that helps them control their performance.

Figure 2
A Regulatory Checklist

Planning
1. What is the nature of the task?
2. What is my goal?
3. What kind of information and strategies do I need?
4. How much time and resources will I need?

Monitoring
1. Do I have a clear understanding of what I am doing?
2. Does the task make sense?
3. Am I reaching my goals?
4. Do I need to make changes?

Evaluation
1. Have I reached my goal?
2. What worked?
3. What didn't work?
4. Would I do things differently next time?

Research by King (1991) found that fifth-grade students who used a checklist similar to Figure 2 outperformed control students on a number of measures, including written problem solving, asking strategic questions, and elaborating information. King concluded that explicit prompts in the form of checklists help students to be more strategic and systematic when solving problems. In a related study, Delclos and Harrington (1991) examined fifth and sixth-grader's ability to solve computer problems after assignment to one of three conditions. The first group received specific problem solving training, the second received problem solving plus self-monitoring training, while the third received no training. The monitored problem solving group solved more of the difficult problems than either of the remaining groups and took less time to do so. Although the self-monitoring group did not use an explicit checklist as did King (1991), steps in the self-monitoring process were quite similar to those used by King. Together, these studies provided experimental support for the utility of regulatory checklists.

Fostering Conducive Environments

Metacognitive skills do not exist in a vacuum. All too often, students possess knowledge and strategies that are appropriate for a task, but do not use them One reason is that students fail to engage and persist in a challenging task, or fail to attribute their success to the use of strategies and self-regulation. Sometimes students do not make the effort needed to do well at a task because they believe that intellectual ability, and specifically a lack of it, makes extra effort useless.

A number of recent motivational theories have addressed these issues directly. In general, successful students have a greater sense of self-efficacy, attribute their success to controllable factors such as effort and strategy use, and persevere when faced with challenging circumstances (Graham & Weiner, 1996; Schunk, 1989). However, one of the most salient characteristics of successful learners is their goal orientation (Dweck & Leggett, 1988). Students with mastery orientations seek to improve their competence. Those with performance orientations seek to prove their competence. A number of studies indicate that high-mastery students are more successful overall because they persevere, experience less anxiety, use more strategies, and attribute their success to controllable causes (Ames & Archer, 1988).

These findings raise concerns about the kind of goal orientations teachers promote in the classroom. Placing a strong emphasis on performance may lead to performance goals (Midgley, Anderman, & Hicks, 1995). In contrast, focusing on increasing one's current level of performance, rewarding increased effort and persistence, and strategy use may create a mastery environment. One potential advantage of classrooms that promote mastery is that students may acquire a broader repertoire of strategies, may be more likely to use strategies, and acquire more metacognitive knowledge about regulating strategy use (Schraw et al., 1995).

PROMOTING GENERAL SKILLS

One of my goals in writing this paper was to argue in defense of general cognitive skills. While most subject areas rely in part on specific skills that are of little use in other domains (e.g., using the quadratic formula), there are a large number of general strategies that aid learning in any domain. Using SEMs and RCs help promote knowledge about individual strategies, as well as metacognitive knowledge about how to use those strategies. Teacher and student modeling provide knowledge about how experts, or those who are more expert than the observer, think about problems and attempt to solve them. Modeling of regulatory skills such as planning, monitoring, and self-evaluation are especially important. Every teacher should make a concerted effort to model explicitly these behaviors.

There are many other skills that help students to think better that I did not discuss. One example are critical thinking skills such as evaluating evidence (Halpern, 1989). Another example are scientific reasoning skills such as hypothesis testing (Kuhn, 1989). These skills can be taught, and when they are, are of tremendous benefit to all students. Research suggests that many students can improve with respect to critical and scientific thinking, given three conditions (Kuhn, 1989; Rogoff, 1990). One is that they spend a sufficient amount of time applying the targeted skills in a meaningful context. A second is that they have the opportunity to observe skilled experts using the skills. A third, and one that is especially important for developing metacognitive awareness, is to have access to an expert's reflection on what he or she is doing, and how well it is being done.

Educational research and practice strongly supports the notion of general cognitive skills instruction. High quality instruction enables students of all ages to construct domain specific and domain-general strategies, metacognitive knowledge about themselves and their cognitive skills, and how to better regulate their cognition. The starting point in this endeavor is for teachers (or expert students) to ask themselves what skills and strategies are important within the specific domain they teach, how they constructed these skills within their own repertoire of cognitive skills, and what they can tell their students about using these skills intelligently.

CONCLUSIONS

Metacognition is essential to successful learning because it enables individuals to better manage their cognitive skills, and to determine weaknesses that can be corrected by constructing new cognitive skills. Almost anyone who can perform a skill is capable of metacognition--that is, thinking about how they perform that skill. Promoting metacognition begins with building an awareness among learners that metacognition exists, differs from cognition, and increases academic success. The next step is to teach strategies, and more importantly, to help students construct explicit knowledge about when and where to use strategies. A flexible strategy repertoire can be used next to make careful regulatory decisions that enable individuals to plan, monitor, and evaluate their learning.

These goals can be met through a variety of instructional practices. My own preference is for an interactive approach that blends direct instruction, teacher and expert student modeling, reflection on the part of students, and group activities that allow students to share their knowledge about cognition. Currently, there are a number of successful programs to use as illustrative models (see, for example, A. Brown & Palincsar, 1989; R. Brown & Pressley, 1994; and Cross & Paris, 1998). All of these programs indicate that metacognitive knowledge and regulation can be improved through classroom instructional practices, and that students use these newly acquired skills to improve performance.

GREGORY SCHRAW
Department of Educational Psychology
The University of Nebraska-Lincoln
Lincoln, Nebraska

REFERENCES

Ackerman, P. C. (1987). Individual differences in skill learning: An integration of the psychometric and information processing perspectives. *Psychological Bulletin*, 102, 3-27.

Alexander, J. M., Carr, M., & Schwanenflugel, P. J. (1995). Development of metacognition in gifted children: Directions for future research. *Developmental Review*, 15, 1-37.

Ames, C., & Archer, J. (1988). Achievement in the classroom: Student learning strategies and motivational processes. *Journal of Educational Psychology*, 80, 260-267.

Astington, J. W. (1993). *The child's discovery of mind*. Cambridge, MA: Harvard University Press.

Baker, L. (1989). Metacognition, comprehension monitoring, and the adult reader. *Educational Psychology Review*, 1, 3-38.

Bereiter, C., & Scardamalia, M. (1987). *The psychology of written composition*. Hillsdale, NJ: Erlbaum.

Brown, A. (1987). Metacognition, executive control, self-regulation, and other more mysterious mechanisms. In F. Weinert & R. Kluwe (Eds.), *Metacognition. motivation. and understanding* (pp. 65-116). Hillsdale, NJ: Erlbaum.

Brown, A. L., & Palincsar, A. S. (1989). Guided, cooperative learning and individual knowledge acquisition. In L. B. Resnick (Ed.), *Knowing and learning: Essays in honor of Robert Glaser*. (pp. 393-451). Hillsdale, NJ: Erlbaum.

Brown, R., & Pressley, M. (1994). Self-regulated reading and getting meaning from text: The Transactional Strategies Instruction model and its ongoing validation. In D. H. Schunk and B. J. Zimmerman (Eds.), *Self-regulation of learning and performance: Issues and educational applications.* (pp. 155-180). Hillsdale, NJ: Erlbaum.

Butler, D. L., & Winne, P. H. (1995). Feedback and self-regulated learning: A theoretical synthesis. *Review of Educational Research,* 65, 245-282.

Cross, D. R., & Paris, S. G. (1988). Developmental and instructional analyses of children's metacognition and reading comprehension. *Journal of Educational Psychology,* 80, 131-142.

Delclos, V. R., & Harrington, C. (1991). Effects of strategy monitoring and proactive instruction on children's problem solving performance. *Journal of Educational Psychology,* 83, 3542.

Dweck, C. S., & Leggett, E. S. (1988). A social-cognitive approach to motivation and personality. *Psychological Review,* 2E, 256-273.

Ericsson, K. A., & Smith, J. (1991). *Toward a general theory of expertise: Prospects and limits.* Cambridge, England: Cambridge University Press.

Ericsson, K. A., Krampe, R. T., & Tesch-Romer, C. (1993). The role of deliberate practice in the acquisition of expert performance. *Psychological Review,* 100, 363-406.

Garner, R. (1987). *Metacognition and reading comprehension.* Norwood, NJ: Ablex Publishing.

Garner, R. (1990). When children and adults do not use learning strategies: Toward a theory of settings. *Review of Educational Research,* 60, 517-529.

Glaser, R., & Chi, M. T. (1988). Overview. In M. Chi, R. Glaser, and M. Farr (Eds.), *The nature of expertise* (pp. xv -xxviii). Hillsdale, NJ: Erlbaum

Graham, S., & Weiner, B. (1996). Theories and principles of motivation. In D. Berliner and R. Calfee (Eds.), *Handbook of educational psychology,* (63-84). New York: Macmillian.

Halpern, D. F. (1989). *Thought and Knowledge: An introduction to critical thinking* (2nd edition). Hillsdale, NJ: Erlbaum.

Hartman, H. J., & Sternberg, R. J. (1993). A broad BACEIS for improving thinking. *Instructional Science,* 21, 401-425.

Jacobs, J. E., & Paris, S. G. (1987). Children's metacognition about reading: Issues in definition, measurement, and instruction. *Educational Psychologist,* 22, 255-278.

Jonassen, D. H., Beissner, K., & Yacci, M. (1993). *Structural knowledge: Techniques for representing, conveying, and acquiring structural knowledge.* Hillsdale, NJ: Erlbaum.

Karmiloff-Smith, A. (1992). *Beyond modularity: A developmental perspective on cognitive science.* Cambridge, MA: MIT Press.

King, A. (1991). Effects of training in strategic questioning on children's problem-solving performance. *Journal of Educational Psychology,* 83, 307-317.

Kuhn, D. (1989). Children and adults as intuitive scientists. *Psychological Review,* 96, 674-689.

Kuhn, D., Schauble, L., & Garcia-Mila, M (1992). Cross-domain development of scientific reasoning. *Cognition and Instruction,* 9, 285-327.

Midgley, C., Anderman, E., & Hicks, L. (1995). Differences between elementary and middle school teachers and students: A goals theory approach. Journal of Early Adolescence, 15, 90-113

Montgomery, D. E. (1992). Young children's theory of knowing: The development of a folk epistemology. *Developmental Review,* 12, 410-430.

Pintrich, P. R., & DeGroot, E. (1990). Motivational and self-regulated learning components of classroom academic performance. *Journal of Educational Psychology,* 82, 33-40.

Pressley, M., & Ghatala, E. S. (1990). Self-regulated learning: Monitoring learning from text. *Educational Psychologist,* 25, 19-33.

Pressley, M., Borkowski, J. G., & Schneider, W. (1987). Cognitive strategies: Good strategy users coordinate metacognition and knowledge. In R. Vasta & G. Whitehurst (Eds.), *Annals of Child Development* (Vol. 5, pp. 89-129). Greenwich, CT: JAI Press.

Reynolds, R. E. (1992). Selective attention and prose learning: Theoretical and empirical research. *Educational Psychology Review,* 4, 345-391.

Rogoff, B. (1990). *Apprenticeship in thinking: Cognitive development in social context.* New York: Oxford University Press.

Schneider, W., & Pressley, M. (1989). *Memory development between 2 and 20.* New York: Springer-Verlag.

Schmuck, R. A., & Schmuck, P. A. (1992). *Group processes in the classroom* (6th edition). Debuque, IA: Wm. C. Brown Publishers.

Schon, D. (1987). *Educating the reflective practitioner*. San Francisco: Jossey-Bass Publishers Schraw, G. (1994). The effect of metacognitive knowledge on local and global monitoring. *Contemporary Educational Psychology*, 19, 143-154.

Schraw, G., & Dennison, R. S. (1994). Assessing metacognitive awareness. *Contemporary Educational Psychology*, 19, 460-475.

Schraw, G., & Moshman, D. (1995). Metacognitive theories. *Educational Psychological Review*, 7, 351-371.

Schraw, G., Dunkle, M. E., Bendixen, L. D., & Roedel, T. D. (1995). Does a general monitoring skill exist? *Journal of Educational Psychology*, 87, 433-444.

Schraw, G., Horn, C., Thorndike-Christ, T., & Bruning, R. (1995). Academic goal orientations and student classroom achievement. *Contemporary Educational Psychology*, 20, 359-368.

Schunk, D. H. (1989). Self-efficacy and achievement behaviors. *Educational Psychology Review*, 1, 173-208.

Siegler, R. S., & Jenkins, E. (1989). *How children discover new strategies*. Hillsdale, NJ: Erlbaum.

Swanson, H. L. (1990). Influence of metacognitive knowledge and aptitude on problem solving. *Journal of Educational Psychology*, 82, 306-314.

CHAPTER 2

METACOGNITION IN BASIC SKILLS INSTRUCTION

ANNETTE F. GOURGEY

ABSTRACT. Metacognition is increasingly recognized as important to learning. This chapter describes self-regulatory processes that promote achievement in the basic skills of reading and mathematical problem solving. Self-regulatory behaviors in reading include clarifying one's purpose, understanding meanings, drawing inferences, looking for relationships, and reformulating text in one's own terms. Self-regulatory behaviors in mathematics include clarifying problem goals, understanding concepts, applying knowledge to reach goals, and monitoring progress toward a solution. The chapter then describes the author's experiences integrating metacognition with reading and mathematics instruction and highlights students' reactions to learning to think metacognitively.

Professionals in teacher education are increasingly acknowledging the importance of metacognition for learning. The APA's Guidelines for the Teaching of Educational Psychology define learning as a process of creating meaningful representations of knowledge through internally mediated processes including self-awareness, self-questioning, self-monitoring, and self-regulation (APA Division 15 Committee on Learner-centered Teacher Education for the 21st Century, 1995). This position is based on accumulated findings of years of research on teaching and learning.

Stahl, Simpson, and Hayes (1992) have advocated that basic skills instruction adopt a cognitive-based philosophy that emphasizes the development of comprehensive strategies for thinking and independent learning. This would include teaching students metacognitive skills of knowing when and how to use different learning strategies; how to plan, monitor, and control their learning; and how to transfer learning skills acquired in the classroom to other contexts. Educational research corroborates theories that emphasize the interaction of cognitive, metacognitive, and affective components in learning. Thus, education that targets only content or discrete skills ignores many components now recognized as essential to a deeper learning that enables students to link school instruction with real-world behaviors and to retain and transfer knowledge (Hartman & Sternberg, 1993; Sternberg, 1986; Wagner & Sternberg, 1984).

What, exactly, are the components that are so essential to learning in the basic skills? This chapter describes current theory and research on the metacognitive

H.J. Hartman (ed.), Metacognition in Learning and Instruction, 17–32.

strategies considered especially important for developing a firm foundation for learning in the areas of reading and mathematical problem solving, followed by examples from the author~s classroom experience.

GENERAL METACOGNITIVE PROCESSES

Metacognition is most broadly defined as awareness and control of one's learning (Baker & Brown, 1984). Flavell (1979) described metacognition as awareness of how one learns; awareness of when one does and does not understand; knowledge of how to use available information to achieve a goal; ability to judge the cognitive demands of a particular task; knowledge of what strategies to use for what purposes; and assessment of one's progress both during and after performance. Whereas cognitive strategies enable one to *make* progress--to build knowledge-- metacognitive strategies enable one to *monitor and improve* one's progress--to evaluate understanding and apply knowledge to new situations. Thus, metacognition is vital to cognitive effectiveness.

Sternberg (1981, 1986) outlined in detail the metacognitive skills that are essential to intelligent functioning but are rarely acknowledged or measured by standard intelligence tests. Metacognitive processes are internal, "executive" processes that supervise and control cognitive processes. They enable one to plan, monitor, and evaluate performance throughout the execution of a task. Through metacognition, one can define the nature of a task or problem; select a useful mental and physical representation; select the most useful strategy for executing the task; allocate resources such as time; activate relevant prior knowledge; pay attention to feedback on how the task is proceeding; and translate feedback into improved performance, either during execution or in a plan for the future. Metacognition enables one to use knowledge strategically to perform most efficiently.

An example contrasting the mathematical problem solving behavior of novices and experts illustrates how metacognitive skills make performance more efficient. In analyzing the problem solving strategies of students and mathematicians, Schoenfeld (1987) found that novice students quickly chose a solution strategy and then spent all their time executing it, rarely stopping to evaluate their work to see if it was leading to the goal. Lacking self-monitoring and self-regulation, they wasted much time on "wild goose chases," solution strategies that led them in the wrong direction. Even when they had adequate mathematical knowledge to solve the problem, they were unable to activate it constructively. In contrast, mathematicians spent most of their time analyzing the problem and making sure that they understood it. They tried many more approaches, constantly asking themselves if their strategy was working and changing it immediately if it was not. Even when the mathematicians' knowledge of the topic was rusty, they were able to activate what they knew by evaluating whether their work made sense. As a result of their greater capacity for clarifying the problem and for monitoring the usefulness of their efforts, the actual solution was worked out quickly and accurately.

Hartman and Sternberg (1993) expanded the profile of metacognitive skills into a comprehensive model describing the interaction of cognitive, metacognitive, and affective components of learning. Their BACEIS model (Behavior, Attitudes, Cognition and the Environment as Interacting Systems) describes an internal supersystem consisting of interrelated cognitive and affective supersystems. The cognitive supersystem includes cognition (acquisition and processing of information) and metacognition (executive management and strategic knowledge); both underlie learning and thinking. The affective supersystem includes motivation, affective self-regulation (self-regulation of values, expectations, and beliefs), and attitudes, also essential to effective functioning. In addition to the internal supersystem is an external supersystem consisting of the environmental context. Within this is an academic system (classroom, curricular, and teacher characteristics) and a nonacademic system (cultural, economic, and familial factors). This represents the most complex view yet presented of the many factors which interact to influence intellectual performance and acknowledges the importance of the cognitive, affective, and environmental context in which metacognitive skills function. Indeed, research has documented the interaction of metacognitive knowledge with motivation to be responsible for one's learning, values about the task, feelings of self-competence, and attributions of success (Palincsar & Brown, 1989).

METACOGNITION IN READING

Research on metacognition in reading comprehension has identified self-regulatory processes that improve achievement and instructional practices that develop them. Palincsar and Brown (1984, 1989) described six strategies consistently found to monitor and foster comprehension: (1) clarifying the purpose of reading to determine the appropriate reading strategy; (2) activating relevant background knowledge and linking it to the text; (3) allocating attention to the important ideas; (4) evaluating content for internal consistency and compatibility with prior knowledge; (5) self-monitoring (e.g. by self-questioning) to verify comprehension; and (6) drawing and testing inferences. Metacognitively oriented readers are aware of both their own learner characteristics and the task demands, are able to select, employ, monitor, and evaluate their use of strategies, and are able to recognize and repair comprehension failures. They have a strong sense of the "meaningfulness" of reading, appreciation of the value of self-testing, and recognition of the need to vary their strategies depending on their purpose (Palincsar & Brown, 1984, 1989).

Long and Long (1987) corroborated these findings in their comparison of the behaviors of more and less successful college readers. More successful readers see knowledge as an organization of concepts rather than as isolated facts; they strive to understand meanings and relationships rather than to recall details; and they test themselves to confirm that they know and remember what they have read. Moreover, they actively interact with the text rather than passively review and underline it: they anticipate test questions, paraphrase, summarize, take notes, relate the text to their experience, make inferences beyond what is stated, and visually represent concepts. Self-questioning plays a strong role in these students' comprehension monitoring and self-testing.

The common thread underlying this research is that to learn best, students must take an active role. Many studies have found that metacognitive activities that are externally imposed (i.e., the teacher generates questions or dictates strategies to use for clarification) are less effective than those generated by the students themselves (Wagner & Sternberg, 1984). This stands to reason, since the point of metacognition is sel/-regulation, not regulation by others. Consequently, it is recommended that instruction encourage students to generate and use their own strategies and self-questions; this approach has been found more effective for promoting independent learning and transfer (Hartman, 1994; Palincsar & Brown, 1984; Paris, Wixson, & Palincsar, 1986; Wagner & Sternberg, 1984).

Questioning, especially when directed toward higher-order thinking, plays a central role in comprehension, comprehension monitoring, self-testing and self-control (Davey & McBride, 1986; Palincsar & Brown, 1984; Paris et al., 1986). Questions generated by students promote active thinking and learning more than those created by teachers (Aldridge, 1989; Hartman, 1994; Paris & Myers, 1981).

Studies have found that certain types of question-generation training can have meaningful effects on students' metacognitive reading strategies. For example, Davey & McBride (1986) successfully trained sixth-grade students to generate, evaluate, and answer questions about the meaning of a text passage. Students who received training in forming "think" as well as "locate" questions generated better questions and had better comprehension and comprehension monitoring than students who did not receive training.

In order to teach students to think more actively and inferentially about reading, Aldridge (1989) had college students generate predictive and self-testing questions in response to a psychology textbook passage. In answering their questions, students differentiated between "knowledge" questions and "analytic" questions, constructed concept maps of the material, and discussed the implications of the ideas in the text. Through this process they learned to focus on meaning rather than mere recall, to regulate their efforts to understand the passage, to form external representations of the concepts, and to use study time more efficiently--all recognized characteristics of metacognitively skilled learning (Sternberg, 1986). These findings are consistent with those of other programs that successfully improved the comprehension of middle school, high school, and college students through self-questioning training, and support the observation that the more that students interact with the material, the better they learn it (Long & Long, 1987).

A powerful method for improving reading comprehension through comprehension monitoring and self-questioning is Palincsar and Brown's reciprocal teaching model (Hartman, 1994; Palincsar & Brown, 1984). In reciprocal teaching, the teacher models and explains four reading strategies and then supervises student practice of the strategies, gradually guiding students toward first participating in and then leading a small group. The ultimate goal is for students to become proficient enough to regulate their use of comprehension strategies and to generate their own feedback.

The four reading comprehension strategies taught in reciprocal teaching are questioning, summarizing (self-review), clarifying, and predicting. Students read a segment of text silently; then the leader asks a question that a teacher might ask about the passage and summarizes the content. The group discusses the passage and clarifies any confusion, and then the leader makes a prediction about the future content of the passage. The process is repeated for the next segment, with a different leader. The teacher leads the first round and then prompts students who take turns leading. In this manner, the group engages in dialogue about the meaning of text; instruction is "scaffolded," meaning that the teacher initially offers much support but gradually reduces it as students become more proficient. With practice, students improve their ability to ask clear questions and to summarize main ideas, and take a more active role in leading group discussions. After group dialogue, students are encouraged to continue to practice the strategies on their own (Hartman, 1994; Palincsar & Brown, 1984).

The reciprocal teaching technique is designed to help students generate and answer their own questions, to differentiate important content from trivial details, to monitor comprehension and find ways to clarify misunderstanding, and to activate prior knowledge and create expectations about future content. It has been demonstrated to be an effective method for improving comprehension and strategies for self-regulated reading (Hartman, 1994).

In summary, research has documented the importance of self-regulation of reading to improved comprehension. Self-regulatory behaviors include clarifying the purpose of reading, understanding meanings, drawing inferences, looking for relationships rather than memorizing isolated facts, and actively interacting with text by reformulating it in one's own terms--in other words, actively using one's skills for building understanding. Reading instruction that includes the metacognitive skills of self-questioning, summarizing, comprehension monitoring, clarification, and prediction has proven to be more effective for improving comprehension than instruction that does not explicitly teach these skills.

METACOGNITION IN MATHEMATICAL PROBLEM SOLVING

Metacognition in mathematics is, in principle, the same as metacognition in reading. That is, once students have acquired the basics (computation in mathematics as compared with decoding in reading), their ability to think in the domain is based on clarifying goals, understanding important concepts, monitoring understanding, clarifying confusion, predicting appropriate directions, and choosing appropriate actions. These metacognitive processes, unlike expertise in a specific area, transcend subject-matter boundaries (Schoenfeld, 1989). In fact, it has been suggested that effective learners see all knowledge acquisition as a form of problem solving (Bransford, Sherwood, Vye, & Rieser, 1986).

Research comparing experts and novices sheds light on the cognitive and metacognitive processes necessary for effective problem solving. Expert problem solvers form internal representations of different problem types called "schemata," based on organization of their domain-related knowledge. When asked to categorize a wide variety of physics problems. experts grouped them by their underlying principles based on laws of physics, whereas novice students grouped them by surface features such as references to pulleys and other physical objects. As schemata influenced choice of solution strategies, the students were also less knowledgeable about how to solve the problems (Chi, Feltovich, & Glaser, 1981; Silver, 1987).

Likewise, high-proficiency students sorted mathematical word problems based on underlying concepts; low-proficiency students were distracted by surface details which led them to use inappropriate solution strategies (Silver, 1979). Incorrect problem definition inevitably leads to incorrect solution both because students are misled by a faulty conception of the problem and because they fail to realize that it is faulty--a combination of cognitive and metacognitive breakdown (Bransford *et al.,* 1986; Silver, 1987).

Schoenfeld (1985) presented a comprehensive theory of the interaction of cognitive and metacognitive processes in mathematical problem solving. He identified four categories of knowledge and behavior: *resources* (mathematical knowledge), *heuristics* (problem-solving techniques), *control* (metacognition), and *belief systems* (attitudes). Whereas instruction tends to focus on the first two categories, student failures in problem solving can often be traced to malfunctions in the latter two categories. That is, students may possess the requisite knowledge but fail to use it appropriately because they neither know how to monitor and evaluate their decisions nor realize that it is advantageous to do so.

Whimbey and Lochhead (1986) also outlined skills necessary for successful problem solving, confirming the interrelationship between cognitive and metacognitive processes. Good problem solvers take great care to understand the relationships among the facts in a problem; check themselves for accuracy; break complex problems down into simpler steps; never make blind guesses without examining their reasoning; create internal and external representations of the problem; and self-question and answer to clarify their thoughts.

A common pattern of poor metacognition is seen in the example above of novice students who seize on a solution strategy and fail to ask themselves if the strategy is leading to their goal (Schoenfeld, 1987). Students frequently perform inappropriate operations because they have not clarified the relationships among the facts in the problem, so they fail to consider exactly what needs to be done and why. This lack of careful attention to sense-making and clarification often leads to impulsive and illogical attempts at solution, such as stating that a shipment of walnuts alone weighs more than the walnuts plus the crates they are packed in (Whimbey & Lochhead, 1986).

In videotaping students solving problems aloud in pairs, Schoenfeld (1985) observed that even when students had demonstrated mastery of course material, they still failed to solve familiar problems correctly. In a typical session, students solving a standard geometry problem chose a solution method immediately, without discussing why the method was appropriate. When they encountered difficulties they did not stop to consider whether they were on the right track. They were also unable to generate alternative ideas and to evaluate which ones might be worth pursuing. Moreover, when students got stuck, they often abandoned their approach without reflecting on what had gone wrong--and abandoned good ideas along with bad ones. Good control does not require that one always make the right decisions, but does require that one be able to recover from a false start, to realize that a strategy is not working, and to consider alternatives. In short, the students had the resources to solve the problems, but were unable to apply them successfully because they lacked the knowledge of how to regulate their thinking.

Observation of a math professor solving the same problem showed that even when resources are poor, good control can lead to success. The professor had not used geometry in ten years and did not remember the material on which the students had received high grades.

Yet the professor clarified the goal of the problem before attempting to solve it and then evaluated every hunch according to whether it was likely to lead to that goal. He actively looked for alternative ideas, discarded poor ideas rapidly, and used logic to derive principles he had forgotten. The outcome was that, although his solution was inelegant by a geometry expert's standards, he managed to solve the problem correctly (Schoenfeld, 1985).

How were the students able to achieve good grades in mathematics courses and then demonstrate such poor ability to solve the same problems? Since the same problem types are usually tested together within a particular lesson, students can apply procedures mechanically without having to understand them well; and instruction often focuses on performing techniques but neglects *when* and *why* to use the different ones. It is the context, rather than students' self-regulation, that keeps them on track. As a result, they may fail to internalize the skills that would enable them to analyze a problem and to draw upon their knowledge to solve it (Schoenfeld, 1985, 1989).

In order to improve metacognitive skills Schoenfeld developed courses in problem solving strategies. One approach involved instructing students to systematically analyze and simplify problems, explore alternative approaches and reformulations, and verify solutions. A model for effective problem solving was presented that included procedures for monitoring and evaluating one's work. These principles were then applied in large- and small-group problem solving sessions which focused on the spirit more than the details of the model. The role of the instructor was to oversee the problem-solving process and interpose questions to remind students to self-monitor, such as, "What are you doing and why?" "How far will this approach get us?" and "Is this working, or should we try something else?" The hands-on sessions helped students to experience the need to monitor their progress and to consider alternative approaches, practices they might not have understood if they had merely been told to do so in a traditional lecture. Results showed significant improvement in students' ability to solve problems, including less familiar ones, and more frequent self-monitoring statements in videotaped problem-solving sessions. Students also showed an increased ability to focus on "deep structure" rather than surface details, consistent with the findings on experts versus novices (Schoenfeld, 1985, 1987).

In another approach, Schoenfeld had students analyze videotapes of other students solving problems inefficiently. The observers, all math majors with good grades, had been resistant to criticism of their own problem-solving behavior--until the tapes made them aware of just how rarely *any* students self-monitor and self-question, and what the consequences are. After critiquing other students' ineffective problem solving, they became more receptive to examining and changing their own behavior. Schoenfeld also recommended that instructors, rather than present their own problem solutions in final, polished form, allow students to see the full range of instructors' false starts, self-questions, experimentations, and insights, so that students get a more realistic picture of what the problem-solving process is about. By modeling only our successes, we give students the false idea that expert thinking is always correct and therefore needs no self-monitoring (Schoenfeld, 1987).

Another successful method for teaching students to improve their problem-solving performance is think-aloud pair problem solving (Whimbey & Lochhead, 1986). In this method one partner reads a problem and thinks aloud through the solution. The listener's role is to monitor the solver's cognitive and metacognitive progress by checking for accuracy and making sure that the solver vocalizes every step in his or her thinking. The listener may ask questions that prod the solver to explain his or her reasoning or may point out the presence of an error without correcting it. After the problem is completed, the two switch roles. Pair problem solving and other cooperative methods resemble reciprocal teaching for reading comprehension as a method for actively engaging both speaker and listener in thinking and self-regulated learning (Hartman, 1994). These methods are successful because they encourage students to self-monitor, to clarify their thinking, and to think about why their strategies are useful (Bransford et al., 1986; Silver, 1987).

To summarize, effective problem solvers, like effective readers, clarify goals, seek to understand concepts and relationships, monitor their understanding, and choose and evaluate their actions based on whether the actions are leading toward their goals. Cognition about mathematics (knowledge of mathematical concepts) interacts with metacognition (control of one's understanding and use of solution strategies). Classroom instruction frequently focuses on mathematical knowledge but neglects the role of metacognition in problem solving. But instruction that emphasizes understanding problem meanings and monitoring strategy choices improves students' success as well as their ability to transfer these skills to less familiar problems. According to Schoenfeld (1987), this broader view of mathematics instruction introduces students to "a culture of mathematics" (p. 214) as mathematicians live in it, that links the classroom to their real-world experience.

APPLICATIONS TO INSTRUCTION

The next section describes the author's experiences integrating metacognitive skills with reading and mathematics instruction. Students were black, Hispanic and white college freshmen required to take an introductory course in thinking skills for reading and problem solving because they scored just below the college's basic skills proficiency standards. The descriptions illustrate the actual day-to-day practice of teaching metacognitive skills to students unfamiliar with them and show ways that students respond to this kind of instruction.

Reading Comprehension

In order to develop skills for self-questioning, comprehension monitoring, and clarification, students read and analyzed a passage called "Unequal Access to the Human Inheritance" from the book *The Population Explosion* (Ehrlich & Ehrlich, 1991). Prior to reading, the students brainstormed questions on the content of the passage; most asked some variation of the following: (1) What access are they talking about? (2) How is it unequal? (3) What is the inheritance? The class also discussed the purpose for reading, in particular, the difference between reading for memorization and reading for understanding. This led to a definition of comprehension monitoring for them to try out as they read: All readers occasionally lose their understanding while reading and must find ways to reestablish it; how do they know when this has happened?

Students then had to read the passage to find the answers to their questions. Along with the assignment to find the *information* in the passage, two questions were posed to help them to become aware of *their strategies* for comprehension monitoring and clarification: (1) Did any parts of the passage confuse me? (2) What did I do to clarify the confusion?

All students had difficulty understanding the meaning of "human inheritance." These prompts helped them to retrace their thinking as they read: What did they do first when they became aware of being confused? Did it help? What did they do next? Students then had to describe their process in writing to be shared with the class, first in small-group discussion and then in the larger group.

Each student had followed a different sequence of steps. Most either reread the text or read on for additional information. Some thought about what "inheritance" meant (either a bequest or genes) and a few looked up the word in a dictionary. Some formulated hypotheses about the meaning and then reread or scanned the text for relevant words. Many asked a classmate for help. One especially articulate student described his thinking as follows:

I looked up the definition for inheritance then looked for some aspect of the passage that could be passed on. I also had to underline, and read over the passage. I next identified two items in paragraph three and thought how and if they could be inherited. These two phrases were "material possessions" and "absolute poverty." I then said that material possessions could definitely be inherited, but absolute poverty was not a possession, but a human obstacle. Then I said that if parents are poor their children are thus born poor. So in nations where the majority of adults are poor and their birth rate is high, that will be a vast number of children born poor. So in fact those children would indeed be inheriting poverty.

Another student felt this still did not capture the authors' meaning. Considering the book title as well, he reformulated the question as, "What human inheritance is accessed unequally?" and answered, the resources of the world are distributed unequally depending on whether people live in rich nations, where the birth rate is low, or poor nations, where the birth rate is high.

Afterward, the class discussed what the experience of metacognitive reading was like. Reaching a satisfactory understanding of the passage took about four class sessions. My prompting during the process revealed that the students were all capable of reasoning out the meaning of a difficult text; however, self-questioning and self-monitoring were arduous and uncomfortable for them, and they needed to be prodded to carry them out. One student remarked that it was hard for her to monitor her thinking because "it goes too fast for me to remember"; nevertheless, with prompting she was able to record her thoughts. Even when they were aware of the steps in their thinking, the students thought these were too trivial to be worth recording, and had to be assured that the process of arriving at the answers was as important as the answers themselves. I suspected that they also feared what they would find if they looked too closely at their intellectual limits, so I felt the need to encourage them and reassure them that I, too, had found the passage difficult. This underscores the importance of affective issues in intellectual performance (Hartman & Sternberg, 1993).

However, despite these difficulties the results were extremely positive. After being guided through the process of generating questions, making predictions, and monitoring and checking their comprehension, the students improved both in their use of a variety of strategies and in the accuracy of their comprehension. They found, to their surprise, that they could do more of their own thinking as they read than they had realized; one student remarked that generating her own questions had forced her to think harder about what information was really important. They also found that they could learn alternative strategies by hearing each other's different ways of approaching the same passage. Thus, they learned not only the correct answers but how to find them on their own. Moreover, they realized the value of self-testing to verify their understanding and of active reading to sustain their interest and attention. These results are consistent with those found for reciprocal teaching (Hartman, 1994; Palincsar & Brown, 1984, 1989). The lesson for me as their instructor was that for metacognitive training in reading to be successful, students require much practice, encouragement to make the effort, and explanation and experience of its usefulness.

Mathematical Problem Solving

Consistent with the findings described earlier (Bransford *et al.,* 1986; Schoenfeld, 1985, 1987; Whimbey & Lochhead, 1986), my students appear to perceive mathematics as isolated skills rather than as concepts that can be applied to their real-world experience. When asked to solve a math problem, they immediately perform operations without thinking carefully about what the problem is asking for and whether the operations are appropriate. As a result, their answers frequently do not make sense; yet students often have to be forced to examine their reasoning and to connect the problem with their concrete experience before they can see their errors. The following example is typical:

> George Smith planted 311 young white pine trees on a two-acre plot. How many trees did he plant per square yard?

Once students have found the total number of yards in two acres (8,960), they automatically divide this larger number by the smaller one (311), resulting in almost 30 pine trees per square yard. Requiring students to write out their solution steps in complete sentences makes many of them aware of what they have done and why. However, some still do not see the impossibility of this answer until they are taken outside to look at a white pine tree and an area of one square yard. Clearly, some method for getting students to connect mathematical problems with their prior knowledge and experience is needed, so that they will see that strategic thinking and self-monitoring in mathematical situations are both possible and useful.

While physical, concrete experience of mathematical problems is not always feasible, it is possible to help students reason about problems rather than approach them mechanically. One such exercise required students to solve, in small groups, a real-life problem about building a well cover out of wood. The problem was presented with clues in the form of questions they could ask themselves to guide the problem-solving process (see Table 1). A sample plank of wood was available to help students appreciate the physical reality of the problem.

The first response I observed was that students rushed to begin calculations before reading the self-questioning prompts. None had stopped to think carefully about what the well cover was supposed to look like, much less to draw a picture of it to be sure that they understood what they were supposed to find. After I called their attention to the self-questions (What questions do I have to answer? What does the cover look like?), students slowed down, albeit reluctantly. Some productive debate then occurred about how to represent and solve the problem, though some students still looked to others for direction. My role was to observe the groups and to ask them periodically what they were doing, if they agreed that they were on the right track, and if they were sure that they had not left anything out.

Table 1. Metacognitively Guided Problem Solving
The Problem: Old Farmhouse

I've just bought an old farmhouse and want to renovate it for a home. There's an old well on the property, about 20 feet in circumference and more than 20 feet deep. There's no water in it, but it's still dangerous, particularly to my pets. So I want to make a square wooden cover for it. I'm advised to get standard thickness 1" by 6" treated lumber for all of the construction: several planks will go across the top of the well, reinforced by two crosswise pieces and one plank across the diagonal. There will be some wastage, because I can't piece together small pieces of wood for the construction.

The lumber comes in three lengths: 8'   @ $9.00 a piece
                                            10' @ $10.50
                                            12' @ $12.00

-       What will be the exact dimensions of the cover?
-       How much will the lumber cost?

Here are some questions you can ask yourself as you solve this problem.

a.   What is the first question that I have to answer? What is the second? Can I restate them in my own words?
b.   What does the cover look like? Am I sure that I understand how it is to be built?
c.   What shape is the well? How wide is it? What information do I need in order to figure out its width? Where can I get this information?
d.   Now let's draw the well opening and mark its dimensions. I will have to draw planks of wood over the opening and mark their dimensions until the opening is covered. Counting up the planks, how many will I need? How long do they have to be? Am I sure that I have followed the sketch exactly? Is there anything that I left out?
e.   What is the smallest length of wood I will need to buy in order to make the cover I have drawn? How many planks of each size will I need and how much does each one cost? What is the total cost?

Now, look back over each step in the long process of solving this problem. Do they all make sense? Are you satisfied that you have answered the questions? What, by the way, *were* the questions you were supposed to answer? Did you remember them throughout the process? If not, did you go back and refresh your memory?

'This problem was written in collaboration with Delbert L. Earisman, Upsala College.

After doing some calculations, one student suddenly exclaimed, "Hey, I forgot what I'm trying to find out! " I asked if others had had the same experience; several had. Had they gone back and reviewed the questions or the goals of the problem? Most had not. This led to a discussion of two major pitfalls in problem solving: (1) forgetting to clarify your goal before beginning to solve the problem, and (2) forgetting to check periodically to see whether your work is leading toward the goal. Eventually the groups were able to solve the problem collaboratively. Although some complained about the tediousness of always having to stop and review the problem and their steps in solving it, there was satisfaction with the finished product-a solution that was thorough and that they were confident was correct.

In another class I had students collectively generate their own steps in solving word problems. They formulated this list: (1) Identify the question you have to answer; (2) lay out all the information given and decide what you need to find out; (3) choose a method for solution; and (4) check your work to see that it makes sense and that it answers the question. While they worked on problems, I reminded them periodically to go back to their model and ask themselves if they had done all that they needed to do. Typically, students fall short on steps 1 and 4--the ones that most clearly reflect the need to monitor their understanding--presumably because traditional math classes so often emphasize techniques but pay insufficient attention to when and why to use them (Schoenfeld, 1985). But with repeated practice students began to ask themselves these questions without being reminded. As with reading, students solving math problems can learn to work metacognitively; but they often require a great deal of practice as well as encouragement to make the effort, and only after seeing the results in their learning do they acknowledge that the effort was worthwhile.

CONCLUSIONS

Research as well as personal experience have demonstrated that students who use metacognitive strategies, notably identifying goals, self-monitoring, self-questioning, reasoned choice of behaviors, and self-assessment, are more academically successful than students who do not use these strategies. Moreover, students can be taught to improve metacognitive proficiency through repeated guided practice.

Informal observations of students' reactions to metacognitive training in reading and mathematics raise some issues about acquisition of these skills. Students who are not used to thinking metacognitively sometimes resist having to do so, especially if they have been passive learners for many years. They do not understand *how* to be more active in their learning or why it is important, and feel uncomfortable with the extra effort required. Improving these students' metacognitive skills is possible but requires patience and persistence on the part of both instructor and students. Researchers have noted that students need scaffolded instruction providing strong initial support that is gradually withdrawn as they become more proficient at self-regulation (Hartman, 1994). When we combine this finding with the those on motivation to take responsibility, values, and self-efficacy, we can appreciate the complexity of the interrelationships among cognitive, metacognitive, and affective components of learning (Hartman & Sternberg, 1993; Palincsar & Brown, 1989).

To take this further, students who are reluctant to use metacognitive skills may, as in the anecdotes described, be afraid to test the limits of their intelligence, or may react defensively to criticism of their customary behavior (Schoenfeld, 1987). This fear may explain in part the rush to compute mathematical answers without taking the time to understand the problem. Awareness of students' anxiety about monitoring their learning is essential to helping them overcome resistance to changes that are difficult but ultimately beneficial. This, too, supports the importance of the affective context (Hartman & Sternberg, 1993).

Finally, not only may affect influence metacognition, but metacognition may influence affect. The anecdotes suggest that students with poor metacognitive skills are not only passive, but dependent on others. A frequent clarification strategy in both reading and mathematics is to ask someone else for help; if help is not readily available, they will often abandon the effort rather than struggle with it. Perhaps the lack of an internal dialogue driven by self-questioning is at the root of this dependency, as they lack a method for constructing and internalizing their own understanding. For these students, metacognitive development might benefit not only their achievement, but their self-efficacy and motivation to learn as well, as it empowers them with the tools to rely on their own intellectual resources and to discover new intellectual capabilities.

ANNETTE F. GOURGEY
The City University of New York

REFERENCES

Aldridge, M. (1989). Student questioning: A case for freshman academic empowerment. *Research and Teaching in Developmental Education,* 5(2), 17-24.
APA Division 15 Committee on Learner-centered Teacher Education for the 21st Century (1995). Learner-centered psychological principles: Guidelines for the teaching of educational psychology in teacher education programs. *NEP/15 Newsletter for Educational Psychologists,* 19(1), November, 4-5, 8.

Baker, L., & Brown, A. L. (1984). Metacognitive skills and reading. In P. D. Pearson, R. Barr, J. L. Kamil, & P. Rosenthal (Eds.), *Handbook of reading research.* New York: Longman Press

Bransford, J., Sherwood, R., Vye, N., & Rieser, J. (1986). Teaching thinking and problem solving: Research foundations. *American Psychologist,* 41(10), 1078-1089.

Chi, M. T. H., Feltovich, P. J., & Glaser, R. (1981). Categorization and representation of physics problems by experts and novices. *Cognitive Science, 5,* 121-152.

Davey, B., & McBride, S. (1986). Effects of question generation training on reading comprehension. *Journal of Educational Psychology, 78,* 256-262.

Ehrlich, P. A., & Ehrlich, A. (1991). *The population explosion.* New York: Simon & Schuster.

Flavell, J. H. (1979). Metacognition and cognitive monitoring: A new area of cognitive developmental inquiry. *American Psychologist,* 34(10), 906-911.

Hartman, H. J. (1994). From reciprocal teaching to reciprocal education. *Journal of Developmental Education, 18(1),* 2-8, 32.

Hartman, H., & Sternberg, R. J. (1993). A broad BACEIS for improving thinking. *Instructional Science, 21,* 401-425.

Long, J. D., & Long, E. W. (1987). Enhancing student achievement through metacomprehension training. *Journal of Developmental Education, 11(1),* 2-5.

Palincsar, A. S., & Brown, A. L. (1989). Instruction for self-regulated reading. In L. B. Resnick & L. E. Klopfer (Eds.), *Toward the thinking curriculum: Current cognitive research.* Alexandria, VA: Association for Supervision and Curriculum Development Yearbook.

Palincsar, A. S., & Brown, A. L. (1984). Reciprocal teaching of comprehension-fostering and comprehension-monitoring activities. *Cognition and Instruction,* 1(2), 117-175.

Paris, S. G., & Myers, M. (1981). Comprehension monitoring, memory, and study strategies of good and poor readers. *Journal of Reading Behavior, 13(1),* 5-22.

Paris, S. G., Wixson, K. K., & Palincsar, A. S. (1986). Instructional approaches to reading comprehension. *Review of Research in Education, 13,* 91-128.

Schoenfeld, A. H. (1989). Teaching mathematical thinking and problem solving. In L. B. Resnick & L. E. Klopfer (Eds.), *Toward the thinking curriculum: Current cognitive research.* Alexandria, VA: Association for Supervision and Curriculum Development Yearbook.

Schoenfeld, A. H. (1987). What's all the fuss about metacognition? In A. H. Schoenfeld (Ed.), *Cognitive Science and Mathematics Education.* Hillsdale, NJ: Lawrence Erlbaum Associates.

Schoenfeld, A. H. (1985). *Mathematical problem solving.* New York: Academic Press.

Silver, E. A. (1987). Foundations of cognitive theory and research for mathematics problem solving instruction. In A. H. Schoenfeld (Ed.), *Cognitive Science and Mathematics Education.* Hillsdale, NJ: Lawrence Erlbaum Associates.

Silver, E. A. (1979). Student perceptions of relatedness among mathematical verbal problems. *Journal for Research in Mathematics Education, 10,* 195-210.

Stahl, N. A, Simpson, M. L., & Hayes, C. G. (1992). Ten recommendations from research for teaching high-risk college students. *Journal of Developmental Education,* 16(1), 2-10.

Sternberg, R. J. (1981). Intelligence as thinking and learning skills. *Educational Leadership,* 39(1), 18-20.

Sternberg, R. J. (1986). *Intelligence applied: Understanding and increasing your intellectual skills.* New York: Harcourt Brace Jovanovich.

Wagner, R. K., & Sternberg, R. J. (1984). Alternative conceptions of intelligence and their implications for education. *Review of Educational Research,* 54(2), 179-223.

Whimbey, A., & Lochhead, J. (1986). *Problem solving and comprehension.* Hillsdale, NJ: Lawrence Erlbaum Associates.

CHAPTER 3

DEVELOPING STUDENTS' METACOGNITIVE KNOWLEDGE AND SKILLS

HOPE J. HARTMAN

ABSTRACT. Recent research highlights the importance of both metacognitive knowledge and metacognitive skills in learning. This chapter reviews some of the recent literature on metacognition in learning and describe some methods of helping students acquire strategic metacognitive knowledge and executive management metacognitive skills to improve their learning. Topics focused on include reading metacognition, graphic organizers, self-assessment, self-questioning, and thinking aloud, all of which can be used across content domains.

This chapter discusses research on metacognition in learning and tutoring and describes ways to help students develop and apply metacognitive knowledge and strategies. In this chapter, a strategy is defined as a conscious, deliberate use of a specific method, whereas a skill is defined as a refined strategy which is used selectively, automatically and unconsciously as needed. From an information processing perspective, metacognitive, executive control processes, which guide the flow of information through the mind and regulate cognition, explain why some students learn and remember more than others (Woolfolk, 1998). High achieving students have been found to possess more metacognitive awareness and engage in more self-regulatory behavior than low achieving students. Indeed, metacognition in general has been found to be an important characteristic of expertise (Meichenbaum & Biemiller, 1998; see Sternberg, Chapter 12). The kinds of metacognition discussed in this chapter can "make or break" academic success; they are the kinds of knowledge and strategies that successful people tend to figure out for themselves and that some people must be taught. When used extensively and in varied contexts, metacognitive knowledge and strategies can be used automatically in skilled performance.

Use of metacognition has been demonstrated to be essential to learning. General strategic, metacognitive knowledge and strategies, and domain-specific knowledge have been shown to have important roles in thinking and problem

33

H.J. Hartman (ed.), Metacognition in Learning and Instruction, 33–68.
© 2001 *Kluwer Academic Publishers. Printed in the Netherlands.*

solving (Bransford, Sherwood, Vye and Rieser (1986). Extensive research and the componential subtheory of Sternberg's triarchic theory of intelligence suggest that high-achieving students are more metacognitive than low-achieving students (Sternberg, 1985). Zimmerman (1990) characterizes the metacognitive processes of self-regulated learners in terms of planning, setting goals, organizing, self-monitoring and self-evaluating at various times during the learning process. Zimmerman (1995) points out that it is not enough for students to have metacognitive knowledge (or skills); they also must self-regulate its use when confronted with stress, competing attractions and fatigue. Context-dependent motivational issues, such as effort, self-efficacy, persistence and task choice are also important determinants of self-regulation. Metacognition is necessary, but not sufficient, for academic success.

Research on learning emphasizes the importance of attention to higher level thinking (including problem solving, metacognition, and critical thinking) and affect (including motivation, self-concept, affective self-regulation and attributions) in addition to the traditional focus on content and basic skills. Learning is best when it is active, meaningful, retained over time, and transfers to a variety of contexts. A vitally important but often neglected aspect of learning is that often students have the requisite knowledge and skills for performing complex tasks but do not use them; i.e, the skills remain inert. Sometimes this is because students are not motivated or confident to apply them, and sometimes students simply do not recognize that the situation calls for use of particular knowledge and skills. That is, students may have declarative and procedural knowledge, but not the contextual or conditional knowledge needed for application and transfer (Hartman & Sternberg, 1993). Garner's (1990) theory of settings suggests that the nature of strategic activity often varies with the context. She notes that children and adults often fail to use the strategies at their disposal because minimal transfer, attributions and classroom goals do not support strategy use, the knowledge base is not adequately developed, and learners tend to use primitive routines and show poor cognitive monitoring. According to Garner's theory of settings there are at least six contextual factors that affect strategy use. These factors include strategies being too tightly linked to particular situations, lack of knowledge about the relationship between strategy use and task demands, and classroom settings that do not value the effortful application of strategies.

Although over the past two decades research has documented the important role of metacognition in learning, many students are unaware of the concept of metacognition and do not reflect on their thinking and learning strategies and attitudes and how they might be improved. Knowing about your own knowing or thinking about your own thinking - metacognition- includes thinking about your own thinking *processes* and the *products* of your thinking. Two fundamental aspects of metacognition are *awareness* of and *control* over one's thinking. Two basic types of metacognition are *executive management* strategies for planning, monitoring, evaluating and revising one's thinking processes and products, and *strategic knowledge* about what information and strategies/skills one has (declarative), when and why to use them (contextual/conditional), and how to use them (procedural). Some metacognition is domain-general, applying across subjects and situations; and some is domain-specific, applying selectively to particular subjects and situations (see Schraw, Chapter 1 and Wolters & Pintrich, Chapter 6). Research suggests that the development of metacognition begins by five to seven years of age and is enhanced during and through schooling (Flavell, 1985; Flavell, Green, & Flavell, 1995; Garner, 1990).

Cognitive (worker) skills perform the intellectual work decided on by the metacognitive bosses. Examples of cognitive skills include encoding (registering information), inferring, comparing, and analyzing. Metacognition refers to "thinking about thinking, " such as deciding how to approach a task. Metacognitive (boss) skills involve executive management processes such as planning, monitoring and evaluating. Although cognitive skills are important, Wagner and Sternberg (1984) argue that teaching needs to emphasize metacognitive skills because:

1. Teaching specific strategies, such as the order in which to perform a particular task, will not give students the skills they need in the long run. Students must learn general principles such as planning, and how to apply them over a wide variety of tasks and domains.

2. Both the long-term benefits of training in cognitive skills and the ability to apply cognitive skills to new tasks appear to depend, at least in part, on training at the metacognitive level as well as at the cognitive level. Metacognitive knowledge and skills are needed for effective cognitive performance.

3. Generally students have a history of blindly following instructions. They have not acquired the habit of questioning themselves to lead to effective performance on intellectual tasks.

4. Students with the greatest metacognitive skill deficiencies seem to have no idea what they are doing when performing a task.

5. Students have metacognitive performance problems of: a) determining the difficulty of a task; b) monitoring their comprehension effectively, i.e. they don't recognize when they don't fully understand something (e.g. task directions, information in textbooks); c) planning ahead (e.g. what they need to do and how long each part should take); d) monitoring the success of their performance or determining when they have studied enough to master the material to be learned; e) using all relevant information; f) using a systematic step-by-step approach; g) jumping to conclusions; and h) using inadequate or incorrect representations.

6. Metacognitive skills and knowledge, as important as they are, are not often taught in most areas of the curriculum.

SELF-ASSESSMENT

Because mastery of course content is often assessed by students' performance on multiple-choice tests, students' ability to assess whether they have selected the right answer may help students attain the goal of earning the best grade possible. Self-regulating students engage in learning activities with specific goals in mind, observe their performance as they work, evaluate progress in attaining their goals and react by continuing or changing their approach as needed, depending upon the value of the task and upon perceived self-efficacy (Schunk 1991). Students who observe and evaluate their performance accurately may react appropriately by keeping and/or changing their study strategies to achieve the goal of maximizing their grade in a course or on a test. In order to study students' evaluation of their academic performance students were given a group-administered metacognitive assessment procedure (Hartman, 1995). Students were 49 freshmen taking a required course in World Arts at a large, urban, ethnically diverse university. High-achieving students were expected to show better metacognition, defined as accurate final grade predictions, than low-achieving students. Moreover, prediction inaccuracy, defined as the difference between predicted and actual grades, was expected to be negatively related to final grades. The results supported the expected relationship between achievement and metacognition; both the predicted grades and the prediction difference correlated significantly with final grades.

A related study by Prohaska (1994) found that at the beginning of the semester, high-GPA students made more accurate predictions of their grades in psychology than low-GPA students. Low-achieving students overestimated their grades more than high-achieving students. High GPA students were more confident about their grade estimates than were low GPA students. Other research showed that both low- and medium-ability students overestimated virtually all of their grades with confidence (Prohaska & Maraj, 1995).

The results suggest that many students could benefit from improved awareness of factors affecting their grades and strategies they can use to get better grades, so that as self-directed learners they can make appropriate efforts to attain the grade goals they have set for themselves. (See the error analysis and question analysis methods discussed later in this chapter as examples.)

CULTURAL INFLUENCES

Research demonstrates cultural and social influences on students' self-perceptions. For example, self-concept is affected by factors including social influences, such as peers and significant others; physical considerations, such as physical appearance and ability; and gender (Shavelson & Bolus, 1982; Skaalvik

& Rankin 1990). In a study of predictors of college graduation, Tracey & Sedlacek (1987) found a differential impact of academic self-concept as a function of ethnicity. Although it was a useful predictor of success for white students, it was not useful for black students. Research suggests there are ethnic differences in locus of control (Kumea-Shorter, 1976 ; Lao, Chuang, & Yang, 1977; & Cole, Rodriguez and Cole, 1978). Mestre (1989) cites research identifying cultural factors that affect mathematics learning. He believes comprehensive attempts to improve math education for minorities must take into account cultural, linguistic, socioeconomic, and attitudinal factors. Cognitive style research has demonstrated that variations within ethnic groups are generally greater than variations among them. Various cultures tend to show considerable similarities in their cognitive styles. (Shipman & Shipman, 1985).

According to Anderson (1988), most minority college students are inadequately prepared to compete with better educated, more affluent students. Unfortunately, most colleges respond by retention programs than emphasize only remediation and counseling. These programs have not been very successful with ethnic minorities in part because of the ethnocentric assumption that minorities have the same cognitive framework as whites. Anderson believes this assumption leads retention program developers to base their approaches on learning theories derived from Anglo-European views about learning, achievement, and cognitive functioning. These programs rarely attempt to identify the learning preferences and cognitive assets of non-white students. Minority students are expected to adapt to the instructional program rather than the instructional program adapt to meet students' needs. The culture of the classroom may conflict with students' cultural styles. For example, while college classrooms often emphasize competition and individual achievement, students from non-western cultures may be more accustomed to group cooperation and value group achievement. Often minority student differences are equated with deficiencies.

How do students from different ethnic backgrounds compare and contrast on metacognitive variables that affect academic performance? The BACEIS model (described in the Preface and later in this chapter) suggests that there may be cultural differences in metacognition and the relationship between metacognition and other variables that affect academic performance. Supporting these predictions is research suggesting that problem-solving metacognition is related to students' academic self-concepts, and that culturally distinct ethnic groups vary on these measures and their interactions (Hartman, Everson, Tobias & Gourgey, 1996). Analysis of variance showed there were significant main effects due to ethnicity in self-reports of metacognition; black students reported the most use, Asian students reported the least use, and Hispanic students were in the middle. There was also a significant interaction between gender and ethnicity in metacognition. Black females reported more use of metacognition than black men, while Asian and

Hispanic men reported more use of metacognition than women in their respective groups. The finding regarding Asian students' reports of relatively little use of metacognition may be a reflection the Asian practice of self-criticism.

The cultural background of students and teachers appears to have a variety of effects on academics. Cognitive developmental theories describe cultural acquisitions as cognitions that develop in people because the society requires or emphasizes them. For non-native speakers of English, linguistic diversity may affect students' academic performance as well as teachers' attitudes and expectations. Cultural factors, such as ethnic or gender stereotypes, may also trigger certain teaching behaviors, such as lowering standards or expectations, thereby affecting the quality of instruction, and in turn academic achievement.

Upon awareness of the high failure rate of black students in freshman calculus, Treisman (1985) examined the academic behavior of black and Chinese students and found that black students, unlike Chinese, rarely studied with classmates. Chinese students often worked in informal study groups. Cooperative work with a shared purpose, which research suggests creates an environment rich in metacognitive processing, enables Asians to share their mathematical knowledge, check out their understanding and approaches, and critique each other. Consequently, cooperative learning facilitates both content acquisition and metacognition. Additionally, while black students worked approximately eight hours a week on math, Chinese students worked around fourteen hours per week on the same tasks. Finally, black students rarely utilized the free tutoring provided on campus because they viewed themselves as self-reliant, which was one of their greatest strengths before college. Treisman used these findings to design an academic support Workshop program in which black students worked collaboratively on difficult problem sets for six to eight hours per week. He found that black Workshop participants, on average, consistently earned one full grade higher than black students who did not participate in the workshops. Retention was also improved. Workshop participants' persistence rate was 76% after the first two years in college, while the persistence rate of non-Workshop participants was 57%. The results suggest that metacognitive strategies of students from one cultural background may have benefitted students from a different cultural background, thus cultural practices may influence metacognitive learning.

Cultural variables, such as those observed by Treisman, can affect thinking and learning. Another major cultural factor that impacts education is when the students' native language is different from the language of instruction, which can affect students' ability to acquire knowledge through reading, as well and their ability to communicate what they have learned through writing.

METACOGNITIVE READING STRATEGIES

When sitting at home reading an assignment in history, science, or English, to what extent do students understand what they read in their texts? As they progress from one course or grade level to the next, to what extent do they have the reading abilities that their instructors generally assume?

Alexander's (1995) Domain Model of Learning suggests self-regulation, such as metacognition, is affected by the level of one's knowledge in a particular domain. Novice learners are likely to engage in metacognitive activities less often and less successfully than learners with more subject area knowledge, who are at the competence stage of learning in a domain. What are the implications for students who must learn the subject area by reading about it in a language different from their native tongue? Some students will compound lack of prior knowledge in a subject with minimal knowledge of the language in which it is written. To what extent does the use of successful metacognitive reading strategies transfer across languages?

Baker (1989) reviewed some recent studies with adult readers. She found that in general, good readers, who are good students, appear to have more awareness and control over their own cognitive activities while reading than do poor readers. In her characterization of the "expert reader", Baker noted that research on metacognitive strategies shows that they interact with domain-specific knowledge. For example, experts and novices in specific domains differ in how they budget and regulate their reading time. Domain-knowledge sometimes includes metacognitive knowledge of the relative effectiveness of various strategies. Studies comparing good and poor readers identify a variety of metacognitive skills that enhance reading comprehension. According to Brown (1980) and others, good readers regularly plan, attend to task demands, predict, use strategies to increase their comprehension and meet task requirements, check, monitor, reality test, control and coordinate their learning. Four effective reading comprehension strategies found by Jones, Amiran and Katims (1985) were: organizational, contextual and reflective thinking, and imagery strategies. Long and Long, (1987) reported that good comprehenders in college are more mentally active while reading than are poor comprehenders. Good comprehenders engage in mental interactions with the text through visualizing, self-questioning, and inferring. Although poor comprehenders engage in some metacognitive activities, such as skimming, rereading and pointing to key words, they perform behaviors similar to those of good comprehenders, but without mentally activating operations needed for understanding.

Metacognitive reading skills include: skimming, activating relevant prior knowledge, constructing mental images, predicting, self-questioning, comprehension monitoring, summarizing and connecting new material with prior knowledge. Students cannot be expected to be competent with these skills because they are rarely taught and not everyone develops them independently. They need to be explicitly and continually addressed, practiced, polished and internalized. Improvements in these skills can lead to dramatic improvements in academic achievement. Students who are aware and in control of their metacognitive reading behaviors are at a distinct advantage because many of them involve monitoring one's comprehension, taking steps to clarify difficulties and restoring the comprehension process when it has broken down. Effective instruction in metacognitive reading skills requires that teachers explain the skills or strategies, model them for students, give examples, explain when, why, and how to use them, emphasize the value of flexibility in selecting specific skills to fit the particular context , provide guided practice on a range of texts, and give corrective feedback. Palincsar and Brown's (1984) reciprocal teaching procedure is specifically designed to develop four metacognitive reading skills: questioning, clarifying, summarizing and predicting. Through reciprocal teaching, eventually students are able to apply these metacognitive reading strategies on their own as self-regulating readers.

Research on college reading and study skills notes that there is a trend across studies showing that students' perception of their own control over learning has important implications for student performance in a wide range of areas (Maxwell, 1993). Students' perceptions of control tend to affect their time management, use of reading strategies, and test taking:. "...previous research on control theory suggests that unless students perceive that they have some control over and can influence their environment, their capacity to learn from instruction is limited" (110, p. 9).

In their critique of research on comprehension enhancing activities, Paris, Wixson and Palincsar (1986) note that not enough attention has been paid to students' self regulation of strategies they have been taught to use. They add that research has not told us much about what teachers need to do to ensure that students find these activities meaningful and internalize them, rather than following them blindly. They describe efforts to make readers more aware of the strategies they use and to foster more self-control in using them. A classic study in this genre (Brown, Campione and Day, 1983) compares three instructional conditions: 1. **blind** training, in which subjects are not told about why the activities they have been asked to perform are useful, 2. **informed** training, in which learners are induced to use a strategy and told why it is useful, and 3.**self -control** training, in which they are explicitly taught how to monitor and self-regulate their use of a reading strategy. Such research suggests that understanding the value of a strategy can give students a **personal rationale** for using it, which facilitates the continued use of the strategy (Paris, Wixson and Palincsar, 1986). This genre of research has demonstrated that reading is enhanced and reading strategies tend to transfer when strategy training is accompanied by self-control training (Garner, 1987).

Garner's (1987) review of research on metacognitive strategy training in reading discussed efforts to improve comprehension through text reinspection. Garner identifies two main components of text reinspection: noting that one does not remember what one has read, and deliberately reprocessing segments of the text to provide the information. Garner and her associates found that to use this strategy successfully, readers need conditional metacognitive knowledge, i.e., knowing when and where to use text reinspection. Duffy, Book and Roehler(1983) found that explicit explanations created student awareness ,which in turn, stimulated student achievement. Garner argues that explanations about reading comprehension strategies should include: why the strategy should be learned; what the strategy is, how to use it, when and where to use the strategy and how to evaluate strategy use. Elementary school teachers do little direct instruction in how to comprehend text (Durkin, 1981). The tendency is for teachers to give students unguided practice. Finally, Garner reviewed the literature on text summarization, including the work of Brown and her associates on what students at different ages do and don't do: e.g. use of deletion rules, topic sentence invention rule, condensing, and revising. Garner (1987) found both high school and college students rarely integrate units of textual information, which would help produce succinct summaries.

Training studies have demonstrated that students can learn to use metacognitive strategies which can lead to better performance. Tobias (1987), using an aptitude-treatment-interaction (ATI) research paradigm focusing on mandatory text review, showed that unstrategic readers with low prior domain knowledge can be made to successfully review and refine their comprehension upon giving the wrong answers to adjunct questions. The results suggest that low-achieving students can be taught to use metacognitive strategies, such as text reprocessing, that may ultimately improve their reading comprehension. Knowledge about when to use strategies is an especially important form of metacognition (Pressley, 1984).

Research indicates that metacognitive knowledge about imagery is an important factor affecting its use. Images provide meaningful representations of material to be learned (Kulhavy & Swenson 1975; Paivio, 1971) . Such meaningfulness may facilitate both learning and retention. Kulhavy and Swenson (1975) investigated whether giving students instructions about images increased semantic recall of what they learned. The instructions they used told their subjects to form mental pictures of the events and activities in each paragraph before answering the question. Subjects in the image-instructed condition were told to use a specific strategy - mental pictures- and they were shown **when** to use the strategy. Embedded within the experimental booklets for these subjects, typed at the bottom of each page was, "Form a mental picture of these events before turning the page" (p. 49). Control subjects were just told to read the material and answer each question correctly. The material was carefully constructed for this study. It consisted of 20 prose paragraphs on "The Island of Ako and Its People," and two questions on each paragraph. Essentially all of the nouns in the paragraphs and questions had concrete environmental referents. Image-instructed subjects performed better than controls on the first test, but the difference was not statistically significant. However, image-instructed participants performed significantly better than controls on the delayed test. The image instructions with strategic metacognitive knowledge about imagery increased the amount of text-content available over time.

In addition to this specific, conditional or contextual information about strategy use, individuals may need to know other information about using the strategies. What good is it to tell a subject when to form a mental image if the subject doesn't know exactly **what** is meant by a mental image?. The strategic knowledge base must include extensive declarative information, facts about the world in general and the particular domain, like the imagery strategy and its application to reading. For example, many students equate imagery with mental pictures and do not realize that mental images can be auditory, olfactory or from any of the senses - not just vision. Declarative knowledge interacts with strategy execution; it is often needed to implement the appropriately identified strategy. Knowing that images may be auditory can stimulate students to construct auditory images while reading. Finally, it may be important for a person being instructed to know step-by-step procedures for how to create one and regulate its use. Students can benefit from hearing an expert reader think aloud while constructing and using mental imagery in reading. Self-regulation includes the ability to monitor and evaluate strategy use. Readers may decide to supplement an auditory image with an olfactory image.

METACOGNITION IN TUTORING

Tutoring has a long history as an instructional method for developing students' knowledge and skills. Theoretical models of tutoring that include metacognitive factors affecting the tutoring process have been used to design tutoring programs and to plan tutor training that is designed to help students become self-directed learners (Hartman, 1990, 1993; Rings & Sheets, 1991; Condravy, 1995). In one tutoring model that emphasizes student development and metacognition, the student development component suggests that tutors should learn how to help students monitor their progress. It also suggests that tutors should confront students who fail to take responsibility for their own learning, and should help students develop effective communication skills and learn about instructional support and other campus resources. The metacognitive component suggests that tutors should teach students a problem solving model with four components: *individual learner characteristics* of motivation, learning styles and culture; *task*, or specific learning goals; *strategies*, including predicting test questions, categorizing information, and managing time; and *materials*, including use of print and media. Tutors should help students become aware of the components of the model and help them implement specific strategies designed to meet their individual learning goals (Rings & Sheets, 1991).

Another tutoring model describes good teaching as helping students "discover what the learning process is about so that they can become lifelong learners" in addition to helping them master content (Gourgey 1992, p. 67). Her tutoring model is intended as a guide for the tutoring process and as a blueprint for tutor training. Its components are dialogue, developing metacognitive skills, response to affective (emotional) needs and reeducation about the learning process. Gourgey notes that often students need reeducation about the learning process because they have unrealistic expectations and do not "appreciate the importance of intellectual struggle, incubation, and understanding ideas rather than just following procedures" (p. 67).

When Condravy (1995) asked tutors to identify methods that were most effective for promoting learning, tutors' responses showed the need to address emotional, cognitive and metacognitive aspects of learning. After completing a nine-hour training program, Condravy's tutors reported spending most of their teaching efforts on students' metacognitive needs, followed by emotional needs, especially motivation, and, finally, students' cognitive needs.

Research by Hostetter (1994) focused on teaching metacognitive strategies to international students who were repeating a developmental reading course. Tutors were trained to tutor metacognitively, to plan, monitor and evaluate their tutoring sessions and to teach students metacognitive reading strategies, such as comprehension monitoring and identifying error patterns so they could change them. The tutorials followed a structured format consisting of: warm-up, mental preparation for testing, testing, discussing passages, and discussing questions and answers. The results suggest that students who received metacognitive tutoring improved in reading comprehension and did better than students who did not receive metacognitive tutoring.

Many students experience academic difficulty because they constantly focus on retaining subject matter content without first learning the intellectual skills needed to support that effort. In order for the students to function intelligently, teachers (including tutors) need to develop both cognitive and metacognitive skills as well as positive affect of emotions, attitudes and motivation.

THE BIG PICTURE:
THE BACEIS MODEL OF IMPROVING THINKING

The B A C E I S model of improving thinking (Hartman & Sternberg, 1993), described in the Preface, underlies the organization of this book as well as my teaching and research. The BACEIS model is a comprehensive framework of factors internal and external to the student which affect a student's academic performance. Factors internal to the student are cognition and affect; factors external to the student are academic and nonacademic environments. The BACEIS acronym stands for the following: **B**=behavior, **A**=affect, **C**=cognition, **E**=environment, **I**=interacting, **S**=systems (Figures 1 & 2). The model suggests that internal factors of cognition and affect are related to each other and are also related to interacting external factors from academic and nonacademic environments. The combination of these factors and their reciprocal influences has implications for successful performance of academic work. Such information may be useful for understanding students' academic performance and for designing instruction which improves it. To promote intellectual development, a teacher (or tutor) may intervene at any point in this complex array.. The cognitive part of the internal supersystem is made up of two parts: cognitive and metacognitive. The cognitive component has three major applications: critical thinking, creative thinking and learning strategies. The affective part of the internal supersystem consists of motivation, affective self-regulation and attitudes. The external supersystem consists of the academic environment (teacher characteristics, content, class environment & instructional techniques) and nonacademic environment (socio-economic status, family background and cultural forces). These environmental factors interact with each other and with the rest of the BACEIS system components. The combination of these interacting variables leads to behavioral consequences regarding intellectual performance.

DEVELOPMENT OF METACOGNITIVE STRATEGIES

This section describes some of the techniques I have used to develop metacognition in tutors and tutees in the tutoring and cooperative learning program I directed and in my undergraduate educational psychology students who are preparing to become teachers. Consequently, what these students learn is intended to have two functions: to develop their own ability to learn metacognitively, and to learn strategies for developing metacognition in their current (from their fieldwork experience) and future students.

ANTECEDENTS
(Internal & External Supersystems)

INTERNAL SUPERSYSTEM

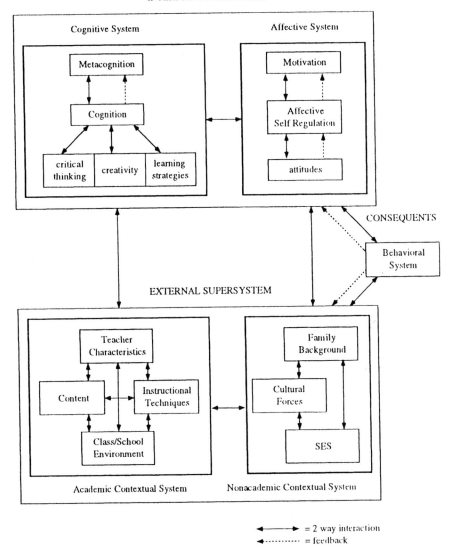

Figure 1. BACEIS model components

(*Hartman & Sternberg,* 1993)

ANTECEDENTS - INTERNAL SUPERSYSTEM

Keisha's Cognitive System	Keisha's Affective System

Metacognition
- skim, image
- monitor comprehension
- self question, look back

Cognition
- encode information
- clarify
- infer

Motivation
- interested in content and wants to answer questions correctly
- wants to please parents and teachers

Affective Self Regulation
- expects to be good reader
- values reading

Critical Thinking	*Creativity*	*Learning Strategies*	*Attitudes*
-evaluates alternative energy sources	-designs new way to purify gasoline	-selective attention	- good reading self concept -curious about content due to father's occupation - persists when reading difficult material

EXTERNAL SUPERSYSTEM

Keisha's Academic Contextual System	Keisha's Non-academic Contextual System

Teacher characteristics
-reading specialist
-extensive teaching experience
-positive towards students
-diverse teaching repertoire

Content (text)
-gasoline emissions
-ozone in atmosphere
-cars v. mass transit
-alternative energy sources

Class Environment
-students challenge authority
-resources accessible
-content at appropriate level

Instructional Techniques
-reciprocal teaching
-imagery formation

Family Background
-native speakers of English
-family reads and discusses books at dinner
-brothers/sisters good readers
-father owns gas station

Cultural forces
-need reading as survival skill in society (signs, labels, job applications)
-television inhibits reading

Socio-economic Status
- money for books, newspapers
-leisure time for readings
-father's income crucial to support family

BEHAVIORAL CONSEQUENTS

Keisha correctly answers comprehension questions, paraphrases text, self regulates reading; writes essay, rejects author's conclusion, proposes new technology

Figure 2. Application of BACEIS model to reading. (*Hartman & Sternberg,* 1993)

Reading Metacognition

There are many techniques I have used to help students develop their metacognitive reading skills. Some of these techniques are identified in Figure 2, which applies the BACEIS Model to the improvement of Keisha's reading comprehension in a classroom lesson about energy, fuel and the environment. One of the first homework assignments in my undergraduate educational psychology class requires students to define ten strategies and reflect on their use of these strategies in reading Chapter 2 of our educational psychology text and in general (Table 1).

Table 1 Reading Metacognition Homework

Define each term, then look back at what you have read so far in this chapter and analyze your use of metacognitive reading strategies. Indicate (Yes/No) which of the strategies below you used when reading this material and indicate your general use of each of them when reading.

Metacognitive Reading Strategies

Strategy	Definition	Used Here	Generally Use
1. skim		yes no	yes no sometimes
2. Predict		yes no	yes no sometimes
3. Image		yes no	yes no sometimes
4. check comprehension		yes no	yes no sometimes
5. clarify		yes no	yes no sometimes
6. self test on content		yes no	yes no sometimes
7. review		yes no	yes no sometimes
8. summarize		yes no	yes no sometimes
9. activate prior knowledge		yes no	yes no sometimes
10. connect prior knowledge to new information		yes no	yes no sometimes

Then there is an in-class cooperative learning activity in which groups of students compare their definitions of the metacognitive reading strategies, tally the results of their use of these strategies, compile the results across groups to develop a class-wide profile and discuss the implications on two levels: the reading strategies that they use, from their perspectives as learners, and the class's reading strategies, from their perspectives as teachers.

Another technique is to teach students the difference between reader and writer-based summaries (Anderson & Hidi, 1988/1989) and give them extensive practice and feedback preparing reader-based summaries. These are emphasized because my students often have difficulty differentiating the author's main ideas from their own, and they tend summarize from a writer-based perspective, often missing important ideas on the topic due the students' subjectivity.

A third technique is Reciprocal Teaching. Reciprocal Teaching is a cooperative learning method of improving reading comprehension that can also be used in individual tutoring/teaching. In reciprocal teaching a teacher/tutor and a group of students take turns leading discussions about specific segments of text using reading strategies of questioning, clarifying, summarizing and predicting (Palincsar & Brown, 1984). Instructional techniques involved are: demonstrate, or model and explain; practice with feedback; dialogue, or "simple conversation with a purpose" (Palincsar, Ransom & Derber, 1988/89, p. 37); scaffold, or provide students with temporary support; and take turns leading text dialogues. The combination of these techniques leads to student self- regulation or self-management of reading comprehension. A review of research on reciprocal teaching (Rosenshine & Meister, 1994) shows two different forms of the method used in studies by the developers and their associates; one involves explicit instruction in the reading strategies *before* the dialogues begin. Consistent with this method is a five-stage sequence of reciprocal teaching instruction: (1) teacher demonstration; (2) student learning and guided practice in using the four comprehension strategies; (3) coordinated practice using the strategies with segments of text in small groups led by the teacher, where students alternate with the teacher leading text dialogues based on the four reading strategies; (4). practice using the strategies in small groups of students with the teacher only observing and guiding as needed; and (5). student competence and self-regulation. These are described in more detail in Hartman (1994). Students learn to use Reciprocal Teaching to improve their own reading comprehension and to improve that of their current and/or prospective students.

A fourth technique I use to improve students' reading metacognition is teaching them to create graphic organizers (external, visual representations) summarizing the main points from our textbook. One procedure for teaching students to create graphic organizers is discussed in the next section.

After teaching students these various metacognitive reading strategies, I encourage them to experiment with them in all of their classes to determine which work most effectively for them in different subjects and situations.

Graphic Organizers

Graphic representations can be used to understand text and solve a variety of problems. Graphic organizer techniques can help students analyze text and see how it is structured. Networks of related ideas (schemata) that the reader brings to the text set up expectations that influence understanding and interpretations of what is read. (See Chapter 9 for an example of a concept map). If there is a mismatch between the reader's and writer's ideas, comprehension can break down. Learning to understand the structure of ideas in a text can improve comprehension (Mulcahy, 1987). For example, teaching students *story grammars*, e.g., a novel usually has a protagonist, antagonist, climax, and denouement helps the reader set up appropriate expectations that make the text easier to understand. Several of these organizer techniques have been found to be especially useful for reading text. Some graphic organizers that can be used to understand text are flow charts, concept maps, Venn diagrams and tree diagrams. Jones et. al. (1988/89) identified other graphic organizers found to be useful for reading text: network trees, fishbone maps, cycles, spider webs, continua/scales, series of events chains, compare/contrast matrices and a problem/solution outlines (Jones et. al., 1988/89). "A good graphic representation can show at a glance the key parts of a whole and their relations, thereby allowing a holistic understanding that words alone cannot convey "(Jones, Pierce and Hunter, 1988/1989, p. 21).

Creating Graphic Organizers through Scaffolding

After years of simply modeling for students how they can create graphic organizers as learning strategies with only moderate success, I changed to a scaffolding approach, which has been much more effective for developing this metacognitive strategy. Scaffolding means providing support (models, cues, prompts, hints, partial solutions) to students to bridge the gap between what students can do on their own and what students can do with guidance from others. The goal of scaffolding is for students to become independent, self-regulating thinkers who are more self-sufficient and less teacher-dependent. Scaffolding is an especially effective teaching approach for developing higher level cognitive strategies (Rosenshine & Meister, 1994) and is discussed in greater detail in Chapter 8, "Teaching Metacognitively". I use the following steps in my scaffolding plan for teaching students to create effective graphic organizers:

1. I show and explain a variety of traditional examples of graphic organizers, such as those identified above, and more innovative, untraditional types, such as ocean scenes, ladders, and our galaxy. Students learn about three uses of graphic organizers: for teaching, learning, and assessment. For half of our midterm and final exam questions students have to create graphic organizers of their answers. I ask students about their past experience with graphic organizers, and usually find out that few students have had experience creating their own graphic organizers, but most students recognize them as something they have seen.

2. Students read about what graphic organizers are, when, why and how to use various types of them. One source (Jones, et. al. 1988/89) provides information on why and how to create graphic organizers to comprehend text and it provides illustrations of a spider map, continuum/scale, series of events chain, compare/contrast matrix, problem/solution outline, network tree, fishbone map, human interaction outline and cycle. Another source focuses on concept maps and Vee diagrams (Novak, 1998).

3. As a homework assignment students are given a partially completed matrix to finish (Table 2). Students are expected to use the information provided as a model for their completions. Many students need explicit instructions to write their own "How" in the second row and their own "What, Why and How" in the third row. I give students feedback on what they write and where they write it. For example, it's not uncommon for students to put information on "why" an idea is important in the section on "how" they might use it, and vice versa.

4. The next homework assignment requires students to complete an empty matrix entirely on their own. Students get feedback, as before.

5. For the next homework assignment students create their own graphic organizers, but it can't be a matrix . Then I give students additional examples of standard and innovative models and specific criteria for constructing and evaluating graphic organizers. Students evaluate their own homework graphic organizers using these criteria. These criteria are:
    a. neat and easy to read
    b. ideas are expressed clearly
    c. ideas are expressed completely
    d. content is organized clearly and logically
    e. labels/other strategies (colors, lines) to guide reader's comprehension
    f. main ideas, not minor details, are emphasized
    g. it is visually appealing
    h. the reader doesn't have to turn the page to read the words

6.   Have students develop a graphic organizer in a cooperative learning group, but they can't use a matrix. Metacognitive processing tends to spontaneously occur during cooperative learning (Artzt & Armour-Thomas, 1992). Students discuss the advantages and disadvantages of different structures, they discuss what concepts to include and exclude, and they self-regulate their attempts to meet the criteria identified above. Once their graphic organizers are completed, the groups show their graphic organizers to the other groups which give them feedback based on the criteria identified above. I supplement the groups' feedback with my own comments, as needed.

7.   For homework, students develop graphic organizers completely on their own, but not using the matrix format. Group members give each other feedback on the extent to which they have met the established criteria.

8.   Finally students are expected to be able to create and critique their own graphic organizers. Because half of the midterm and half of the final exam in our course require students to put their answers in the form of graphic organizers, students know they are accountable for their mastery and the ability to self-regulate their development.

Modeling Metacognition

An important strategy for developing metacognitive knowledge and skills is for teachers to provide models of metacognition in everyday-life and/or school. Modeling is based on Bandura and Walters's (1963) theory which highlights the importance of observation, identification, imitation and motivation in learning. The previous section on scaffolding the creation of graphic organizers involves repeated and varied modeling. Teachers can think out loud to externalize their thought processes, serving as an "expert model," so students can hear effective ways of using metacognitive knowledge and skills. Modeling is often a component of scaffolding, as can be seen by reviewing the first steps of both Reciprocal Teaching and Cognitive Behavior Modification. Many students appreciate seeing models of higher-level metacognitive strategies, especially those involving everyday life experience. Table 3 shows one way I have modeled executive management metacognition in everyday life. Table 4 shows one way I have modeled strategic metacognitive knowledge for reading and writing strategies.

Table 2

Partially Completed Graphic Organizer

Complete the graphic organizer below using ideas from this chapter of our text. Tell
what the ideas are, *why* they're useful and *how* you might use them. Part is filled
out for you as a model; please complete the rest of it based on information from
Chapter 2 of our text. Add your own "*how*" to the second row and your own "*what,
why* and *how*" in the third row.

WHAT is the idea?	WHY is it useful?	HOW might I use it?
Reader-based summary	To make sure I have identified, understand and can remember the author's main ideas.	After reading a chapter of a textbook, I'll look for the author's signals about the main ideas, identify the most important ones, check my understanding by briefly writing them in my own words. I'll be objective and selective.
Writer-based summary	To remember the ideas I'm personally most interested in.	

Table 3
Model: Executive Management Metacognition in Everyday Life

<u>Planning: Decision Making</u>
Identify and define the problem or task.
Get Michael an excellent doctor who knows about his disease and can follow up on
the specialist's recommendations; Michael's doctor of 20 years didn't.
Diagram or represent the problem or task internally and/or externally.
Create visual image of the x-ray of Michael's liver that the specialist showed me as
he said Michael should get on a transplant list and start taking Actigall.
Create along with that a visual image of his doctor of 20 years
Select processes needed to perform the task.
    Identify potential sources of the information.
    Contact those sources to see who they recommend in our area.
    Choose a doctor and make an appointment.
Explore alternative approaches and select the best.
    Make sure we look at more than one type of source.
    Don't just rely on people we know, use the Internet to identify top people in the
    New York area.
Sequence the processes and approaches into an effective order.
    First make phone calls to 3 people we know because we can do that right away
    Schedule time to search the Internet.
    Search the Internet.
Budget time and resources for performing the task.
    Spend minimal time on each of the 3 phone calls, 5 to 10 minutes each.
    Plan to spend at least two hours searching the web.
Anticipate potential difficulties and how to overcome them.
    If our sources don't pan out, see if they can give us leads.
    Identify other possible doctors in case the first one doesn't work out.

<u>Monitoring: Checking Implementation in Progress</u>
Comprehension
    Do I really understand what kind of doctor Michael needs?
    How well do I understand the timing of his need for a new doctor?
Approach
    Are we going about this doctor search in the right way?
    Are there other ways we could be looking for a doctor?
Memory
    What other people, organizations or institutions do I know of that might help
us find a liver specialist familiar with PSC?

(Table 3 continued)
 Evaluating: Assessing Implementation
Use internal and external feedback to judge your own performance.
The doctor from the first hospital was good because he got Michael on Actigall right away.
The doctor from first hospital was disappointing because he had no interest in putting Michael on the transplant list and I didn't like his "bedside manner".
Use judgements from internal and external sources to plan future performance.
If it were me, I'd get a new doctor. How does Michael feel? I'll ask him. Michael feels the exact same way. New doctor it is!
Develop and implement specific action plans to improve your performance.
We'll contact the doctor from the second hospital who published an article on Michael's disease and who spoke recently at a local conference on liver diseases. After we see him, we'll evaluate him to see if we want to stay at the second hospital or try a third.

Table 4
Models of Strategic Metacognitive Knowledge

WHAT (FACTS)	WHEN & WHY (CONTEXT)	HOW (PROCEDURES)
Clarify is to fix up understanding or to make clear.	When something is confusing/ unclear, vague, ambiguous; to attain comprehension.	Use context clues in the text. Look back. Look ahead. Ask questions.

Revise is to change or modify.	After writing a draft. To improve a paper.	Get feedback on a draft.
		    Internal (self)
		    External (others)
		Use feedback to correct, refine, elaborate, delete.

When providing models such as those in Tables 3 and 4, I generally explain each component and ask questions to monitor and evaluate students' understanding of the concepts. Then I try to elicit students' own examples of each component of the model and have students work in groups, giving each other feedback on the quality of the examples as I circulate among the groups providing individualized feedback.

Teachers can use the think-aloud method (discussed later in this chapter) to serve as expert models showing students how to use metacognitive knowledge and strategies when working on a variety of tasks; for example, to let students see and hear how they plan, monitor, and evaluate their work and how they would approach tasks like their students'. When the thinker-talker is the subject-matter expert, the process allows the expert to model their own thinking for students. This modeling shows how to think about the material (knowledge, skills, procedures etc.). It lets students hear what goes on in an expert's head when a text is read, a homework assignment is attacked, study for a test is planned, an essay is written, an error is found, or a problem is solved. It also should include statements from the expert that externalize her/his feelings so that students can learn how to self-regulate their own emotions. When modeling academic performance, it's a good idea to intentionally make occasional mistakes, so that students can observed becoming aware of them and strategies for recovering from them and self-correcting. Meichenbaum and Biemiller (1998) state that think-aloud modeling may be in the form of self-questions (e.g., Did I carefully check my work?) or self-instructional directive statements (e.g., That's not what I expected. I'll have to retrace my path). They recommend that teacher use think-aloud modeling for showing students how to: summarize, access prior knowledge, self-monitor, obtain help, and self-reinforce. This modeling should involve communicating with students so that the lesson is an interactive dialogue instead of a monologue, and modeling should be gradually phased out as student competence and responsibility increase.

Self-questioning

Questioning and self-questioning strategies are effective ways of promoting self-directed learners. Self-questioning can guide the learner's performance before, during, and after task performance; it can improve self-awareness and control over thinking and thereby improve performance; self-questioning can .improve long-term retention of knowledge and skills; it can improve the ability to apply and transfer knowledge and skills students learn; and finally, it can improve attitudes and motivation as a result of improved performance. Research on self-questioning shows that questions created by the student are much more effective than questions given to the student by someone else Model self questioning, and discuss and illustrate how it is used in school and everyday life situations. Self-questions such as " Have I left out anything important?" can help a student self-direct in identifying the omission of important points or examples. Ask students questions such as "How do you prepare for a test? How would you plan, monitor, and evaluate a surprise party?"and have students generate and use their own self- questions. The more students practice generating and using self-questions in diverse situations the more likely they are to develop the habit of self- questioning so it becomes a skill, which is used automatically and unconsciously as the situation requires. The I DREAM of A approach to writing (Hartman, 1993) and to solving math/science problems (Hartman, 1996; see Chapter 9) is designed to help learners become more self-directed. If students can't do this individually, try doing it in pairs or small groups. Teachers (or tutors) can listen to students executing tasks while using their self-questions and give them feedback on their questions and answers. They can encourage students to keep a readily accessible prompt sheet for their own self-questions to stimulate their thinking of the kinds of questions to ask in a particular situation. It is important to regularly have students adapt their self-questions to the needs of the specific subject and task and not impose preformulated questions on them.

Teachers should not be satisfied with putting students in situations which require them to use self-questioning (or any strategy they want students to use). **Practice isn't enough.** It is also important to provide **explicit instruction** in when, why and how to use self-questioning; students need to understand the rationale and effective procedures for self-questioning so that they can recognize appropriate contexts for its use, so that they have criteria for evaluating their self-questioning, and so they can self-regulate its use.

Table 5 shows some of the types of self-questions students can ask to plan, monitor and evaluate their thinking in a range of academic domains. By focusing on a range of subjects students can see some of the similarities and differences in metacognition across subjects. Perceiving the similarities may promote positive transfer and perceiving differences may inhibit negative transfer of metacognitive strategies. Teachers should give students examples of questions like these to stimulate students' thinking about the kinds of questions they may use in different subjects, but teachers should emphasize that students need to create their own questions that are situation- and task-specific. Teachers and tutors should be sure to emphasize the value of student-generated, task-specific questions rather than pre-formulated questions.

Assessment and Error Analysis

Students often joke about their graded papers being put in the "circular file". Many students waste a valuable resource their teachers give them that could help them to improve their future performance - feedback - both oral and written. In most classes there are several opportunities for students to obtain information from the teacher on their mastery of course concepts and skills. Yet frequently written feedback ends up ignored and only the grade is noted. Students should be encouraged to reflect on what feedback they've received, how that feedback is best interpreted and how it can be used to improve their future performance.

However, assessment is most effective when it also includes students' self-monitoring and self -evaluating so that they can manage their own learning. One method I use to promote student self-monitoring and self-evaluating is error analysis. Metacognitive knowledge about error analysis includes:

1) Declarative knowledge: Error analysis is a systematic approach for using feedback metacognitively to improve one's future performance. It involves obtaining strategic metacognitive knowledge about one's mistakes and recycling that knowledge for self-improvement.

2) Conditional/Contextual Knowledge: Error analysis has several potential benefits. First, it gives students a second opportunity to master important material. Second, it develops students' metacognition, both strategic knowledge and executive management, as students evaluate their test performance, identify errors and possible errors patterns, and plan for the future   For example, it can help students anticipate their specific likely errors and self-correct them before turning in a test. Third, it helps internalize students' attributions so that they recognize that their educational outcomes (grades) are a result of their own efforts, actions and strategies - factors within their control- rather than attributing their performance to external factors outside their control, like the professor or bad luck. This could improve students' feelings of self-efficacy, their academic self-concept in the specific subject area, and perhaps transfer to their general academic self- concept.

3) Procedural knowledge: Error analysis requires identifying what the correct information/answer/approach is, and identifying what errors, omissions, etc., were made, determining why they occurred, and planning how to prevent them in the future. When doing error analyses my students are required to: 1. Identify what their wrong answer was and what is the correct answer (declarative knowledge). 2. Determine specifically why they got the answer wrong (contextual knowledge) and 3. Formulate an action plan on how they have now learned and understood the material and how they will remember this information (procedural knowledge).

Table 5

Sample Student Self-Questions for Managing School Subjects

Thinking Objective	PLANNING	MONITORING	EVALUATING
Reading	What do I already know about this topic? What am I expected to learn from this reading? How much time should it take for me to read this?	Is there anything I don't understand? Can I figure it out on my own? Which ideas are most important? How can I remember what I've read so far?	Did I understand and remember everything? Which reading strategies worked best this time? How can I read with better understanding next time?
Writing	What is the purpose of this essay? What should be in the introductory paragraph? How should I put these ideas in the best order?	Am I elaborating on all of my main points? How clearly am I expressing my ideas? Am I making any spelling or grammar mistakes?	What was best about my paper? Why did I make those spelling and grammar errors? How can I best prevent those mistakes next time?
Mathematics	What do I have to find? Have I ever solved a problem like this before? What formula should I use?	Is my diagram of the problem right? Am I using the right formula? Am I making any careless mistakes?	Does my answer make sense? Is the right answer? Did I use an appropriate method to solve this problem?
Social Studies	What causes of World War 11 am I supposed to remember? Which are the key events I need to understand? How can I make sure I will remember them for the essay exam?	Am I confusing the political causes with the social causes ? What do they mean by the law of supply and demand? Am I giving up-to-date answers to the questions on current events?	Did I correctly identify all the important causes of World War 11? What else should I have included in my discussion of the critical events? What did I learn from this history lesson that applies to the world today?
Science	How can I design research to test this hypothesis? What are all of the critical variables that need to be considered? Which variables need to be controlled?	Does the research design validly test this hypothesis? Should I try a different approach? Am I recording all the observations accurately?	How effective was my experimental design? Were my conclusions justified by the results? How could I be a more accurate observer and recorder next time?

Preliminary analysis of the quality of students' error analyses suggests declarative information is relatively easy for students to produce, contextual knowledge is moderately difficult, and procedural knowledge is the most difficult for students to generate. Sample error analyses (additional procedural knowledge) are in the Appendix.

Error Analysis Model
1.   **What answer I had AND what the answer really was. OR WHAT I did wrong AND what I should have done.**
2.   **WHY did I choose the wrong answer?   OR Why did I do it wrong?**
3.   **HOW will I remember what I now know is the correct answer? OR How will I make sure I don't make the same mistake again?**

In all three steps the student must focus on the specific content involved in the errors rather than focus on general causes of errors, such as not studying enough.

After taking exams, I teach students error analysis procedures and require them to perform error analyses as homework assignments. Occasionally, for each written error analysis a student performs correctly, the student may recapture half of the points that were lost for each test item, if it appears that the student has now mastered the material and understands his or her mistakes.

When reviewing this chapter for the book, Gourgey introduced me to a more comprehensive method used in medical education for test error metacognition that emphasizes students' mastery of the topic. Pelley & Dalley's (1997) "question analysis" is intended to help students make a broader analysis of test questions than just a literal interpretation because a narrower, more literal interpretation can constrain their studying and limit   learning. Their procedure has four steps: identifying topics, understanding the correct answer, understanding wrong answers, and rephrasing the question. Pelley and Dalley encourage students to ask questions such as, "How would I have had to study to know that the correct answer was right?" "How would I have had to study to know that each wrong answer was wrong?" Focusing on the topic rather than the question helps students understand material more deeply, so they understand how ideas are interrelated, and therefore students are able to correctly answer more and different questions.

Thinking Aloud

As mentioned in the section on modeling, thinking aloud is an excellent technique for developing metacognitive knowledge and strategies. It is a fundamental component of Cognitive Behavior Modification (Meichenbaum, 1977), Pair-Problem Solving (Whimbey and Lochhead, 1981) and the I DREAM of A approaches to writing (Hartman, 1993) and problem solving (Hartman, 1996).

When teaching my students to think aloud, I provide them with strategic metacognitive knowledge about this technique so that they can use it in appropriate situations and with proper procedures. The section below provides a detailed example of strategic metacognitive knowledge I give to students to maximize the effectiveness of their use of thinking aloud.

WHAT is Think Aloud?

It is a technique of externalizing one's thought processes as one is engaged in a task that requires thinking. The thinker says out loud all of the thoughts and feelings that occur when performing a task (e.g. solving a problem, answering a question, conducting an experiment, reading through lecture/textbook notes etc.) . It is a method that can be used by a teacher or tutor, two students working together, or a student working alone. Using the think-aloud process with two students - where one serves as the THINKER while the other serves as the analytical LISTENER - is known as "pair-problem solving" (Whimbey & Lochhead, 1982). The thinker verbalizes out loud ALL the thoughts that arise in the process of completing an academic task. The listener actively attends to what the thinker says, examines the accuracy, points out errors, and keeps the thinker talking aloud.

WHEN should the Think Aloud process be applied?

- When the teacher wants to demonstrate to the student what and how to think about academic content and strategies.
- When the teacher wants to help guide the student in learning what and how to think about academic material and tasks.
- When the teacher wants to diagnose or assess what and how the student thinks and knows.
- When there is a desire to become more thorough, precise and systematic when performing tasks that require thinking.
- When the teacher wants the student to become more aware of and more in control of his or her own knowledge, skills and attitudes.

WHY should Think Aloud be used?
- It helps prevent passivity and rote learning.
- It helps students communicate to the teacher what they know and how they approach academic tasks. This helps the teacher identify and diagnose misunderstood or misused concepts, rules, facts, important omissions and inadequate or incomplete knowledge, approaches, or skills.
- It helps students think more precisely, carefully, and systematically.
- It helps students examine their own knowledge, skills and attitudes.
- By hearing themselves think, they become more aware of their strengths and weaknesses.
- Through combining this self-awareness with feedback from the listener, students can check their own performance and make appropriate changes as needed.
- It increases students' control over themselves as learners and can improve their academic (and nonacademic) performance.
- Students working together can discover errors, misconceptions, disorganizations, and other impediments to intellectual performance.

HOW to do the Think-Aloud process

How to Think Aloud: Problem Solver's Task
1.Translate your thoughts (ideas; images etc.) into words and recite them aloud.

2. Verbalize aloud all the steps you go through when solving problems. Don't censor. No thought or step is too small, easy, obvious or unimportant to verbalize.

3. Verbalize all the thinking you do before you start to solve the problem (e.g. what you are going to do, when, why, and how). Even second-guessing yourself is important to verbalize aloud, e.g., "What's the best way to solve this problem? I think I should use that long, complicated formula we were using a couple weeks ago. What was it called, the quadratic equation?. No, maybe not. Maybe I'm supposed to use the formula we did in class yesterday".

4. Verbalize all thoughts as you proceed, e.g., "OK, I'm almost through with this division problem. Now that I have my answer, all I have to do is multiply to check and see if my answer is right." Verbalize <u>ALL</u> the thinking done before, during, and after work. The verbalization must include plans of what to do, when certain steps are taken, why steps are used (not used), and how to proceed with each thought. For example, I think I should use that long, complicated formula we were talking about a couple of weeks ago. No, maybe not. Maybe I'm supposed to use that new one we covered in class today."

How to Listen Analytically: Listener's Task

The following guidelines for listening while engaged in pair-problem solving are adaptations of Whimbey & Lochhead (1982).

1. Think along with the problem solver. Follow every step and make sure you understand every step. If not, ask a question. Have the problem solver identify and define important terms, variables, rules, procedures etc. Make sure the problem solver vocalizes all the steps and does all the work. If the problem solver skips over a step without thinking aloud, ask her or him to explain the missing thought.

2. Do NOT work on the problem independently. Listen to and work along with the problem solver.

3. Never let the problem solver get ahead of you. Whenever necessary, ask the problem solver to wait so you can check a procedure or computation etc. and catch up. If the problem solver is working too fast, slow her or him down so you can follow carefully, analytically, and accurately.

4. Check the problem solver at every step. Don't wait for his or her ultimate solution or answer. Check everything - each computation, diagram, procedure, etc. In the back of your mind, constantly ask yourself, "Is that right? Did I check that?" To promote precise thinking, have the thinker carefully define important terms and variables.

5. If you find an error, avoid correcting it. Point it out and try to get the problem solver to self-correct. If he or she gets stuck, ask questions to guide thinking in the right direction. If necessary, give suggestions, hints or partial answers; only give the answer as a last resort. Let the problem solver know that you are not trying to be difficult, you are trying to help him or her become an independent problem solver. If no amount of suggestion helps the thinker and you must give information or demonstrate a procedure, assign a similar task as follow up and require the thinker to do it aloud. Let students know that by doing these things, you're not being picky or critical, you're helping them to become more self-directed learners and to develop important academic knowledge, skills and attitudes.

The teacher observes each pair, monitors progress, and provides feedback on the process. To make sure listeners really do their job, periodically teachers should ask listeners to summarize the steps the problem solvers used. The following activities were suggested by Larcombe to help student pairs in elementary grades or remedial high school students learn to externalize their mathematical thought processes: 1) Students take turns describing the rules they use. 2) Students describe to each other how the parts fit together when doing a construction task. 3) Working with concrete objects at first, students can describe operations used when calculating,   and   4) One student must guess an object, a mathematical representation or a graphic based on another student's description.

There are several limitations of the Think Aloud method. Knowing how to use Think Aloud effectively includes the thinker's awareness of the types of difficulties that might be encountered (awareness) so that they can be prevented or at least overcome. The following factors may cause some student difficulties: belief that rote learning (memorization without understanding) is acceptable; lack of familiarity with the academic content, inadequate skills for executing the academic task; inadequate knowledge and skills of either or both the thinker and listener; the need for more practice in using the technique; the cultural background of the student, leading some students to be reluctant to reveal private thoughts; and that thinking and listening are faster than speaking.

Having this strategic metacognitive knowledge about the Think-Aloud technique makes students are more likely to use it because understanding the conditions and context of its use, i.e., why it's a useful strategy, makes it more meaningful, and because by having procedural knowledge, they know what methods to use when applying it in various situations.

SUMMARY AND CONCLUSION

Metacognition is an essential ingredient of self-directed and self-regulated learning. There are numerous forms of metacognition that can be used in academic learning and everyday life. With extensive and varied use, metacognitive strategies and knowledge can be refined and used automatically as needed in skilled performance. However, because not all students develop and use metacognition spontaneously, teachers need to provide students with explicit instruction in both metacognitive knowledge and metacognitive strategies. The most important point is that through practice of self-regulation, students can develop voluntary control over their own learning. Teachers can enhance students' awareness and control over learning by teaching them to reflect on how they think, learn, remember and perform academic tasks at all stages before, during and after task execution. Finally, and most importantly, teachers should repeatedly emphasize, and demonstrate through actions, that students are responsible for and can control their own outcomes in their education and their everyday lives.

HOPE J. HARTMAN
Department of Education
The City College of City University of New York
Department of Educational Psychology
Graduate School and University Center
City University of New York

REFERENCES

Alexander, P. (1995). Superimposing a situation-specific and domain-specific perspective on account of self-regulated learning. *Educational Psychologist.* 30(4) 189-193.

Anderson, J. (1988). Cognitive Styles and Multicultural Populations. *Journal of Teacher Education.* January/February. 2-9.

Anderson, V. & Hidi, S. (1988/1989). Teaching students to summarize. *Educational Leadership,* 46(4), 26-28.

Bandura, A. & Walters, R. H. (1963). *Social learning and personality development.* New York: Holt, Rinehart & Winston

Bransford, J. & Stein, B. (1984). *The IDEAL Problem Solver.* New York: W. H. Freeman & Co.

Cole, D., Rodriguez, J. & Cole, S. (1978) Focus of control in Mexicans and Chicanos: the Case of the Missing Fatalist. *Journal of Consulting and Clinical Psychology,* 46(6), 1323-1329.

Condravy, J. (1995). Tutors learn about learning: An assessment. *Research and Teaching in Developmental Education.* 11(2). 43-56.

Durkin, D. (1981). Reading comprehension instruction in five basal reader series. *Reading Research Quarterly,* 16, 515-544

Flavell, J. 1985. Cognitive Development. (2nd. Edition). Englewood Cliffs, NJ: Prentice Hall

Flavell, J. Green, F. L. & Flavell, E. R. (1995). Young children's knowledge about thinking. Monographs of the Society for Research in Child Development. 60(1) (Serial No. 243).

Garner, R. (1990). When children and adults do not use learning strategies: Toward a theory of settings. *Review of Educational Research.* 60(4). 517-529.

Garner, R. (1987). *Metacognition and Reading Comprehension.* Norwood, NJ: Ablex Publishing Corporation.

Hartman, H. (1996). Cooperative Learning Approaches to Mathematical Problem Solving. In: *The Art of Problem Solving : A Resource for the Mathematics Teacher.* Alfred S. Posamentier & Wolfgang Schulz (Eds.). Corwin Press, Inc. Thousand Oaks CA (1996) pp.401-430.

Hartman, H. (1995). Factors affecting students' metacognition about their academic performance. Presented at the annual meeting of the American Psychological Association. New York.

Hartman, H. (1994). From Reciprocal Teaching to Reciprocal Education. *Journal of Developmental Education.* 2-6, 8, 32.

Hartman, H. (1993). *Intelligent Tutoring,*, H & H Publishing Co.: Clearwater FL .

Hartman, H. (1990). Factors affecting the tutoring process. *Journal of Developmental Education.* 14(2). 2-4, 6.

Hartman, H., Everson, H., Tobias, S., & , A. (1996.) Self-Concept and metacognition in ethnic minorities: Predictions from the BACEIS model. *Urban Education.* 31(2), 222-238.

Hartman, H. & Sternberg, R. J. (1993). A Broad BACEIS for Improving Thinking , Instructional Science: An International Journal of Learning and Cognition, Vol. 21, No. 5. p. 401-425.

Hayes, J., Flower, L., Schriver, K, Stratman, J. & Carey, L (1987) Cognitive Processes in Revision. In S. Rosenberg.(Ed.) *Advances in applied psycholinguistics: Reading, writing and language processing.* Cambridge, UK

Hostetter, S. A. (1994). Metacognitive Tutoring: Theory and Practice. National Tutoring AssociationNewsletter. 1. 3-4.

Jones, B. F., Amiran, M. R. Katims (1985). Teaching Cognitive Strategies and Text Strategies. In J. Segal, S. Chipman, & R. Glaser (Eds.) Thinking and Learning Skills Relating Instruction to Research. Vol. 1. Hillsdale, NJ: Erlbaum

Jones, B.F., Pierce, J. & Hunter, B. (1988/89). Teaching students to construct graphic representations. Educational Leadership. December/January. 27-31.

Kumea-Shorter, D., (1976). Towards developing Black activists: The relationship of beliefs in individual and collective internal-external control. *Journal of Black Psychology*, 3(1) 59-70.

Lao, R., Chuang, C. & Yang, K. (1977) Focus of Control and Chineese College Students. *Journal of Cross-Cultural Psychology*. 8()3), 299-313.

Maxwell, M. (1993). Are the skills we are teaching obsolete?: A review of recent research in reading and study skills. Fourteenth Institute for Learning Assistance Directors and Professionals. January. Tucson, AZ.

Meichenbaum, D. & Biemiller (1998). Nurturing Independent Learners: Helping studentsake charge of their learning. Cambridge, MA: Brookline Books

Meichenbaum, D. (1978). Teaching children self-control. In B. Kahey & A. Kazdin (Eds.) Advances in child clinical psychology (Vol. 2). New York, Plenum Press.

Mestre, J. (1989). The impact of culture on learning math. College Prep. Vol. 5: Counseling students for higher education. New York: The College Board, Inc.

Novak, J. D. (1998). Learning, Creating and Using Knowledge: Concept maps as facilitative tools in schools and corporations. Mahwah, NJ: Erlbaum

Palincsar, A. & Brown, A. (1984). Reciprocal Teaching of Comprehension Fostering and Monitoring Activities. Cognition and Instruction. 1:117-175.

Palincsar, A., Ransom, K. & Derber, S. (1988/1989). Collaborative Research and Development of Reciprocal Teaching. Educational Leadership. 37-40 .

Pelley, J. W. & Dalley, B. K. (1997). Successful Types for Medical Students. Lubbock, TX: Texas Tech University Extended Learning.

Prohaska, V. (1994). "I Know I'll Get an A": Confident Overestimation of Final Course Grades.

Prohaska, V. & Maraj, F. (1995). Low and medium ability students confidently overestimate all their grades. Presented at the Seventh Annual Convention of the American Psychological Society. New York.

Rings, S. & Sheets, R. (1991). Student development and metacognition: Foundations of tutor training. Journal of Developmental Education, 15(1), 30-32.

Rosenshine, B. & Meister, C. (1994). Reciprocal Teaching: A Review of Research. Review of Educational Research. 64(4). 479-530.

Rosenshine, B. & Meister, C. (1992). The use of scaffolds for teaching higher-level cognitive strategies. Educational Leadership. April. 26-33.

Schunk, D. (1991). Self-efficacy and academic motivation. Educational Psychologist. 26. 207-231.

Shavelson, R. & Bolus, R. (1982). Self-concept:The interplay of theory and methods. Psychology. 74, 3-17.

Shipman, S., & Shipman, V. (1985). Cognitive styles: Some conceptual, methodological and applied issues. Review of Research in Education, 12, 229-291.

Skaalvik, E. & Rankin, R. (1990). Math, verbal and general academic self-concepts: The internal/external frame of reference model and gender differences in self-concept structure. Journal of Educational Psychology, 82(3) 546-554.

Tracey, T. & Sedlacek, W. (1987). Prediction of college graduation using noncognitive variables by race. Assessments for minority populations: Traditional and nontraditional approaches. (Special Issue) Measurement and Evaluation in Counseling and Development, 19(4) 177-184.

Vygotsky, L. (1978). Mind in society: The development of higher psychological processes. Cambridge: MA: Harvard University Press.

Wagner, R. & Sternberg, R. J. 1984). Alternative conceptions of intelligence and their implications for education. Review of Educational Research. 54 (2) 179-223.

Wong, B. (1985). Self-questioning instructional research: A review. Review of Educational Research. 55(2) 227-268.

Woolfolk, A. (1998). Educational Psychology. Boston: Allyn and Bacon.

Zimmerman, B. (1995). Self-regulation involves more than metacognition: A Social Cognitive Perspective. *Educational Psychologist*.30(4) 217-221.

Zimmerman, B. (1990). Self-regulated learning and academic achievement: an overview. *Educational Psychologist*. 24(1) 3-17.

APPENDIX

Sample Error Analyses

Reading Comprehension

Test Item:
The content in paragraph 3 indicates that the writer's belief was:
a). The first stage of the civil rights movement was a failure.
b) Supreme Court decisions do not have as much influence on society as actions by the Congress.
c). Social movements are able to influence the political process.
d). The costs of civil disobedience sometimes outweigh the benefits.

Error Analysis of Item
1. What I got wrong and what the right answer is.
I thought the answer was "a ", but now I know the answer is "c".

2. Why I got it wrong.
I confused my beliefs with what was actually in the text. I though of what the author called "the first stage" as a failure, but the author didn't say or imply that. The author was really trying to make a different point.

3. How I will remember this and prevent future similar mistakes.
My teacher taught me to ask myself questions about what I read. So I'll ask myself a question like, "Is this what I think or is this what the author is really saying?"

Math problem
Subtract
        2668
      -1629
        1049

1. What I got wrong and what the right answer is.
The answer 1049 is wrong. The correct answer is 1039.

2. Why I got it wrong.
I forgot to change the "6" in the tens column to a "5" after borrowing to subtract 9 from 18 in the ones column.

3. How I will prevent mistakes like this in the future.
From now on, instead of trying to remember I borrowed in my head, I will cross out the number I borrowed from, and write the new number above it.

For example,

$$\begin{array}{r} 5 \\ 2668 \\ -\ \underline{1629} \\ 1039 \end{array}$$

Essay

1. What I got wrong and what I should have done.
There were two major things wrong with my paper. First, I didn't elaborate on my ideas enough. I should have developed the ideas in my topic sentences more and given more examples to support my points.
The paper was not as well organized as it should have been. In some paragraphs the ideas I started off with were not related to later ideas in the paragraph. Then in the next paragraph I would pick up on ideas I started in the previous one. I should have followed through with related ideas in the same paragraph instead of jumping around.

2. Why I did this wrong.
I was so concerned about coming up with ideas and getting them on paper that I didn't pay that much attention to where the ideas were and how organized it was.

3. How I will prevent similar mistakes in the future.
I'm going to make a checklist to use when I revise and proofread my papers. One thing on the checklist will be: Development of Ideas. Another thing will be organization of ideas.

Error Analysis of Research Report

1. What I got wrong and what I should have done.
I lost credit because I did not cite the sources of my information in the text. I should have put the authors' names and publication years at the end of the information I got from them.

2. Why I did this wrong.
In high school we didn't have to do this so I didn't know it was the correct procedure. I didn't understand "plagiarism". I also didn't read the assignment sheet carefully enough to see this was required. I just read it to get a general idea of what was expected and missed some details.

3. How I will prevent similar mistakes in the future.
I'll remember to cite my sources in the text because I'll think about how I would feel if someone took my ideas and didn't give me credit for them.
I'll also read my assignment sheets more carefully, looking for specific details instead of general ideas.

Biology test item

Which of the following is correct for the **resting** membrane potential of a typical neuron?
a) It is negative outside compared to inside.
b) It depends on high permeability of the membrane to sodium and potassium ions.
c) It carries impulses from one region to another.
d). It results from the unequal distribution of ions across the membrane.

Error Analysis of Item
1. What I got wrong and what the right answer is.
I thought the answer was "b", but now I know the answer is "d".

2. Why I got it wrong.
I know there was high permeability to potassium but I forgot it was impermeable to sodium.

3. How I will remember this and prevent future similar mistakes.
I'll remember that the resting potential of a neuron depends upon the **imbalance.** The unequal distribution of ions results from the difference in permeability between sodium and potassium. The membrane is highly permeable to potassium, but it is impermeable to sodium. This causes it to be negative inside compared to the outside.
I'll also try to use the process of elimination more so I can rule out some of the answer choices.

CHAPTER 4

THE ABILITY TO ESTIMATE KNOWLEDGE AND PERFORMANCE IN COLLEGE: A METACOGNITIVE ANALYSIS

HOWARD T. EVERSON   SIGMUND TOBIAS

ABSTRACT. While in college students learn a great deal of new knowledge, and over time successful students learn to update their knowledge as new concepts, facts, and procedures are acquired. The metacognitive ability to accurately estimate one's knowledge was hypothesized to be related to academic achievement in college. The two studies reported in this paper examined the relationship between a measure of metacognitive word knowledge (the KMA) and performance in college. Using undergraduate GPA in a number of academic domains as criterion measures, this research provides support for the validity of the KMA as a predictor of success in college. Suggestions for further research relating performance on the KMA to learning in complex domains are offered.

Metacognition has been defined as the ability to monitor, evaluate, and make plans for one's learning (Flavell, 1979; Brown 1980). The literature in this area identifies two distinct aspects of metacognition, knowledge about cognition and the regulation of cognition, with both viewed as important for effective learning (Brown, 1987; Garner and Alexander, 1989; Jacobs and Paris, 1987). Indeed, researchers have reported differences in metacognitive abilities between capable and less capable learners (see, for example, Baker, 1989; Brown and Campione, 1986; Garner and Alexander, 1989; Pressley and Ghatala, 1990). In general, students with effective metacognitive skills accurately estimate their knowledge in a variety of domains, monitor their on-going learning, update their knowledge, and develop effective plans for new learning. Though widely recognized as important, assessing individual differences in metacognition has proven to be both difficult and time consuming (O'Neil, 1991; Schwartz and Metcalfe, 1994), and remains an obstacle to the advance of research.

Typically, assessments of metacognition rely either on inferences from classroom performance, or ratings based on interviews of students who are questioned about their knowledge and cognitive processing strategies, or on analyses of "think-aloud" protocols (Meichenbaum, Burland, Gruson, & Cameron, 1985). Recently, a number of self-report measures of metacognition (Everson,

69

H.J. Hartman (ed.), Metacognition in Learning and Instruction, 69–83.

Hartman, Tobias, and Gourgey, 1991; O'Neil, 1991; Pintrich, Smith, Garcia, and McKeachie, 1991; Schraw and Dennison, 1994) have been developed. For the most part, these measures are more efficiently administered and scored than "think aloud" protocols. Unfortunately, the use of self-report measures raises questions of validity (see Schwartz and Metcalfe (1994) for a review of these methodological issues). In light of these concerns, it is not surprising that little research has been conducted on the metacognitive processes related to learning in adults, looking, for example, at those in college or in advanced instructional or training programs, where instructional times less easily accommodates research. Thus, more efficient measures of metacognition are needed not merely to satisfy psychometric standards (although important), but because they would permit research in settings where instructional time is less flexible, such as college classrooms and training courses. In this paper we introduce a method for assessing students' knowledge monitoring ability (referred to as the KMA) and relate those scores to their learning and performance in college. Before presenting our results, it may be useful to establish the context for investigating the relationship between metacognition and complex learning in environments such as college and industry-based training courses.

METACOGNITION AND LEARNING

In college students learn a great deal of new knowledge, and are faced, at times, with classroom and laboratory situations that require them to learn material and apply problem solving skills in new and innovative ways. The literature on human metacognition makes a compelling case for its importance in these learning and training environments (Bjork, 1994; Davidson, Deuser, and Sternberg, 1994). Accurate monitoring of new learning enables students with effective metacognitive strategies to concentrate on new content and adjust their learning goals. In college classrooms or advanced training programs, for example, the learner usually has to master a great deal of new knowledge in a limited amount of time. Moreover, learning in classrooms or other structured training environments is often dynamic, with knowledge and information being acquired and updated frequently. Clearly, those who accurately distinguish between what they have already mastered and what is yet to be learned have an advantage in these situations, since they can be more strategic and effective learners. Yet many students have ineffective metacognitive strategies. It is important, therefore, to evaluate students' metacognitive abilities and target instruction to the development of these key learning strategies.

Monitoring Knowledge

Given the premise outlined above, we assumed that knowledge monitoring accuracy, an ability presumably involved in the regulation of cognition, would be related to learning in complex environments and reflected in indices such as students' grades in college. Thus, we developed a technique for assessing this metacognitive dimension that conjointly evaluates students' self-reports of their knowledge in a particular domain (e.g., verbal) and their performance on an objective measure of knowledge in that domain (see, for example, Tobias et al., 1991; Everson, Smodlaka, and Tobias, 1994; Tobias and Everson, 1996; Tobias and Everson, in press). The basic strategy is to assess knowledge monitoring by evaluating the differences between students' estimates of their knowledge in a particular domain (both procedural and declarative) and their actual knowledge as determined by performance on a test. In the prototypical KMA, students are asked to estimate their knowledge (e.g., in the verbal domain they identify words they know or do not know from a word list, or in mathematics its is problems they expect they can solve) and these estimates are contrasted with their performance on a standardized test containing many of the same words or math problems. Differences between students' estimates and their test performance provide an index of knowledge monitoring ability. This method is similar to methods used in research on metamemory (Nelson and Narens, 1990), reading comprehension (Glenberg, Sanocki, Epstein and Morris, 1987), and psychophysics (Green and Swets. 1966). A brief description of our use of the KMA in an earlier study (Everson et al., 1994) serves as an illustration.

In an effort to understand better the relationship between metacognition and reading comprehension, the KMA was administered to 169 college students. Each was given a list of 33 words and asked to indicate the words they knew and did not know. This was followed by a vocabulary test based on the same words. The KMA generated four scores, including estimates that the word was: a) known and correctly identified on a subsequent vocabulary test [+ +]; b) known, yet incorrectly identified on the test [+ -]; c) unknown, yet correctly identified on the test [- +]; and d) unknown and incorrectly identified on the test [- -]. Within this framework the [+ +] and the [- -] scores represented accurate metacognitive estimates of vocabulary word knowledge, while the two other measures [+ -, and - +] represented inaccurate knowledge monitoring estimates. The results indicated that college students' accurate metacognitive judgments, both the + + and - - scores, were positively correlated with their scores on a standardized measure of reading comprehension (i.e., the Descriptive Test of Language Skills, 1979), E = .46 and -.43, respectively. Encouraged by these findings, we adapted the KMA for use in an extensive program of research (Tobias and Everson, 1996; Tobias and Everson, in press).

In light of the importance of verbal reasoning and general word knowledge in a variety of college courses such as English, humanities, and the social and behavioral sciences, we expected KMA scores in the verbal domain to be related to grades in those courses. Thus, the purpose of the two studies reported below was to examine the empirical relationships between and among the KMA scores and indices of learning in college, i.e., grade point averages in various courses, and to investigate whether KMA scores would at all predictive of achievement in courses requiring general verbal abilities.

STUDY I

Participants

The sample consisted of 139 students attending a large urban university, though only 84 participants completed all the materials during two sessions. A portion of the sample (11%) were students seeking a college degree in nursing. The nursing students (N = 47; N = 33 with complete data) were recruited from a class serving as the orientation course in a nursing program. The remainder (N = 92; N = 51 with complete data) were recruited from a freshman orientation course.

Materials

A revised version of the KMA developed in prior research (Everson et al., 1994) was used in this study. In addition to minor editorial revisions of the expository text, a narrative version of the passage was also developed in order to examine the effect of situational interest on metacognition. A total of 38 words was defined in the revised versions of the text, 19 words were explicitly defined (e.g., "Coronary or heart disease...."), and another 19 received implicit definitions (e.g., "Epidemiologist who have compared the prevalence of heart disease in the United States and in other countries..."). Explicit or implicit definitions were determined by two independent judges who rated all words. When there was any disagreement about a particular word, the judges conferred and the passage was modified to eliminate the disagreement. The word list and vocabulary task were also modified to contain an equal number of explicitly and implicitly defined words. A multiple choice vocabulary test was developed, containing the correct choice and three distractors for the 38 items on the word list.

Procedures

The KMA word list and vocabulary test, coefficient alpha = .80 (Cronbach, 1951), were administered first in a group session. The two versions of the text were then randomly assigned to students in a second experimental session, followed by a re-administration of the KMA word list and vocabulary test. In each instance, the experimental materials were administered during class in the presence of the instructors.

Results and Discussion

The correlations between total score on both administrations of the vocabulary test, based on the 84 students who completed the test on both administrations, was $r =$ .75. (This correlation, however, should not be interpreted as an estimate of test-retest reliability (Crocker and Algina, 1986), because students read the text passage, from which the meaning of the words could be inferred, immediately before the second administration of the vocabulary test.) Students' estimated word knowledge and performance on the vocabulary test were determined for both administrations. Two scores were computed for each administration: the total number of correct (words in the [+ +] and [- -] categories) and incorrect estimates (words in the [+ -] and the [- +] categories). Preliminary analyses revealed no differences between students assigned to the expository or narrative text versions, or between ex- and implicitly defined words. Therefore the data for both text versions and both types of words were pooled in subsequent analyses. For this sample of 84 students, the mean total score increased from 23.3 (SD = 6.0) for the first vocabulary test to 26.0 (SD = 6.6) for the second, t (83) = 5.53, $p < .001$. Thus, students clearly learned the meanings of some words once they read the passage and updated their word knowledge. The correlations between the correct and incorrect estimates on both administrations of the words and students' GPA in English, humanities, sciences, social sciences, and combined GPA were computed and are shown in Table 1.

Since 92 participants were freshmen in their initial term of college, the overall GPA for this group was based on an average of only 12.1 credits (SD = 5.6), whereas the nursing students had a mean of 56.4 credits (SD = 28.3). Therefore, the correlations are presented for each group separately, as well as for the total sample. Table 1 also shows the correlations for metacognitive estimates and vocabulary raw scores, (i.e., the number correct on the vocabulary test), separately. Finally, the different number of cases in the various cells of Table 1 should also be noted. The correlations shown in Table 1 are generally positive and frequently significant, ranging in magnitude from low to moderate. The results support the concurrent validity of the KMA with respect to its relationship to learning in college. As expected, relationships between knowledge monitoring scores and GPA in English were generally highest, followed by humanities courses and the combined GPA, while correlations with social science and science GPAs were generally lower. The largely non-significant relationships with social science courses were surprising, since it had been assumed that these courses usually contained material and vocabulary which was less technical or unfamiliar to students than natural science courses. Perhaps grades in these courses, like those in the natural sciences, reflected greater domain specific knowledge than found in the English and humanities courses.

Table 1
Correlations between KMA Scores, Vocabulary Raw Scores, and GPA in Different Academic Areas.

Variables

| Group | | *Administration 1* | | | *Administration 2* | |
		Correct *Estimate*	*Raw* *Score*		*Correct* *Estimate*	*Raw* *Score*
Total GPA	N	r	r	N	r	r
Total	101	.20*	.01	94	.09	-.00
Freshmen	65	.09	-.25	61	-.10	-.21
Nurses	36	.28*	-.37*	33	.19	.17
English GPA						
Total	72	.30**	.19	63	.19	.05
Freshmen	53	.31**	.10	48	.00	.16
Nurses	19	.25	.33	19	.45*	.44*
Humanities GPA						
Total	82	.26**	.04	74	.13	.00
Freshmen	52	.12	-.21	46	-.11	.22
Nurses	30	.48*°	.40*	28	.35	.24
Science GPA						
Total	65	.18	-.01	63	.03	-.07
Freshmen	28	.11	-.30	27	-.28	-.47
Nurses	37	.26	-.42*	36	.18	.26
Social Science GPA						
Total	64	.18	.26	63	.24*	-.26*
Freshmen	26	.15	.10	29	.14	.18
Nurses	38	.09	-.31	34	.14	.10

* $p < .05$
** $p < .01$

The significance of the correlations reported in Table 1 varies widely, probably as a function of at least three factors. First, the number of cases in each cell differs due to students' absence from either administration of the materials, leading to variability in the predictors. Second, it is well known that college grades are often unreliable (Werts, Linn & Joreskog, 1978; Willingham, Lewis, Morgan, & Ramist, 1990), reducing the magnitude of any correlations with them. Third, students completed a varying number of courses in each area, thus GPAs may have been based on one, or a few courses in some fields reducing the stability of the criterion. The reliability of the grades may have been reduced further by three factors: a) students took dissimilar courses in each of the areas shown in Table 1; b) when similar courses were taken they were taught by different instructors; and c) the differences in students' major fields of study. As expected, the correlations between KMA scores and grades in English were generally higher, and more frequently significant, than those of any other subject. The findings indicate that the metacognitive knowledge monitoring scores are related to students' ability to learn materials from somewhat different domains than the ones on which the KMA was based.

It was assumed in this study that having the chance to update one's word knowledge before estimating it would be more similar to students' learning in their classes than merely estimating prior word knowledge. Therefore, relationships with grades were expected to be higher for the second administration than from the first. The findings did not support these expectations. While the increase in vocabulary score after reading the text was statistically significant. it indicated that less than three new words were learned from the text passage. Perhaps such modest acquisition was dissimilar to the amount of learning in college courses, leading to lower relationships with metacognitive monitoring scores on the second administration of the procedure. Similarities between the knowledge monitoring task and school learning might have increased if students were instructed to study the passage more intensely, or asked to pay special attention while reading words they had previously seen on the vocabulary test. Such instructions may have increased the correlations with GPA for the second administration. It remains for further research to explore that possibility.

The results shown in Table 1 also indicate that the correlations with number correct on the vocabulary scores were generally similar to the relationships with correct knowledge monitoring estimates. Due to the varying Ns in the different cells, the differences in the correlations were examined with a test developed by Hotelling (Tukey, 1977). For the correlations with GPA based on the both administrations, using the total group, the KMA scores were higher seven times (one difference was significant at $p < .05$), while the correlations based on raw scores were higher three times (none significantly so). For freshmen, the correlations with the KMA scores were higher twice, but not significantly so, while correlations with raw vocabulary score were higher eight times (two were significant at $p < .05$) Finally, for nursing students.~ correlations with scores were higher five times (none significant), while relationships based on raw vocabulary scores were higher five times (one significant $p < .05$). In contrast to the findings from earlier studies (Tobias, et al., 1991; Tobias & Everson, 1996; Tobias & Everson, in press), the KMA scores appeared to add little independent variance to the relationship with grades beyond that accounted for by the number correct on the vocabulary test.

STUDY II

The preceding study was concerned with the issue of concurrent validity and examined the correlations of KMA with students' prior learning in college. To extend this work we undertook a second study that investigated the KMA's predictive validity, by examining whether the metacognitive estimates would predict how well entering students would perform academically during their first year of college.

Procedures and Participants

The materials used in Study II were identical to those used in Study I. They were administered while students attended a pre-freshman skills program before beginning their first semester of college. Achievement was determined by obtaining students' grade point averages (GPAs) at the end of their first year of college in the same subjects examined in the prior study: English, humanities, sciences, and social sciences, as well as the combined GPA. The sample consisted of 115 students (59 female) participating in a skills program intended for students considered at risk of doing poorly in their first year of college.

Each participant completed all of the study materials and took similar types of courses. High- and low-achievement groups were created by dividing students at the GPA median for the different academic areas and for the combined GPA. Then differences in knowledge monitoring ability between the groups were examined. Mixed between- and within-subjects analyses of variance were computed to determine the significance of the differences in estimates of word knowledge between groups above and below the GPA median. At the conclusion of the freshman year, it was determined that 95 of the 115 original participants had completed some courses at the college.

Results and Discussion

The number of correct estimates students made of their word knowledge was determined. As in the prior studies, correct estimates were defined, by combining the [++] and [- -] categories. Preliminary analyses again indicated that there were no differences between the results obtained for the expository and narrative passages, nor between the words defined explicitly or implicitly. Therefore, these data were pooled for the succeeding analyses.

ANOVA indicated that, as expected, students above the median GPA (N = 48) made significantly more accurate overall estimates of their knowledge (M_H = 49.2), F (1, 93) = 6.42, $p < .05$, on both administrations than those below the median (N = 47, M_L = 45.8,); the size of that effect, determined by eta² (η^2; Kennedy, 1970) was .065. Also as expected, there was a significant difference between the mean of the first administration (M_1 = 22.9) and the mean of the second administration (M_2 = 24.5) of the word list and vocabulary test, F (1,93) = 14.95, $p<.01$, η^2 = .138, though there was no interaction between these variables. A similar analysis was computed using the number right on both administrations of the vocabulary test as the dependent variable. That analysis indicated that the mean differences between the high (M_H = 43.2) and low GPA groups (M_L = 39.3) on the vocabulary test were not significant, F (1, 93) = 2.73, η^2 = .029, while the differences between the means of the first (M_1 = 17.7) and second administrations (M_2 = 24.5) were highly significant F (1, 93) = 198.04, $p < .001$, η^2 12 = .68. Again, there were no interactions between the variables.

High- and low-achieving groups in English, humanities, science, and social science courses were also identified by dividing the students at the median GPA for each of these subject areas and examining the significance of differences on the number of correct estimates of word knowledge. In English, the overall differences in the accuracy of the estimates between students above (M_{EH} = 48.9) and below the median (M_{EL}= 45~4) were significant, F (1, 82) = 6.18, $p = .02$; η^2 = .07, as were the differences between the first (M_{E1} = 45.6) and second administrations (M_{E2} = 48.7), F (1, 82) = 1 1.92; $p < .01$; η^2 = 127). Furthermore, there was an interaction between groups and administrations, F (1, 82) = 4.41, $p < .05$; η^2 = .051. The interaction, as shown in Figure 1, suggests that while the accuracy of both groups' estimates of known and unknown words increased from the first to the second administration, higher achieving students made greater gains.

A similar analysis was computed for number correct on both vocabulary test administrations. The finding indicated that the difference between the high- (M_{EH} = 42.9) and low-GPA groups (M_{EL}= 38.9), F (1, 82) = 5.43; η^2 = .062, was slightly smaller than that determined when the KMA scores were used, but there was a stronger effect for differences between the first (M_{E1} = 18.0) and second administrations (M_{E2} = 23.6), F (1, 82) = 169, $p < .001$; η^2 =.673; there was no evidence for interaction in these results.

Similar analyses were made for students above and below the median in humanities courses (Art, History, Music, Philosophy, World Civilization, World Humanities, and World Arts). Differences between the means of the high (M_{HH} =

49.4) and low humanities GPA groups (M_{HL} = 45.3) were also significant, F (1, 81) = 7.96, p < .01; η^2 =.089, as were the differences between first (M_{H1}= 23.0) and second administrations (M_{H2} =24.5), F (1, 81) = 9.94, p < .001; η^2 =.109; there was no interaction. The same type of analysis was also computed for number correct on the first and second vocabulary tests; again it revealed somewhat smaller differences between the high- (M_{HH} = 43.1) and low GPA groups (M_{HL} = 39.0), F (1, 81) = 4.18, p < .05; η^2= .049) and larger differences between the first (M_{H1} = 17.8) and second administration (M_{H2} = 23.4), F (1, 81) = 179.2, p < .001; η^2= .689, than the results for knowledge monitoring scores. There were no significant differences between the science or the social science GPA groups using either the knowledge monitoring scores or the vocabulary raw scores.

The relationships between metacognitive scores and GPA were generally similar to those reported in Study I, supporting the predictive validity of the KMA scores. In contrast with Study I, in which both the KMA scores and the vocabulary raw scores had fairly similar patterns of relationship, the metacognitive scores had a significant effect on overall GPA, whereas the raw scores did not. Furthermore, the KMA scores accounted for more variance between groups than did the number correct on the vocabulary test in two of three other comparisons, supporting the construct validity of the procedure.

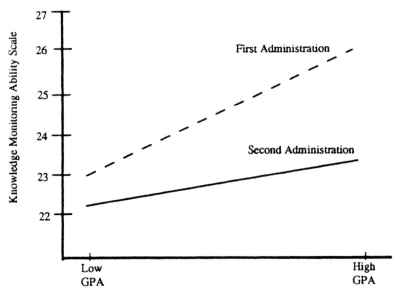

Figure 1. Interaction of English GPA groups, correct KMA estimates, and test administrations.

GENERAL DISCUSSION

The findings of the two studies summarized above provide support for the validity of the KMA, both in terms of the construct of metacognitive knowledge monitoring and the predictive validity of the assessment procedure. The results suggest that the procedure has some generality across different samples of college students, various types of content, as well as different types of vocabulary. In general, the KMA scores seemed to more successfully differentiate the capable students, whose grades were above the median, from those less able than did the raw vocabulary scores, replicating the findings reported elsewhere (Tobias and Everson, 1996). The knowledge monitoring scores accounted for anywhere from 1 to 4 percent more variance than did similar analyses using the raw vocabulary scores.

It was also interesting that the analysis of differences in the raw vocabulary scores between the first and second vocabulary test administrations always accounted for substantially more variance than did a similar analysis based on knowledge monitoring scores. The latter finding is reasonable and supports the construct validity of the KMA in that most students learned some new words from reading the passage, though their knowledge monitoring ability was not equally enhanced. However, it should be noted that the results for the English grades indicated that there were greater increases in knowledge monitoring ability for capable students than for their less able peers (see Figure 1). These findings suggest that while all students increased both their demonstrated knowledge of vocabulary and their knowledge monitoring ability from the first to second administration, the increases monitoring ability were greater for more capable students (i.e., those whose English grades were above the median). Apparently there was a greater degree of improvement in such students' metacognitive skills than in those of their less able colleagues.

Research has indicated that vocabulary test scores are one of the most powerful predictors of school learning (Breland, Jones' & Jenkins, 1994; Just & Carpenter, 1987). KMA scores combine both students' estimates of what they know and their actual knowledge. Thus, the + + score is a composite of both actual word knowledge, determined by the raw score on the vocabulary test, and the students' correct estimates of that knowledge. Each of the studies described above examined whether the KMA estimates contributed independent information beyond that accounted for by students' actual word knowledge. Operationally, this question was analyzed by comparing the variance accounted for by correct estimates (+ + and - - combined) with the variance accounted for using only the number correct on the vocabulary test (++ and -+). In general, the effect size for actual word knowledge alone was greater (about 13%) than for the knowledge estimates. It is not unusual for knowledge of vocabulary, even in unrelated academic domains, to be an important predictor of students' grades in college. Vocabulary scores based on words not directly related to a particular course or curriculum have been shown to be powerful predictors of all types of classroom learning (Breland, et al., 1994; Just and Carpenter, 1987). Further research is obviously needed to clarify these effects.

Learning in complex domains such as science and engineering, or making diagnoses in medicine or other fields, often requires that students bring substantial amounts of prior learning to bear in order to understand and acquire new knowledge or solve problems. Some prior learning may be recalled imperfectly, or may never have been completely mastered during initial acquisition. Students who can accurately distinguish between what they know and do not know should be at an advantage while working in such domains, since they are more likely to review and try to relearn imperfectly mastered materials needed for particular tasks, compared with those who are less accurate in estimating their own knowledge. In view of the fact that the existing knowledge monitoring scores accounted for little variance in science grades, it would be useful to develop a KMA procedure in the science domain to determine its relationship to achievement in science and engineering.

Further research is also needed to determine the relationships between the KMA procedure and self-report measures of metacognition, study skills, and self-regulated learning. These constructs have some similarity to the KMA procedure and positive relationships should be obtained. Finally, the relationship between knowledge monitoring ability and measures of intelligence should be investigated. Sternberg (1991) has suggested that metacognition should be a component of intelligence tests; presumably those who consider metacognition an executive process (Borkowski, Chan, and Muthukrishna, in press) would also agree with that recommendation. Research findings (Schraw, in press) indicate that academically able students have higher knowledge monitoring ability than those less able. Therefore, positive relationships between the KMA procedure and measures of general intellectual ability may be expected.

Several factors are likely to have reduced the magnitude of the effects and the generalizability of the results to other groups of college students. As in the first study, the participants in the pre-freshmen program were considered to be at risk for poor performance in college. This may have reduced the range of achievement for the sample and, therefore, may also have reduced the differences in the knowledge monitoring ability between the groups. Furthermore, even though data were not collected in classes of the pre-freshmen skills program devoted exclusively to English as a Second Language (ESL), some of the students were enrolled in both ESL and other courses, and thus ended up as part of the sample. The presence of non-native English speakers could also have reduced group differences in this study. Further research limited to native English speakers may reduce the variability among participants and narrow the group differences.

It should be noted that many of the students in this sample took less than a full-time schedule of courses. That fact is likely to have decreased the reliability of the GPA, because it was based on fewer courses and credits than is usually the case after a year of college. This may also limit the generalizability of the results to other groups, in addition to reducing the magnitude of the findings by decreasing the potential variability of the GPA. Therefore, in order to increase both the reliability and variability of the criterion, it would be useful to investigate the predictive validity of the KMA procedure for a large number of full-time students.

HOWARD T. EVERSON
The College Board, New York

SIGMUND TOBIAS
Educational Psychology
Fordham University

REFERENCES

Baker, L. (1989). Metacognition, comprehension monitoring, and the adult reader. *Educational Psychology Review*, 1, 3-38.

Bjork, R.A. (1994). Memory and metamemory considerations in the training of human beings. In J. Metcalfe & A.P. Shimamura (Eds.), *Metacognition: Knowing about knowing* (p . 185-206). Cambridge, MA: MIT Press.

Borkowski, JG, Chan, LCS, & Muthukrishna, N. (in press). A process-oriented model of metacognition and executive functioning. In G.. Schraw (Ed.), *Issues in the measurement of metacognition*. Lincoln, NE: Buros Institute / The University of Nebraska Press

Breland, H., Jones, R. J., & Jenkins, L. (1994). *The College Board vocabulary study*. College Board Report No. 94-4. NY: The College Board.

Brown, A. L. (1980). Metacognitive development and reading. In R. J. Spiro, B.B. Bruce, & W.F. Brewer (Eds.) *Theoretical issues in reading comprehension* (pp. 453-481). Hillsdale, NJ: Erlbaum Associates.

Brown, A. L. (1987). Metacognition, executive control, self-regulation, and other more mysterious mechanisms. In F. Weinart & R. Kluwe (Eds.), *Metacognition. motivation. and understanding* (pp. 65-116). Hillsdale, NJ: Erlbaum Associates.

Brown, A .L. & Campione, J. C. (1986). Psychological theory and the study of learning disabilities. *American Psychologist*, 14, 1059-1068.

Crocker, L., & Algina, J. (1986). *Introduction to classical and modern test theory*. Orlando, FL: Holt, Rinehart and Winston.

Cronbach, L. J. (1951). Coefficient alpha and the internal structure of tests. *Psychometrika*, 16, 297-334.

Davidson, J. E., Deuser, R., & Sternberg, R. J. (1994). The role of metacognition in problem solving. In J. Metcalfe & A.P. Shimamura (Eds.), *Metacognition: Knowing about knowing (*pp. 207-226). Cambridge, MA: MIT Press.

Descriptive Test of Language Skills. (1979). Princeton, NJ: The College Entrance Examination Board

Everson, H.T., Hartman, H., Tobias, S., & Gourgey, A. (1991, June). A metacognitive reading strategies scale-Preliminary validation evidence. Paper presented at the annual convention of the American Psychological Society, Washington, DC.

Everson, H.T., Smodlaka, I., & Tobias, S. (1994). Exploring the relationship of test anxiety and metacognition on reading test performance: A cognitive analysis. *Anxiety, Stress, and Coping*, 7, 85-96.

Flavell, J. (1979). Metacognition and cognitive monitoring: A new era of cognitive developmental inquiry. *American Psychologist*, 34, 906-911.

Garner, R., & Alexander, P. (1989). Metacognition: Answered and unanswered questions. *Educational Psychologist*, 24, 143- 158.

Glenberg, A.M., Sanocki, T., Epstein, W., & Morris, C. (1987). Enhancing calibration of comprehension. *Journal of Experimental Psychology: General*, 116 (2), 119-136.

Green, D. M., & Swets, J. A., (1966). *Signal detection theory and psychophysics*. NY: Wiley.

Jacobs, J. E., & Paris, S.G. (1987). Children's metacognition about reading: Issues in definition, measurement, and instruction. *Educational Psychologist*, 22, 255-278.

Just, M.A., & Carpenter, P.A. (1987). *The psychology of reading and language comprehension*. Needham Heights, MA: Allyn & Bacon.

Kennedy, J. J. (1970). The eta coefficient in complex ANOVA designs. *Educational and Psychological Measurement*, 30, 885-889.

Meichenbaum, D., Burland, S., Gruson, L., & Cameron, R. (1985). Metacognitive assessment. In S. R. Yussen (Ed.), *The growth of reflection in children* (pp. 3-27). NY: Academic Press.

Nelson, T.O., & Narens, L. (1990). Metamemory: A theoretical framework and new findings. In G. Bower (Ed.), *The Psychology of learning and motivation* (Vol. 26) NY: Academic Press.

O'Neil, H..F.(1991, August). *Metacognition: Teaching and Measurement*. Paper presented at the annual convention of the American Psychological Association, San Francisco, CA.

Pintrich, P.R., Smith, D.A., Garcia, T., & McKeachie, W..J. (1991). *A manual for the use of the Motivated Strategies for Learning Questionnaire (MSLQ!)*Ann Arbor, MI: National Center for Research to Improve Postsecondary Teaching and Learning.

Pressley, M., & Ghatala, ES (1990). Self-regulated learning: Monitoring learning from text. *Educational Psychologist*, 25, 19-33.

Schraw, G. (in press). *Issues in the measurement of metacognition*. Lincoln, NE: Buros Institute/ The University of Nebraska Press.

Schraw, G., & Dennison, R.S. (1994). Assessing metacognitive awareness. Contemporary Educational Psychology, 19, 460-475.

Schwartz, B.L., & Metcalfe, J. (1994). Methodological problems and pitfalls in the study of human metacognition. In J. Metcalfe & A.P. Shimamura (Eds.), *Metacognition: Knowing about knowing* (pp. 93- 114). Cambridge, MA: MIT Press.

Sternberg, R..A (1991). Toward better intelligence tests. In M.C. Wittrock & E..L. Baker (Eds.), *Testing and cognition* (pp. 31-39). Englewood Cliffs, NJ: Prentice-Hall.

Tobias, S., & Everson, H.T. (in press). Assessing metacognitive word knowledge. In G. Schraw (Ed.), *Issues in the measurement of metacognition*. Lincoln, NE: Buros Institute/ University of Nebraska Press.

Tobias, S. & Everson, H.T. (1996). *Assessing metacognitive knowledge monitoring*. College Board Report No. 96-01. NY: The College Board

Tobias, S., Hartman, H., Everson, H.T., & Gourgey, A. (1991, August). *The development of a group administered, objectively scored metacognitive evaluation* procedure paper presented at the annual convention of the American Psychological Association, San Francisco, CA.

Tukey, J. (1977). *Exploratory data analysis*. Reading, MA: Addison-Wesley.

Werts, C., Linn, R. L., & Joreskog, K.G. (1978). Reliability of college grades from longitudinal data. *Educational and Psychological Measurement*, 38, 89-95.

Willingham, W. W., Lewis, C., Morgan, R., & Ramist, L. (1990). *Predicting college grades: An analysis of institutional trends over two decades*. NY: The College Board.

Acknowledgments

An earlier version of this paper was presented at a symposium entitled Issues in Metacognitive Research and Assessment at the annual meeting of the American Educational Research Association, April 1995, San Francisco, CA., USA.

Preparation of this paper was partially supported by The College Board. Portions of this research were conducted while the second author was a Visiting Faculty Fellow at the Navy Personnel Research and Development Center in San Diego, in a program sponsored by the American Association for Engineering Education, and the U.S. Navy.

PART II: STUDENTS' METACOGNITION AND MOTIVATION

There are two chapters in this section, both of which address affective components of students' academic performance in relationship to metacognition. Affect is the second component of the BACEIS model of improving thinking's internal supersystem. It includes students' motivation, attitudes and affective self-regulation. Affective self-regulation functions in the affective subsystem comparable to metacognition's function in the cognitive subsystem. The two chapters in this section of the book both focus on relationships between metacognition and aspects of motivation, including will and self-efficacy. The affective domain has had a history of (intentional) neglect by many from the cognitive tradition, so these chapters make important contributions to overcoming that gap.

Mayer's chapter emphasizes motivational, cognitive and metacognitive aspects of the types of problem solving that are required in academic situations. Mayer argues that successful problem solving is a function of three components: will, skill, and metaskill. He discusses three sources of motivation: interest, self-efficacy and attributions and he characterizes motivation as "will". The role of will in problem solving is treated in depth. Domain-specific knowledge is an important ingredient of Mayer's conceptualization of skill and Mayer introduces the concept of "metaskill, which problem solvers need to recognize and solve non-routing problems. He also examines metacognitive strategy training in specific content domains: reading, writing and mathematics.

Wolters and Pintrich's chapter makes two distinct contributions: examining connections between affect, metacognition and achievement, and providing empirical support addressing the controversy over whether metacognition is domain general or domain specific. Their research examines contextual or domain-specific differences in seventh and eighth grade students' self-regulated learning and their motivation in mathematics, English, and social studies classrooms. Their research suggests that while there are some subject area differences in cognitive and motivational components of self-regulated classroom learning, they may be less pervasive than similarities across contexts. Thus their research suggests that perhaps the question should be change from "Is metacognition domain general or domain specific?" to "To what extent is metacognition domain general as opposed to domain specific?", thereby converting it from a dichotomy to a continuum.

CHAPTER 5

COGNITIVE, METACOGNITIVE, AND MOTIVATIONAL ASPECTS OF PROBLEM SOLVING

RICHARD E. MAYER

ABSTRACT. This chapter examines the role of cognitive, metacognitive, and motivational skills in problem solving. Cognitive skills include instructional objectives, components in a learning hierarchy, and components in information processing. Metacognitive skills include strategies for reading comprehension, writing, and mathematics. Motivational skills include motivation based on interest, self-efficacy, and attributions. All three kinds of skills are required for successful problem solving in academic settings.

COGNITIVE, METACOGNITIVE, AND MOTIVATIONAL ASPECTS OF PROBLEM SOLVING

Introduction

Suppose that a student learns a mathematical procedure such as how to find the area of a parallelogram. Later, when the student is given a parallelogram problem like the one she has studied, she is able to compute its area correctly. In short, the student shows that she can perform well on a *retention test*. However, when this student is asked to find the area of an unusually shaped parallelogram, she looks confused and eventually answers by saying, "We haven't had this yet." In short, the student shows that she cannot perform well on a *transfer test*, that is, on applying what she has learned to a novel situation.

This pattern of good retention and poor transfer is commonly observed among school students (Wertheimer, 1959). On *routine problems*--that is, problems that are like those they have already learned to solve--they excel; on *nonroutine problems*--i.e., problems that are not like any that they have solved in the past--they fail. Similar examples can be found in other academic domains, including reading and writing. If a goal of education is to promote transfer as well as retention, then this pattern of performance represents a serious challenge to educators.

87

H.J. Hartman (ed.), Metacognition in Learning and Instruction, 87–101.
© 2001 *Kluwer Academic Publishers. Printed in the Netherlands.*

How can students learn in ways that support solving both routine and nonroutine problems? How can teachers promote the learning of transferable problem solving skills? More than 50 years ago, Max Wertheimer eloquently posed the questions that motivate this chapter:

Why is it that some people, when they are faced with problems, get clever ideas, make inventions, and discoveries? What happens, what are the processes that lead to such solutions? What can be done to help people to be creative when they are faced with problems?" (Luchins & Luchins, 1970, p. 1). Although Wertheimer can be credited with posing an important question, he lacked the research methods and cognitive theories to be able to answer it. The mantle of Wertheimer's questioning has been passed to educational psychologists who are concerned with the issue of problem solving transfer (Chipman, Segal & Glaser, 1985; Halpern, 1992; Mayer & Wittrock, in press; Nickerson, Perkins & Smith, 1985; Segal, Chipman & Glaser, 1985). Despite success in understanding how to promote routine problem solving using tried-and-true versions of the drill-and-practice method of instruction, the discipline continues to struggle with how to promote nonroutine problem solving. What does a successful problem solver know that an unsuccessful problem solver does not know? First, research on problem solving expertise (Chi, Glaser & Farr, 1988; Ericsson & Smith, 1991; Mayer, 1992; Smith, 1991; Sternberg & Frensch, 1991) points to the crucial role of domain specific knowledge, that is, to the problem solver's skill. For example, some important cognitive skills for the parallelogram problem include the ability to identify the length and width of the parallelogram, and to perform arithmetic computations such as multiplying length times width to find area. An instructional implication of the skill-based view is that students should learn basic problem-solving skills in isolation.

Unfortunately, mastering each component skill is not enough to promote nonroutine problem solving. Students need to know not only what to do, but also when to do it. Therefore, a second ingredient, suggested by research on intelligence (Sternberg, 1985) and on the development of learning strategies (Pressley, 1990), is the ability to control and monitor cognitive processes. This aspect of problem-solving ability is the problem solver's *metaskill*. For example, in the parallelogram problem, students. An instructional implication of the metaskill approach is that students need practice in solving problems in context, that is, as part of solving a real problem.

A focus solely on teaching problem solving skill and metaskill is incomplete, because it ignores the problem solver's feelings and interest in the problem. A third prerequisite for successful problem solving is suggested by recent research on motivational aspects of cognition (Renninger, Hidi & Krapp, 1992; Weiner, 1986), that is, the problem solver's will. This approach suggests that problem solving skill and metaskill are best learned within personally meaningful contexts, and that the problem solvers may need guidance in their interpretation of success and failure in problem solving.

The theme of this chapter is that successful problem solving depends on three components--skill, metaskill, and will--and that each of these components can be influenced by instruction. When the goal of instruction is the promotion of nonroutine problem solving, students need to possess the relevant skill, metaskill, and will. Metacognition--in the form of metaskill-is central in problem solving because it manages and coordinates the other components. In this chapter, I explore each of these three components for successful problem solving.

The Role of Skill in Problem Solving

Perhaps the most obvious way to improve problem solving performance is to teach the basic skills. The general procedure is to analyze each problem into the cognitive skills needed for solution and then systematically teach each skill to mastery. Although a focus on teaching basic skills may seem to be the most straightforward way to improve problem solving performance, the results of research clearly demonstrate that knowledge of basic skills is not enough. In this section, I explore three approaches to the teaching of basic skills in problem solving that have developed over the years--instructional objectives, learning hierarchies, and componential analysis--and show how each is insufficient when the goal is to promote problem-solving transfer.

Skills as Instructional Objectives

Sally wishes to learn how to use a new word processing system, so she takes a course. In the course, she learns how to save and open a document, how to move the cursor, how to insert text, how to delete text, and so on. For each skill, she is given a demonstration and then is asked to solve a problem requiring that skill. She continues on a skill until she can perform it without error; then, she moves on to the next skill. In this way she learns each of the basic skills involved in using the word processing package.

The approach taken in this instruction is to break the subject of word processing into component skills, and then to systematically teach each skill to mastery. In this approach, any large task can be broken down into a collection of "instructional objectives." Each objective is a single skill, such as being able to move the cursor from the end of a document to some point within the document. Bloom et al. (1956) developed a taxonomy of objectives, and programs of mastery learning were developed to insure that students accomplished each instructional objective (Block & Burns, 1976; Bloom, 1976).

Although mastery programs often succeed in teaching of specific skills, they sometimes fail to support problem-solving transfer. For example, Cariello (reported in Mayer, 1987) taught students to use a computer programming language using a mastery or conventional approach. The mastery group performed better than the conventional group on solving problems like those given during instruction, but the conventional group performed better than the mastery group on solving transfer items. Apparently, narrow focus on master of specific objectives can restrict the way that students apply what they have learned to new situations.

Skills as Components in a Learning Hierarchy

Pat is learning how to solve three-column subtraction problems such as, 524 - 251 =_. First she practices simple subtraction facts (e.g., 5 - 2 =). Then, she moves on to two column subtraction where no borrowing is needed (e.g., 54 - 21=). Next, she learns to solve two-column subtraction problems involving borrowing (e.g., 52 - 25 =). In short, she learns to carry out the simpler computational procedures before moving on to the more difficult ones.

This instructional episode is based on Gagne's (1968; Gagne, Mayor, Garstens & Paradise, 1962) conception of learning hierarchies. A learning hierarchy is a task analysis that yields a hierarchy of subtasks involved in any problem-solving task. Validation of a learning hierarchy occurs when it can be shown that students who pass a higher-level task also are able to pass all prerequisite tasks in the hierarchy (White, 1974). Interestingly, students often are able to pass all prerequisite tasks but still fail to pass the corresponding higher-level task. For example, students who are able to subtract single-digit numbers (such as 6 - 1 = 5 or 15 - 9 = 6) and to regroup two-digit numbers as is required in "borrowing" (such as changing 75 to 6 tens and 15 ones) may not be able to carry out two-column subtraction (such as 75 - 19 =). In this situation, students possess all the basic skills but still cannot carry out the task; what may be missing is the ability to organize and control the basic skills within the context of solving the higher-level task. Thus, research on learning hierarchies shows that possessing basic skills is a necessary, but not sufficient, prerequisite for successfully solving higher-level problems.

Skills as Components in Information Processing

Dan is taking a course to prepare him for college entrance examinations. As part of the training, he learns how to solve analogy problems, such as:

page:book: room (a. door, b. window, c. house, d. kitchen)

The teacher describes and provides practice for each step in the process of analogical reasoning. First, Dan learns to encode each term: The A term is page, the B term is book, the C term is room, and there are four possible D terms. Second, Dan learns to infer the relation between the A and B term: in this example, page is a part of book. Third, Dan learns to apply the A-B relation to the C-D terms: room is a part of house. Finally, Dan learns to respond: the answer is (c).

This instructional episode is based on a componential analysis of analogical reasoning (Sternberg, 1985; Sternberg & Gardner, 1983). In componential analysis, a reasoning task is broken down into its constituent cognitive processes. For example, to solve an analogy problem,, a problem solver needs to engage in the cognitive processes of encoding, inferring, applying, and responding. Training in componential skills, especially inferring and applying, tends to improve students' problem solving performance (Robins & Mayer, 1993). However, expertise in executing the component processes is not sufficient for problem-solving transfer. Based on a series of studies, Sternberg (1985) concludes that in addition to possessing cognitive components, problem solvers need to know how to orchestrate and control the cognitive components in any problem-solving task. Sternberg uses to term *metacomponents* to refer to these required metaskills.

The Role of Metaskill in Problem Solving

The foregoing section provides three examples--from research on instructional objectives, learning hierarchies, and componential analysis--in which cognitive skill is needed but by itself is not sufficient to support problem-solving transfer. In addition to possessing domain-specific skills, problem solvers need to be able to manage their skills; in short, metaskill seems to be an important component in problem solving. Metaskills (or metacognitive knowledge) involves knowledge of when to use, how to coordinate, and how to monitor various skills in problem solving. For example, knowing how to summarize is a skill but knowing that one should take detailed summary notes on to-be-tested lecture requires a metaskill.

An important instructional implication of the focus on metacognition is that problem solving skills should be learned within the context of realistic problem-solving situations. Instead of using drill and practice on component skills in isolation--as suggested by the skill-based approach--a metaskill-based approach suggests modeling of how and when to use strategies in realistic academic tasks. In this section, I explore examples of metacognitive strategy training in reading, writing, and mathematics.

Strategy Training in Reading Comprehension

Mary, a fourth-grader, is a good reader. She can read every word of a story aloud, without making any errors. However, when the teacher asks her what the story was about, Mary does not know what to say. When the teacher asks her a question requiring inference, such as why a character did something, again Mary cannot respond. Thus, even though she possesses the basic skills needed for efficient verbatim reading, she is not able to use what she has read to solve problems.

According to theories of active learning, Mary is not using meaningful reading strategies. For example, Brown & Day (1983) found that children have difficulty summarizing what they have read unless they are taught how to summarize stories. When students are taught how to summarize stories, their ability to answer questions about passages they read improves (Bean & Steenwyk, 1984; Rinehart, Stahl, & Erickson, 1986; Taylor & Beach, 1984). In one study, Cook & Mayer (1988) taught students how to outline paragraphs found in their science textbooks. Students who received this training showed improvements in their ability to answer transfer questions based on the material in new passages.

The procedure used in teaching of reading comprehension strategies involves modeling of successful reading within the context of realistic academic reading tasks. In addition, students receive practice in describing their comprehension processes in the context of a reading task. Rather than practicing of basic component skills in isolation, successful comprehension strategy instruction requires reaming within the context of real tasks. By embedding strategy instruction in academic tasks, students also acquire the metacognitive skills of when and how to use the new strategies.

Strategy Training in Writing

As part of an English class assignment, Peter is writing a persuasive essay. He is careful to spell each word correctly, use appropriate grammar, and write grammatically correct sentences. However, in spite of his excellent knowledge of the mechanics of writing, he produces an unconvincing essay that the teacher rates as low in quality. Peter seems to have the basic cognitive skills needed for writing but is unable to use these skills productively.

According to Hayes & Flower's (1986) analysis of the writing process, composing an essay involves planning, translating, and reviewing. Although Peter has the skills needed for translating--that is actually putting words on the page--he seems to lack planning and reviewing skills. He does not think about what is going to write and he does not monitor whether what he writes makes sense. Through direct strategy instruction, however, students can learn how to plan and revise their essays. For example, several researchers have successfully taught students how to systematically generate a writing plan and how to review and revise what they have written in light of their plan (Fitzgerald & TESL, 1986; Graham & Harris, 1988). Such programs involve modeling of the writing process by experts as well as having students describe their writing process in detail. Importantly, students who receive writing strategy training show improvements in the quality of what they write.

Strategy Training in Mathematics

Marco is working on an arithmetic story problem:

Gas at ARCO costs t.18 per gallon.
This is 5 cents less per gallon than gas at Chevron.
If you want to buy 5 gallons of gas, how much will you pay at Chevron?

He knows how to add, subtract, multiply, and divide. He knows the meaning of every word in the problem. Yet, when he sits down to work on the problem, he produces an incorrect answer. He subtracts .05 from 1.18, yielding 1.13; then he multiplies 5 times 1.13, producing a final answer of 5.65.

Although Marco possesses the basic skills for solving the gas problem, he fails. According to Mayer's (1985, 1992) analysis of mathematical problem solving ability, solving a story problem requires representing the problem, devising a solution plan, and executing the plan. Marco is able to carry out the arithmetic operations needed to execute the solution; however, he seems to misunderstand the problem. It follows that his problem solving performance would improve if he learned how to represent the problem within the context of actually trying to solve it. For example, when Lewis (1989) taught students how to represent story problems using a number-line diagram, students' problem solving performance improved dramatically and they were able to transfer what they had learned to new types of problems.

Similarly, Schoenfeld (1979) successfully taught mathematical problem-solving strategies, such as how to break a problem into smaller parts, and found that the training transferred to solving new types of mathematics problems. These studies show that, in addition to mastering the needed arithmetic and algebraic skills, students need to be able to know when and how to use these skills-- knowledge that Schoenfeld (1985) refers to as *control*. The most successful instructional technique for teaching students how to control their mathematical problem-solving strategies is cognitive modeling of problem-solving in context, that is, having a competent problem solver describe her thinking process as she solves a real problem in an academic setting (Mayer, 1987; Pressley, 1990).

In summary, research on strategy training shows that knowledge of basic skills is not enough for successful performance on complex academic tasks such as reading comprehension, writing, and mathematical problem solving. In each case, students benefitted from training that was sensitive to the metacognitive demands of the task, that is, from learning when and how to apply domain-specific learning strategies. The term "conditional knowledge" can be used to describe this aspect of metacognition.

The Role of Will in Problem Solving

The role of motivation in learning to solve problems has a long history in educational psychology, yet theories of problem solving instruction have not always emphasized the role of motivation. This section examines three approaches--interest theory, self-efficacy theory, and attributional theory. Although they differ in many ways, the three approaches also share a cognitive view of motivation--the idea that the will to learn depends partly on how the problem solver interprets the problem solving situation.

Motivation Based on Interest

In preparation for a physics test, Mary learns to solve every computational problem in her physics textbook involving the laws of motion. In contrast, Betsy has decided to build a roller coaster as a class project and in order to accomplish this goal she finds that she needs to understand the physical laws of motion. Both students learn to solve motion problems but Mary learns based on effort and Betsy learns based on interest.

Who will learn more deeply? More than 80 years, John Dewey (1913) eloquently argued that the interest-based learning of Betsy results in qualitatively better learning than the effort-based learning of Mary. According to Dewey, the justification of educators favoring an effort-based approach is that "life is full of things not interesting that have to be faced,"so teachers should not spoil students by making school a place where "everything is made play, amusement...everything is sugar coated for the child" (Dewey, 1913, p. 3-41. In contrast, the interest-based approach assumes that when a child "goes at a matter unwillingly [rather] than when he goes out of the fullness of his heart" the result is a "character dull, mechanical, unalert, because the vital juice of spontaneous interest has been squeezed out" (Dewey, 1913, p, 3).

Effort theory and interest theory yield strikingly different educational implications. The effort theory is most consistent with the practice of teaching skills in isolation, and with using instructional methods such as drill-and-practice. The interest theory is most consistent with the practice of teaching skills in context, and with using instructional methods such as cognitive apprenticeship. Dewey (1913, p. ix) pleads for the central role of interest in education: "Our whole policy of compulsory education rises or falls with our ability to make school like an interesting and absorbing experience to the child." Rather than forcing the child to work on boring material, Dewey (1913, p. ix) argues that "education only comes through willing attention and participation in school activities."

Although Dewey's writings are based on logical arguments rather than empirical research, modern research includes empirical studies of two types of interest--individual interest and situational interest (Renninger, Hidi, & Krapp, 1 992). Individual interest refers to a person's dispositions or preferred activities, and therefore is a characteristic of the person; situational interest refers to a task's interestingness, and therefore is a characteristic of the environment. In both cases, interest is determined by the interaction of the individual and the situation. Interest theory predicts that students think harder and process the material more deeply when they are interested rather than uninterested. In a recent review of 121 studies, Schiefele, Krapp, & Winteler (1992) found a persistent correlation of approximately $r = .30$ between interest--how much a student liked a certain school subject--and achievement--how well the student performed on tests in a certain school subject. In another set of studies, Schiefele (1992) found that students who rated a passage as interesting engaged in more elaboration during reading the passage and were better able to answer challenging questions than students who rated the topic as uninteresting. These results are consistent with the predictions of interest theory, and show how the learner's cognitive activities on school tasks is related to the specific significance of the material to the learner.

Interest theory also predicts that an otherwise boring task cannot be made interesting by adding a few interesting details. Dewey (1913, p. 1112) warned that "when things have to be made interesting, it is because interest itself is wanting." To test this idea, Garner, Gillingham, & White (1989) asked students to read passages about insects that either did or did not contain seductive details--highly interesting and vivid material that is not directly related to the important information in the text. Similar to the findings of other studies (Wade, 1992), adding seductive details did not improve learning of the important information although the details themselves were well remembered. Wade (1992) suggests that educators should focus on techniques that increase cognitive interest--being able to make sense out of material--rather than emotional interest--overall arousal and excitement. According to interest theory, students will work harder and be more successful on problems that interest them than on problems that do not interest them. For example, in one study, some elementary school children learned how to solve mathematics problems using personalized examples that contained information about the individual student's friends, interests, and hobbies, whereas other students learned from non-personalized examples (Anand & Ross, 1987). Consistent with interest theory, students who learned with personalized examples subsequently performed better on solving transfer problems. Similarly, Ross et al. (1985) compared nursing and education students who learned statistics using examples that either did or did not come from their disciplines. As predicted by interest theory, subsequent transfer performance was best for nursing students who had received medical examples and education students who had received examples based on teaching.

These results are particularly important because they focus on problem-solving transfer. The theme in this line of interest research is that students learn more meaningfully when they are interested in the material. Unfortunately, researchers have not yet been able to clearly specify the mechanism by which interest affects what is learned, or even to clearly specify what interest is. However, on-going research on interest is useful, especially in light of the role that interest seems to play in promoting problem-solving transfer.

Motivation Based on Self-Efficacy

Sally is taking a class on how to use a new graphics program. She has never used graphics program before so she is somewhat nervous and unsure of herself. After a few minutes of hands-on experience, she finds she is able to draw some figures quite easily, so her self-efficacy increases. She looks over to see that other first-time users like herself are also able to use the program to make drawings. Again, her self-efficacy grows because she reasons: "If they can do it, I can do it." Her instructor walks by Sally's computer and says, "You can do this!" This vote of confidence pushes Sally's self-efficacy even higher. Eventually, she loses her initial state of high anxiety, including high heart rate and nausea, and she becomes relaxed in front of the computer. This change in body state signals an increase in Sally's self-efficacy.

Self-efficacy refers to a person's judgments of his or her capabilities to accomplish some task. This scenario exemplifies four sources of self-efficacy, namely, when Sally interprets her own performance, the performance of others around her, others' assessments of her capabilities, and her own physiological state. According to Schunk (1991, p. 209): "...students derive cues signaling how well they are learning, which they use to assess efficacy for further learning." Furthermore, Schunk (1991, p. 209) concludes that "motivation is enhanced when students perceive they are making progress in learning."

Self-efficacy theory predicts that students work harder on a learning task when they judge themselves as capable than when they lack confidence in their ability to learn. For example, Zimmerman & Martinez-Pons (1990) found that students' ratings of their verbal skills was strongly correlated with their reported use of active learning strategies on a verbal task. Pintrich & De Groot (1990) found strong correlations between students' self-efficacy and their use of active learning strategies in various classes. Schunk (1981) reported a positive correlation between self-efficacy and persistence on exercise problems during arithmetic learning. These kinds of results support the prediction that self-efficacy is related to deeper and more active processing of information during learning.

Self-efficacy theory also predicts that students understand the material better when they have high self-efficacy than when they have low self-efficacy. For example, Schunk & Hanson (1985) found that students' ratings of problem difficulty before learning were related to test scores after learning to solve arithmetic problems. In particular, students who expected to be able to learn how to solve the problems tended to learn more than students who expected to have difficulty.

Finally, self-efficacy theory predicts that students who improve their self-efficacy will improve their success in learning to solve problems. Schunk & Hanson (1985) provided self-efficacy instruction to some students but not to others; the instruction involved watching videotapes of students successfully solving arithmetic problems, while occasionally making positive statements such as "I can do that one" and receiving positive feedback from the teacher. Students who received training learned to solve arithmetic problems more effectively than students who did not. These findings support the idea that self-efficacy can influence how students learn to solve problems in an academic setting.

Motivation Based on Attributions

As the teacher passes back the math tests, Joe squirms in his seat. At last, the teacher hands him his paper, and right at the top the teacher has written a failing grade in red. Joe searches for a justification for this outcome. He could attribute the failing grade to his ability: "I'm not very good in math." Instead, he might attribute his failure to lack of effort: "I really didn't study very hard." Perhaps, the cause of his failure is task difficulty: "That was a hard quiz." Alternatively, he might judge the cause of his failure to be luck ("I made some unlucky guesses"), mood ("I just had a bad math day"), or hindrance from others ("The guy in front of me was so loud I couldn't concentrate").

These are examples of attributions that learners may give for their failures or successes on academic tasks. According to attribution theory, the kind of causal ascriptions that a student makes for successes and failures is related to academic performance (Weiner, 1986). In particular, students who attribute academic success and failure to effort are more likely to work hard on academic tasks than students who attribute academic success and failure to ability. Furthermore, students infer that they lack ability when teachers offer sympathy or pity in response to failure whereas students infer the need to work harder when teachers encourage persistence on a task.

When faced with failure on a problem, some students quit whereas others simply work harder. Borkowski, Weyhing & Carr (1988) have devised an instructional program to encourage students to attribute failure to lack of effort rather than lack of ability. Learning disabled students were given strategy training in how to summarize paragraphs and attribution training which emphasized the importance of trying hard and using the strategy. Students who received both types of training performed better on answering transfer questions about passages than students who received only strategy training. These results show that students need to learn cognitive strategies such as effective study aids and motivational strategies such as the belief that academic success depends on effort.

When teachers show a student how to solve a problem, they may be conveying the message that the student is not smart enough to figure out how to solve the problem. For example, Graham & Barker (1990) asked elementary school students to view videotapes in which two students solved math problems on a worksheet and then were told they had done well, correctly answering 8 out of 10 problems. In the videotape, one of the students was helped by the teacher who happened to be walking by his desk, whereas the other student worked on the problems without any hints from teacher. Students viewing the videotape rated the helped boy as less able than the unhelped boy, even though neither student asked for help and both did well on solving the problems.

In a related study by Graham (1984), students were given a series of puzzles to solve, with one minute allowed for each puzzle. If students failed to solve a puzzle within one minute, the teacher told them to stop and then displayed the correct solution. For some students the teacher expressed pity by saying she felt sorry for the student, whereas for others she simply told them they had failed. Pitied students were more likely to cite lack of ability as the cause of their failure than were unpitied students. These studies show that when the teacher provides unsolicited help or expresses pity, students may infer that the teacher has a low opinion of their ability. Students may then come to accept this assessment, which in turn causes them to give up when faced with a difficult academic problem-solving task.

In summary, in this section I have explored three possible sources of motivation to learn, namely interest, self-efficacy, and attribution. In each case, the will to learn can have significant influence on students' problem solving performance. Future research is needed to determine whether any one of these three approaches is sufficient, or whether each contributes something unique to student motivation. In contrast to classic approaches to motivation, these three views of motivation share a focus on the domain specificity of motivation, on connecting motivation with cognition, and on examining motivation in realistic academic settings. In short, research on academic motivation points to the important role of will in problem solving.

CONCLUSION

Tom is working on geometry problem that he has never seen before. He begins enthusiastically, but he soon runs into a dead end. Not knowing what to do, he quits saying, "We haven't had this yet." Why did Tom fail? Perhaps he lacked the cognitive tools he needed, such as basic knowledge of geometry. We give him a short test of basic geometry and find that he is highly knowledgeable, so we rule out cognitive factors as a source of the failure. This leaves two other possibilities-- metacognitive and motivational factors may be involved. On the metacognitive side, Tom may not know how to devise, monitor, and revise a solution plan, so whenever the most obvious plan fails he is lost. On the motivational side, Tom may have a low estimation of his ability to solve this kind of problem, so whenever he runs into trouble he wants to quit.

How can we help students like Tom to become better problem solvers? The theme of this chapter is that three components are needed: skill--domain-specific knowledge relevant to the problem-solving task; metaskill--strategies for how use the knowledge in problem solving; and will--feelings and beliefs about one's interest and ability to solve the problems. According to this view, instruction that focuses only on basic skills is incomplete. Problem-solving expertise depends on metacognitive and motivational factors as well as purely cognitive ones.

Continued research is needed to understand (a) how skill, metaskill, and will together contribute to problem solving; (b) why skill, metaskill, or will alone is not sufficient for far-transfer to occur; and (c) how best to help students acquired needed skill, metaskill, and will for successful problem solving.

RICHARD E. MAYER
Department of Psychology
University of California, Santa Barbara

REFERENCES

Anand, P.G. & Ross, S.M. (1987). Using computer-assisted instruction to personalize arithmetic materials for elementary school children. *Journal of Educational Psychology*, 79, 72-78

Bean, T. W.. & Steenwyk, F..L. (1984). The effect of three forms of summarization instruction on sixth graders' summary writing and comprehension. *Journal of Reading Behavior*. 16, 297-306.

Block, J. .H. & Burns, R..B. (1976). Mastery learning. In L.S. Shulman (Ed.), *Review of Research in Education*. Volume 4. Itsaca, IL: Peacock. Bloom, B.S. (1976). *Human characteristics and school learning*. New York: McGraw-Hill.

Bloom, B.S., Englehart, M.D., Furst, E..J , Hill, W..H & Krathwohl, D. R. (1956). *Taxonomy of educational objectives: The classification of educational goals. Handbook 1: Cognitive domain*. New York: McKay.

Borkowski, J. G., Weyhing, R.S., & Carr, M. (1988). Effects of attributional retraining on strategy-based reading comprehension in learning disabled students. *Journal of Educational Psychology*, 80, 46-53.

Brown, A..L. & Day, J.D. (1983). Macrorules for summarizing texts: The development of expertise. *Journal of Verbal Learning and Verbal Behavior*, 22, 1-14.

Chi, M..T. H., Glaser, R., & Farr, M.. A (Ed.). (1988). *The nature of expertise*. Hillsdale, NJ: Erlbaum.

Chipman, S .F., Segal, J..W. & Glaser, R. (Eds.). (1985). *Thinking and learning skills. Volume 2: Research and open questions*. Hillsdale, NJ: Erlbaum.

Cook, L.. K. & Mayer, R.E. (1988). Teaching readers about the structure of scientific text. *Journal of Educational Psychology*, 80, 448-456.

Dewey, J. (1913). *Interest and effort in education*. Cambridge, MA: Riverside Press.

Ericsson, K. A., Smith, J. (Eds.). (1991). *Toward a general theory of expertise*. Cambridge, England: Cambridge University Press.

Fitzgerald, J. & Teasley, A.B. (1986). Effects of instruction in narrative structure on children's writing. *Journal of Educational Psychology*, 78, 424-432.

Gagne, R..M. (1968). Learning hierarchies. *Educational Psychologist*, 6, 19.

Gagne, R..M., Mayor, J. R., Garstens, H.L., & Paradise, N. E. (1962). Factors in acquiring knowledge in a mathematics task. *Psychological Monographs*, No. 7 (Whole No. 526).

Garner, R., Gillingham, M.G., & White, C. S. (1989). Effects of "seductive details" on macroprocessing and microprocessing in adults and children. *Cognition and Instruction*, 6, 41-57.

Graham. S. (1984). Communicating sympathy and anger to black and white children: The cognitive attributional) consequences of affective cues. *Journal of Personality and Social Psychology*, 47, 40-54.

Graham, S. & Barker, G.P. (1990). The down side of help: An attributional developmental analysis of helping behavior as a low-ability cue. *Journal of Educational Psychology*, 82, 7-14.

Graham, S. & Harris, K..R. (1988). Instructional recommendations for teaching writing to exceptional students. *Exceptional Children*. 54, 506512.

Halpern, D.F. (Ed.). (1992). *Enhancing thinking skills in the sciences and mathematics*. Hillsdale, NJ: Erlbaum.

Hayes, J..R. & Flower, L.S. (1986). Writing research and the writer. *American Psychologist*, 41, 1106-1113.

Lewis, A.B. (1989). Training students to represent arithmetic word problems. *Journal of Educational Psychology*, 79, 363-371.

Luchins, A.S. & Luchins, E. H. (1970). *Wertheimer's seminars revisited: Problem solving and thinking*. Vol. 1.. Albany, NY: State University of New York.

Mayer, R.E. (1985). Mathematical ability. In R. .A Sternberg (Ed.), *Human abilities: An information processing approach* (pp. 127-150). New York: Freeman.

Mayer, R.E. (1987). *Educational psychology: A cognitive approach*. New York: Harper Collins.

Mayer, R.E. (1992). *Thinking. problem solving cognition; second edition*. New York: Freeman.

Mayer, R.E. & Wittrock, M.C. (in press). Problem solving and transfer. In D. Berliner & R. Calfee (Eds.), *Handbook of educational psychology*. New York: Macmillan.

Nickerson, R.S., Perkins, D..N., & Smith, E.E. (Eds.). (1985). *The teaching of thinking.* Hillsdale, NJ: Erlbaum.

Pintrich, P.R. & De Groot, E. V. (1990). Motivation and self-regulated learning components of classroom academic performance. *Journal of Educational Psychology,* ~ 33-40.

Pressley, M. (1990). *Cognitive strategy instruction.* Cambridge, MA: Brookline Books.

Renninger, K. A., Hidi, S., & Krapp, A. (Eds.). (1992) *The role of interest in learning and development.* Hillsdale, NJ: Erlbaum.

Rinehart, S D., Stahl, S.A., & Erickson, L.G. (1986). Some effects of summarization training on reading and studying. *Reading Research Quarterly,* 21, 422-438.

Robins, S. & Mayer, R.E. (1993). Schema training in analogical reasoning. *Journal of Educational Psychology,* 85, 529-538.

Ross, S.M., McCormick, D., Krisak, N., & Anand, P. (1985). Personalizing context in teaching mathematical concepts: Teacher-managed and computer-managed models. *Educational Communication Technology Journal,* 133, 169-178.

Schiefele, U. (1992). Topic interest and level of text comprehension. In K. A. Renninger, S. Hidi, & A. Krapp (Eds.), *The role of interest in learning and development* (pp. I 51 - 182). Hillsdale, NJ: Erlbaum.

Schiefele, U., Krapp, A., & Winteler, A. (1992). In K. A. Renninger, S. Hidi, & A. Krapp (Eds.), *The role of interest in learning and development* (pp. 183-212). Hillsdale, NJ: Erlbaum.

Schoenfeld, A.H. (1979). Explicit heuristic training as a variable in problem-solving performance. *Journal for Research in Mathematics Education,* 1979, 10, 173-187.

Schoenfeld, A.H. (1985). *Mathematical problem solving.* Orlando, FL: Academic Press.

Schunk, D. (1991). Self-efficacy and academic motivation. *Educational Psychologist.* 26, 207-231.

Schunk, D.H. & Hanson, A.R. (1985). Peer models: Influences on children's self-efficacy and achievement. *Journal of Educational Psychology,* 77, 313-322.

Smith, M. U. (Ed.). (1991). *Toward a unified theory of problem solving; Views from the content domains.* Hillsdale, NJ: Erlbaum.

Segal, J W., Chipman, S..F, & Glaser, R. (Eds.). (1985). *Thinking and learning skills. Volume 1: Relating instruction to research.* Hillsdale, NJ: Erlbaum.

Sternberg, R.. A (1985). *Beyond IQ: A triarchic theory of human intelligence.* Cambridge, England: Cambridge University Press.

Sternberg, R..A & Frensch, P.A. (Eds.). (1991). *Complex problem solving: Principles and mechanisms.* Hillsdale, NJ: Erlbaum.

Sternberg, R. .A & Gardner, M. .K.. (1983). Unities in inductive reasoning. *Journal of Experimental Psychology: General* 112, 80-116.

Taylor, B.M. & Beach, R.W. (1984). The effects of text structure instruction on middle-grade students' comprehension and production of expository text. *Reading Research Quarterly.* 19, 134- 6.

Wade, S.. E. (1992). How interest affects learning from text. In K. A. Renninger, S. Hidi, & A. Krapp (Eds.), *The role of interest in learning and development* (pp. 255-278). Hillsdale, NJ: Erlbaum.

Weiner, B. (1986). *An attributional theory of motivation and emotion.* New York: Springer-Verlag.

Wertheimer, M. (I 959). *Productive thinking.* New York: Harper & Row.

White, R. T. (1974). The validation of a learning hierarchy. *American Educational Research Journal.* 11, 121-236.

Zimmerman, B.J. & Martinez-Pons, M. (1990). Student differences in self-regulated learning: Relating grade, sex, and giftedness to self-efficacy and strategy use. *Journal of Educational Psychology.* 82, 51-59.

CHAPTER 6

CONTEXTUAL DIFFERENCES IN STUDENT MOTIVATION AND SELF-REGULATED LEARNING IN MATHEMATICS, ENGLISH AND SOCIAL STUDIES CLASSROOMS

CHRISTOPHER A. WOLTERS   PAUL R. PINTRICH

ABSTRACT. Recent research on self-regulated learning has stressed the importance of both motivational and cognitive components of classroom learning. Much of this research has examined these components without consideration of potential contextual differences. Using a within-subject correlational design, the present study assessed mean level differences in students' task value, self-efficacy, test anxiety, cognitive strategy use, regulatory strategy use, and classroom academic performance by gender and across the subject areas of mathematics, social studies, and English. In addition, the relations among the motivational, strategy use, and performance measures were assessed using multivariate regressions. The participants were 545 seventh and eight grade students (51% females) who responded to a self-report questionnaire. Results revealed mean level differences by subject area and gender in the motivation and cognitive strategy use variables, but not in regulatory strategy use or academic performance. In contrast, results indicated that the relations among these constructs was very similar across the three subject areas examined. Findings are discussed in terms of their importance for understanding the contextual nature of students' self-regulated learning.

Recent research on student academic performance has stressed the importance of considering both motivational and cognitive components of classroom learning. Although there are a number of important motivational components, three have been linked consistently to self-regulated learning including beliefs about one's efficacy to do classroom tasks, value for these tasks, and anxiety (Pintrich & De Groot, 1990; Pintrich, Roeser, & De Groot, 1994; Pintrich & Schrauben, 1992). Two general cognitive components seem to be most important in this research including cognitive strategies designed to increase encoding, retention, and comprehension of classroom material as well as various metacognitive and regulatory strategies that help students monitor and control their own learning (Corno, 1989; Sternberg, 1988; Weinstein & Mayer, 1986; Zimmerman, 1989).

Models of self-regulated learning strive to integrate these different motivational and cognitive components into a comprehensive model of students' classroom academic performance (Garcia & Pintrich, 1994; Zimmerman, 1994). However, most of these models assume that self-regulated learning is a relatively

103

H.J. Hartman (ed.), Metacognition in Learning and Instruction, 103–124.
© 2001 *Kluwer Academic Publishers. Printed in the Netherlands.*

general process that operates in the same fashion across different domains or situations. Very little empirical research has examined how the various components of self-regulated learning may vary as a function of contextual differences. The present study seeks to address this gap in the literature by examining components of motivation and cognition across three different academic subjects using a within-subject design. In particular, the purpose of this study was to examine whether students' level of motivation and cognition varies across domains and if the relations between the motivational and cognitive components of self-regulated learning change as a function of the three domains.

Many motivational processes are thought to be sensitive to features of the task, the classroom, or the context within which a student is engaged. For example, self-efficacy is usually described as being task-specific (Bandura, 1986; Schunk, 1989, 1991) as well as a vital process involved in general self-regulation (Schunk, 1994). In this model, students are thought to generate efficacy judgments for specific classroom tasks and it is assumed that these beliefs will vary as a function of task or classroom features (Pintrich & Schunk, 1996). Task value is usually conceptualized as personal characteristics of the individual in expectancy-value models of motivation (Eccles, 1983; Wigfield, 1994). At the same time, these models assume that individuals will find different domains (i.e., mathematics vs. English) as more or less personally interesting or valued (Wigfield, 1994; Wigfield & Eccles, 1992; 1994). Accordingly, the level of task value should differ as a function of the domain. Anxiety is also viewed as an individual difference variable that may vary by domain with some individuals having more anxiety for a particular domain such as mathematics (e.g., Wigfield & Eccles, 1989). In sum, the influences of each of these motivational components are assumed to depend on features of the task or domain.

The research on the cognitive components suggest these factors also may vary as a function of the task or domain. For example, research on cognitive strategies has found that strategies may not transfer across situations in that the use of cognitive strategies often seems to be dependent on environmental cues and the features of the tasks (Brown, Bransford, Ferrara & Campione, 1983; Schneider & Pressley, 1989). At the same time, however, there are individual differences in students' knowledge and use of cognitive strategies (Siegler, 1988; Sternberg, 1988; 1994) that seem to transcend contextual features. In addition, if the use of cognitive strategies is related to motivational beliefs, as it seems to be (see Pintrich & Schrauben, 1992 for review), then when the level of motivational beliefs vary by domain, it would be expected that the level of cognitive strategy use would also vary.

A similar argument can be made for variations in the use of self-regulation strategies by domains or situations. In some cases, the process of self-regulation has been described as more independent of contextual influences. Self-regulating students are assumed to be aware of and able to control their actions in order to reach learning goals and an important aspect of this awareness and control is the ability to overcome contextual difficulties (Corno, 1989; Zimmerman & Martinez-Pons, 1990). This ability to overcome problems would include the power to create one's own goals for a reaming situation, to muster motivation for that goal, and to enact the cognitive resources necessary to reach the goal. Self-regulated reamers are able to avoid or conquer obstacles that obstruct their reaming goals. Past research on self-regulation has reflected this view by examining self-regulation within a particular context (Pintrich & De Groot, 1990) or without reference to any specific context (Zimmerman & Martinez-Pons, 1990). This view would suggest that there may not be variations in self-regulation by context.

In apparent opposition to this view, Zimmerman (1994) suggests that the nature of the classroom context plays an important role in facilitating self-regulating reaming. Classrooms that do not allow for much choice or control in use of time, choice of strategies to perform tasks, or even which tasks to perform, limit the opportunities for the development and use of self-regulatory strategies. In addition, classroom studies have shown that differences in teachers' instructional methods, including the type of task in which they ask students to engage, can influence the motivational goals that students adopt for their reaming as well as their self-regulated reaming (Ames, 1992; Machr & Midgley, 1991). More generally, work on academic tasks (e.g., Doyle, 1983; Meece, Blumenfeld, & Hoyle, 1988) and research on the nature of the classroom participation structures (Cohen, 1994) has provided evidence that the activities students participate in can have an important impact on students' motivation and level of self-regulated reaming in the classroom.

Most of these classroom studies, however, have not examined subject area or disciplinary differences in these classroom features. Although the contextual differences among classrooms of different academic disciplines may not seem pronounced, there is evidence that significant differences exist among teachers and classrooms representing different academic subjects. For example, it seems that secondary teachers from different subject areas (mathematics, science, social studies, English, and foreign languages) have different views of the nature of the discipline they teach and that these views relate to different instructional beliefs and practices (Grossman & Stodolsky, 1994; 1995; Stodolsky & Grossman, 1995). This research has found that 6 mathematics and foreign language teachers believed that their subject areas were more defined, sequential, and static, while science, social studies, and English teachers perceived their subject areas as more open, less sequential, and more dynamic. This suggests that mathematics classrooms may provide less opportunity for self-regulated learning if Zimmerman's (1994) claims are correct regarding constraints that might be operating on opportunities for self-regulated reaming in many traditional classrooms. In support of this argument,

Stodolsky (1988) found differences between mathematics and social studies lessons in fifth grade classrooms including differences in the nature of instruction and the types of tasks assigned to students. She found that mathematics instruction was more structured, sequential, and less engaging than social studies lessons and that mathematics tasks were often of less cognitive complexity than the variety and diversity found in the social studies tasks. She also found that student involvement, basically measured by an observer's dichotomous rating of "on-task" or "off-task", was higher when cognitive complexity of the task was high. However, this type of observational data did not address the quality of student cognitive engagement in terms of self-regulated reaming or motivation. In this study, we will address this gap in the empirical literature by using students' self-reports of their cognition and motivation in the different subject areas.

In research that has focused on students' motivational beliefs for different subject areas, Eccles and Wigfield and their colleagues have consistently found differences between English and mathematics classrooms in elementary through secondary classrooms. The consistent pattern is that students' expectancies or efficacy beliefs, task value and interest, and anxiety are generally less positive and less adaptive in mathematics classrooms than in English classrooms (Eccles, 1983; 1984; Wigfield, 1994; Wigfield & Eccles, 1992; 1994). However, they have not examined other subject areas in their research, nor have they investigated students' cognitive engagement in terms of self-regulated reaming. Stodolsky, Salk and Glaessner (1991) found that fifth graders' beliefs about mathematics were more likely to be tied to their ability to do the work, while social studies beliefs were related to interest in the activities. Given these results, it seems important to examine students' motivational beliefs and self-regulated reaming in different subject areas.

In addition, differences between disciplines may be more pronounced for some groups of students in comparison to other groups. For example, there is a fair amount of research that suggests there are stable gender differences in males' and females' motivation for mathematics and English courses. Eccles and Wigfield and their colleagues report that males have higher self-competence or efficacy beliefs for mathematics, while females have higher efficacy beliefs for English. They did not find differences in task value beliefs in mathematics, but females had higher value beliefs for English (Eccles, 1983; 1984; Eccles, Wigfield, Flanagan, Miller, Reuman, & Yee, 1989; Wigfield, Eccles, MacIver, Reuman, & Midgley, 1991; Wigfield & Eccles, 1994). In addition, research on self-regulation has found differences in the amount of self-regulation behavior reported by males and females with females showing higher levels of self-regulated reaming (Zimmerman & Martinez-Pons, 1990). Thus, when considering subject area differences in student motivation and cognition, it is important to examine how these differences might interact with gender.

In summary, three basic questions were addressed in this study. First, are there differences in the students' level of motivation and self-regulated reaming for the subject areas of mathematics, social studies, and English? Motivation is defined in terms of self-efficacy, task value, and anxiety, whereas self-regulated reaming is defined in terms of students" cognitive and regulatory strategy use. Based on previous theoretical characterizations and classroom studies of self-efficacy and task value, it was expected that students would report greater levels of self-efficacy and task value in English and social studies than in mathematics (Eccles, 1983; 1984; Stodolsky, 1988; Wigfield, 1994; Wigfield & Eccles, 1992; 1994). Consistent with the anticipated differences in students' motivation, and following Stodolsky's (1988) finding that mathematics instruction was more structured, sequential, less engaging and consisted of less complex tasks than social studies lessons, it was predicted that students would report greater levels of cognitive and regulatory strategy use in social studies, and perhaps English, than in mathematics. In sum, the overall expectation was that students would report a more adaptive motivational and cognitive profile in English and social studies than in mathematics.

A second major research question was, do the relations between these motivational and self-regulated learning constructs vary as a function of subject area? With regard to this question it was predicted that the relation between the motivational, cognitive and achievement factors would be similar across the three subject areas examined. In other words, whereas the level of students' motivation and/or cognitive or regulatory strategy use was predicted to vary across domains, the relations between the motivational and cognitive components was predicted to remain stable. Regardless of subject area, higher levels of task value and self-efficacy were predicted to lead to greater cognitive and regulatory strategy use, whereas higher levels of anxiety were predicted to be negatively related to cognitive and regulatory strategy use.

The final research question was, does gender have a main or interactive effect on students' motivation and cognition in these three different subject areas? Consistent with previous studies by Eccles and her colleagues (e.g., Eccles, 1983; Eccles, et al., 1989) it was predicted that the pattern of mean level differences among the three subjects examined would be different for males and females. Specifically, it was predicted males would report higher efficacy beliefs in mathematics, whereas females would report higher efficacy beliefs in English. Further, based on the work of Zimmerman and Martinez-Pons (1990) it was predicted that females would report higher levels of self-regulation than males.

METHOD

Participants

Participants for the study were 545 seventh and eighth grade students from a junior high school (7-9th grades) in a working class suburb of a midwestern city. There were slightly more females (n = 280, 51%), than males (n = 265, 49%) in the sample. Ages ranged from 11 to 15 years, with an overall mean age of 12.6 years (SD = .66). The majority of subjects (95%) were Caucasian. Seventh and eighth grade students present in school the day and class period that questionnaires were administered participated in the study. However, only students who had valid data for all of the outcome measures were included in the present analyses. All participants were enrolled in mathematics, English, and social studies. There were six teachers for mathematics, six teachers for English, and five teachers for social studies. None of the teachers in the study taught more than one subject area.

Measures

Motivation and Cognition

Students completed a self-report questionnaire adapted from Pintrich and De Groot (1990) and Pintrich, and cognition including the three motivational beliefs of task value, self-efficacy, and test Smith, Garcia, and McKeachie (1993) that assessed different facets of student motivation anxiety and the two cognitive components of cognitive and self-regulatory strategy use. The questionnaire used in this study was different from earlier versions in two ways. First, the current questionnaire included only a subset of all the scales represented on previously-published forms of the Motivated Strategies for Learning Questionnaire (Pintrich, et al. 1993). Second, items on the current questionnaire were selected and/or adapted to reflect better the academic behaviors and experiences of the age group examined. For example, a cognitive strategy use item which referred to underlining important ideas in the textbook was dropped because students in this age group typically do not buy their textbooks and are expected to keep them free of marks. On this questionnaire, students were presented with an item and then asked to respond to the item once for each of four different subject areas including mathematics, English, social studies, and science. Students responded to each item using a seven point Likert scale from (1) "Not at all like me" to (7) "Very much like me".

For this study, the task value scale was composed of nine items that assessed students' instrumental value and interest for the material studied within each subject. Students scoring high on this scale viewed the material within a particular subject as personally useful, interesting, and important. Coefficient alphas for the three subject areas ranged from .77 to .83. The self-efficacy scale included 4 items that assessed students' beliefs about how capable they were of doing the work within each subject area (α's = .80 to .84). Students high on this scale were sure they could learn and understand the material being taught in the class and perform well in the class. The four test anxiety items asked students about affective and physical symptoms of anxiety during tests (α's = .75 to .80). Higher scores on this scale reflected greater anxiety associated with tests and classroom performance. The cognitive strategy use scale included nine items that asked students about their use of different learning strategies (α's = .86 to .87) such as rehearsal and elaboration, whereas the seven self-regulation items asked students about strategies they might use to plan, monitor and control their learning (α's = .69 to .70). Higher scores on these two scales meant that students reported engaging in these strategies more often than students with lower scores on these scales.

Classroom Academic Performance

Classroom performance was measured using teacher reported grades. These grades were assigned by the teachers approximately three months after the questionnaire data were collected but reflected performance throughout the semester. Marks were converted from letter grades to a thirteen point scale with "A+" being equal to 12 and "F" being equal to a 0. In order to minimize teacher effects and differences in grading patterns, classroom grades were standardized within teachers before completing analyses.

Procedures

Students were administered questionnaires in late October. Questionnaires primarily were administered to students during their mathematics and English class periods by members of the research team. In all classes, a brief set of directions, including practice questions, were read aloud, and any questions by the students addressed. Next, all items on the particular questionnaire were read aloud while students followed along and circled their responses in individual test booklets. Classroom grades were collected using official school records at the end of the semester.

Analyses

The first purpose of this paper was to investigate subject area differences in the motivational, cognitive, and academic performance variables. These differences were examined using a repeated measures analysis of variance for each of the six outcome measures described above with subject area as a repeated measures factor. In addition, gender was included as a between subjects factor given our third research question. Multivariate results from these 3 (subject area) by 2 (gender) ANOVAs were used to check for the main effects of subject area, gender, and for a subject area by gender interaction. All significant subject area, or subject area by gender effects then were followed-up using univariate Scheffe confidence intervals. In the presence of an interaction, these post hoc tests were calculated separately for males and females.

After these mean level analyses, we performed analyses designed to investigate our second question concerning the relations among the motivational, cognitive, and performance variables. First, we present the zero-order correlations among each of the six variables within each subject area. Second, we present results from a series of multivariate regressions using the motivational variables and gender to predict the cognitive strategy use, regulatory strategy use, and performance outcomes in mathematics, English. and social studies.

Results

Subject Area Differences in Mean Level

The overall mean scores for each of the outcome measures, as well as the mean scores for both males and females separately, are presented in Table 1. Results from the repeated measures ANOVAs and appropriate follow-up tests are reported first for the motivational variables, then for the two cognitive variables. and finally for students' classroom performance.

Task Value

First, we examined students' value for the tasks in different academic subjects. Results indicated a main effect of subject, $F(2, 542) = 16.22, p < 0.001$, no main effect of gender, $F(1, 543) = 0.01, p > .10$, and a subject area by gender interaction, $F(2, 542) = 6.78, p < 0.001$. Together these results indicate that, although there was a difference in the mean level of task value across subject areas with mathematics generally higher than the other two areas contrary to our expectations (see Table 1), the pattern of these mean differences across subject areas varied for males and females.

The post hoc Scheffe tests indicated that males reported greater levels of task value in mathematics than in English ($p < 0.05$), and social studies ($p < 0.05$). However, there was no difference in the task value expressed for English and social studies ($p < 0$ .05) for males. Females, as expected from the significant interaction effect, expressed a somewhat different pattern of means. Females reported a higher mean level of task value in mathematics than in either English ($p < 0.05$) or social studies ($p < 0.05$). Unlike males, females also reported a higher level of task value in English than in social studies ($p < 0$ .05).

Self-efficacy

The repeated measures ANOVA examining self-efficacy indicated an effect for subject area, $F(2, 542) = 6.90$, $p < 0.001$, and a significant interaction between subject area and gender, $F(2, 542) = 16.57$, $p < 0.001$, but no effect for gender, F $(1, 543) = 2.07$, $p > 0.10$. The main effects for subject area was consistent with our hypothesis and showed that self-efficacy was highest in English compared to mathematics and social studies, but this effect was conditional on a gender by subject area interaction. The post hoc Scheffe tests indicated that males reported similar levels of self-efficacy across all three subject areas. That is, the differences between mathematics, English, and social studies all failed to reach significance (see Table 1). In contrast, females reported, on average, higher levels of self-efficacy in English than in mathematics ($p < 0.05$) or social studies ($p < 0.05$). Females' self-efficacy in mathematics and social studies was similar.

Test Anxiety

Results for students' level of test anxiety indicated a main effect for subject area, $F(2, 542) = 58.06$, $p < 0.001$, a main effect for gender, $F(1, 543) = 10.82$, $p < 0.001$, as well as an interaction between gender and subject area, $F(2, 542) = 14.39, 1, p < 0.001$. The main effect for subject area showed that anxiety was highest in social studies followed by mathematics and then English. However, the gender by subject area interaction indicated that males reported less anxiety in English than in social studies ($p < 0.05$), whereas there was no difference in the test anxiety reported by males in mathematics and English, or between mathematics and social studies (see Table 1). Females reported feeling less anxious in English than in mathematics ($p < 0.05$) or social studies ($p < 0.05$). Also, females were less anxious in mathematics than in social studies ($p < 0.05$).

Cognitive Strategy Use

For students' use of cognitive strategies there was a main effect of subject area, $F(2, 542) = 17.96$, $p < 0.001$, and a main effect of gender, $F(1, 543) = 5.13$, $p < 0.05$. However, unlike the motivational outcomes, the subject area by gender interaction did not reach significance, F(2, 542) = .13, $p > 0.10$. Hence, the relationship among subject areas was similar for males and females and the Scheffe post hoc tests were computed across all students. Summing across both males and females these tests indicated that, on average, students reported greater cognitive strategy use in social studies than in mathematics $(p < 0.05)$, or English ($p < 0.05$). Moreover, students reported greater levels of strategy use in English than in mathematics ($p < 0.05$). These findings were consistent with our hypotheses.

Self-Regulation

With respect to students' use of regulatory strategies, the main effects of subject area, F(2, 542) = .65, $p > 0.10$, and gender, F(1, 543) = 0.12, $p > 0.10$, and the subject area by gender interaction, F(2, 542) = 2.62, $p > 0.05$, all failed to reach significance. Hence, both males and females, on average, reported similar levels of regulatory strategy use across all three subject areas, contrary to our hypotheses.

Classroom Performance

Finally, analyses examining mean level differences in students' grades were completed. Although these analyses indicated no effect of subject area, F(2, 542) =0.08, $p > 0.10$, as would be expected given that we standardized within teachers, and no interaction of subject area and gender, F(2, 542) = 1.46, $p > 0.05$, there was a significant main effect of gender, F(1, 543) = 6.50, $p < 0.05$ On average, across all subject areas, females received higher grades than males (see Table 1).

Subject Area Differences in Relations among Variables

While results from these mean level analyses are helpful for examining differences in the level of motivational, strategy use and performance measures across subject areas, they do not provide any information about the relations among these constructs, or about how these relations might differ among the subject areas. In order to explore the relations among the motivational, strategy use, and performance variables, we next computed the zero-order correlations among variables within the same subject area.

Table 2 presents the zero-order correlations among the motivational, strategy use and performance variables within and across the subject areas of mathematics, English, and social studies. Results from these analyses indicate significant relations among many of the variables within each subject area that parallel previous findings (Pintrich & De Groot, 1990). Within each subject area, the strongest correlation was between the two strategy use variables, with $r = .66, .67$ and $.67$, p's $< .001$, in mathematics, English, and social studies, respectively. More importantly, the pattern of the relations across the three subject areas was similar, suggesting very little in the way of domain differences in the relations. The correlations among the same constructs across different subject areas were all positive and significant (see Table 2). The correlations among the cognitive strategy use and regulatory strategy use variables across subject areas were especially large (r's between .85 and .90), indicating that students tended to report similar levels of strategy use across all three domains.

In order to address our second research question further, we next computed a series of multivariate regression analyses. More specifically, we computed a separate regression equation to predict cognitive strategy use, regulatory strategy use and classroom performance within each subject area. We followed the general strategy of Pintrich and De Groot (1990) by using the motivational beliefs to predict the cognitive outcomes. Independent variables for these nine equations (three each in mathematics, English, and social studies) were gender (dummy-coded) task value, self-efficacy, and test anxiety assessed with respect to each specific subject area. initially, we also included the three cross-product terms for the interactions between gender and each of the three motivational predictors to check for gender by motivation interactions. None of these interactions were significant, so they were dropped from the final analyses and are not reported. Results from these final regression analyses are presented in Table 3, and will be discussed first for cognitive strategy use, then regulatory strategy use, and finally for classroom performance.

Cognitive Strategy Use

Gender, task value, self-efficacy, and test anxiety together accounted for a significant portion of the variance in cognitive strategy use in mathematics, $F(4, 540) = 61.66$, $p < 0.001$, English, $F(4, 540) = 75.12$, $p < 0.001$, and social studies, $F(4, 540) = 62.77$, $p < 0.001$. As presented in Table 3, task value had the greatest individual standardized coefficient in the analyses predicting cognitive strategy use in mathematics, English and social studies. This variable uniquely explained between 15% (English) and 24% (mathematics) of the variance in cognitive strategy use, with greater task value predicting greater use of cognitive strategies. In other words, students who valued and were interested in the subject area reported higher levels of cognitive strategy use in each of the three subjects examined. Self-efficacy and test anxiety also were both significant individual predictors of students' cognitive strategy use in all three subject areas, although to a somewhat lesser degree than task value. After accounting for the other variables in the analyses, self-efficacy uniquely explained between 2% (mathematics) and 9% (English) of the variance in cognitive strategy use, whereas test anxiety uniquely explained approximately 2% of the variance in cognitive strategy use across all three subject areas. In mathematics, English, and social studies, students who reported greater self efficacy and higher levels of test anxiety were more likely to report using cognitive strategies than students who were less efficacious and less anxious. Finally, the standardized coefficient for gender was also significant although this variable uniquely explained less than 1% of the variance in strategy use in each of the three subjects examined after accounting for differences in the three motivational variables. Generally, females reported using cognitive strategies more often than males within each of the three subject areas (see Table 3).

Regulatory Strategy Use

Gender, task value, self-efficacy, and test anxiety together accounted for approximately one-third of the variance in regulatory strategy use in mathematics, F (4, 540) = 74. 81, $p < 0.001$, English, F (4, 540) = 63.87, $p < 0.001$, and social studies, F(4, 540) = 63.87, $p < 0.001$. Task value was the single best predictor of regulatory strategy in all three subject areas. This variable alone uniquely explained between 13% (English) and 22% (mathematics) of the variance in students' reported use of regulatory strategies (see Table 3). Across all three subject areas, students who reported greater task value for the subject area reported using regulatory strategies more often than students with lower task value. The significant coefficients for self-efficacy and test anxiety indicated that these variables also were important predictors of regulatory strategy use. After accounting for the other variables in the analyses, self-efficacy uniquely explained between 1% (mathematics) and 4% (English) of the variance in regulatory strategy use (see Table 3). Similarly, test anxiety by itself explained between 2% (mathematics) and 3% (social studies) of the variance in regulatory strategy use (see Table 3). However, while greater levels of self-efficacy were associated with greater reported use of regulatory strategies, students who reported higher levels of test anxiety were less likely to report engaging in regulatory strategy use across all three subject areas. The standardized coefficient for gender was non-significant in mathematics, English, and social studies.

Performance

With respect to classroom performance, the four predictors together explained a significant amount of the variance in classroom performance in mathematics, F(4, 540) = 31. 04, $p < 0.001$, English, F(4, 540) = 33.99, $p < 0.001$, and social studies, F(4, 540) = 30.61, $p < 0.001$. Unlike the strategy use equations, the standardized regression coefficient for task value indicated that this variable was a non-significant predictor of classroom performance in each of the three subject areas studied (see Table 3). The standardized regression coefficients for both self-efficacy and test anxiety, however, were each significant in mathematics, English and social studies. Self-efficacy, by itself, explained approximately 6% of the variance in classroom grade, even after accounting for students' gender, task value, and level of test anxiety. Similarly, test anxiety uniquely explained approximately 6% of the variance in classroom grade in mathematics, English and social studies (see Table 3). In all three subject areas, students with greater self-efficacy, on average, received higher classroom grades than students with lower self efficacy. In contrast, students who reported higher levels of test anxiety received lower grades than students who were less anxious (see Table 3).

DISCUSSION

This study investigated contextual differences in motivation and self-regulated learning in three different subject areas. With respect to our first research question concerning mean level differences, our findings provide evidence that the motivational aspects of self-regulated learning are, to some degree, context specific. In particular, we found differences in students' reported value and interest for academic tasks, self-efficacy, and test anxiety across the academic subject areas of mathematics, English, and social studies. Moreover, as suggested in our third research question, the nature of these mean level difference was moderated by gender for each of the three motivational constructs examined.

In terms of students' reported value or interest in classroom tasks, students tended to view mathematics as more important, useful and interesting than either English or social studies. Both males and females rated mathematics as the most important, useful, and interesting subject overall. However, there were gender differences in terms of comparisons between social studies and English. For males, English and social studies were perceived in the same way in terms of value and interest, whereas for females, English was rated as more important than social studies (although not as highly as mathematics). These results parallel the findings of Eccles and Wigfield and their colleagues (Eccles, 1983; 1984; Eccles, et al. 1989; Wigfield, et al. 1991; Wigfield & Eccles, 1994) where males and females did not differ in terms of their liking and value for mathematics, but that males usually find English (or reading, in the studies of young elementary children, e.g., Wigfield & Eccles, 1994) as less interesting and important. The consistency in these findings for task value and interest across a number of different studies of both elementary and secondary students suggest that any difficulties females may have in mathematics is not due to variations in their liking or value for mathematics.

However, our results do show that females are less likely to have adaptive levels of efficacy and anxiety in mathematics. In particular, males reported similar levels of self-efficacy across all subject areas, whereas females reported higher levels of self-efficacy in English than in either mathematics or social studies. Finally, with respect to test anxiety, males reported similar levels of test anxiety in mathematics and English, while females reported lower levels of anxiety in English than in mathematics. Again, our results are in line with previous findings of the gender differences in efficacy and competence beliefs for mathematics and English (Eccles, 1983, 1984; Wigfield & Eccles, 1994) suggesting that females do not have as adaptive efficacy beliefs as males. This is particularly troublesome as our results and the work of Eccles and Wigfield and their colleagues also show that there are few gender differences in actual classroom performance or achievement. In fact, in our study, females received higher average grades than males in all three subject areas. This "lack of calibration" (lack of a good match between efficacy beliefs and actual achievement) is a consistent pattern in the research on gender differences with females traditionally underestimating their competence and efficacy relative to their performance in comparison to males (see Phillips & Zimmerman, 1990; Pintrich & Schunk, 1996). Accordingly, any problems females might experience in mathematics seem more likely to stem from less adaptive efficacy and anxiety beliefs than lack of value or interest.

At the same time, it appears that these gender differences in efficacy and anxiety beliefs do not necessarily result in less cognitive strategy use or self-regulation for females. In terms of cognitive strategy use, we found differences in the level of cognitive strategy use across subject areas as predicted. As a group, students reported higher levels of cognitive strategy use in social studies than in English or mathematics, and higher levels in English than in mathematics. In addition, females reported higher levels of cognitive strategy use than males across all three subjects. In contrast and against predictions, the reported level of regulatory strategy use was similar among all subject areas for both males and females. Hence, while students tended to report using more cognitive strategies in social studies, they did not report regulating their learning in social studies any more than in mathematics or English. Of course, given that we standardized grades within teachers, there were no differences by subject area in academic performance.

The finding that students report greater cognitive strategy use in social studies fits neatly with the work of Stodolsky and Grossman (Grossman & Stodolsky, 1994; 1995; Stodolsky 1988) who found that social studies classrooms might offer more diverse and engaging tasks than mathematics classrooms. Taken together, our results on student reports of cognitive strategy use and Stodolsky and Grossman's results on disciplinary differences suggest that the level of self-regulated learning in terms of strategy use can vary as a function of subject area differences in classroom context. Of course, a definitive conclusion awaits studies that combine observation of disciplinary differences in actual classroom tasks and instruction as well as concomitant differences in the level of students' self-regulated learning.

Nevertheless, it seems that level of cognitive strategy use can be sensitive to contextual differences and there is a need for future research to investigate how the different dimensions of the classroom and academic disciplines are linked to self-regulated learning as suggested by Zimmerman (1994).

With respect to our second research question, we found very similar relations among the motivational, strategy use, and performance outcomes across subject areas. Both the correlational and regression analyses indicated that the relations among students' task value, self-efficacy, test anxiety, cognitive strategy use, regulatory strategy use and performance were similar for mathematics, English and social studies. For example, the amount of variance explained by the motivational variables and gender in students' cognitive strategy use, regulatory strategy use and performance were very similar across all three subject areas. Further, in all of the analyses there were no differences in terms of which predictors were significant across subject areas. In mathematics, English, and social studies, task value was the best individual predictor of both cognitive and regulatory strategy use, whereas task value was not a significant predictor of classroom performance. As we have found in other studies (Pintrich & De Groot, 1990; Pintrich, et al. 1994) students who valued and were interested in the content of the subject area were more likely to report using deeper processing strategies and more self-regulatory strategies. Paralleling findings from many different studies (see Pintrich & Schrauben, 1992 for review), students were more deeply cognitively engaged in learning when their interest and value was high.

In contrast, task value was not a significant predictor of actual performance in comparison to self-efficacy. Self-efficacy predicted both strategy use variables as well as classroom performance similarly in all three subject areas. Students who felt they were capable of learning and understanding the material and expected to do well were more likely to report) using a variety of cognitive and self-regulatory strategies. In addition, they also received higher grades. This finding that efficacy predicts actual performance and task value does not, although both predict strategy use, is consistent with previous findings (Pintrich & De Groot, 1990). It appears that task value is related to the initial "choice" of becoming involved in academic tasks in terms of higher levels of cognitive strategy use and self-regulation, but in terms of the ultimate outcome of grades, self-efficacy is more important, as well as actual strategy use (Pintrich & De Groot, 1990).

From a social cognitive and self-regulated learning perspective, it appears that interest and value can help a student choose to become involved in a task, somewhat like a "starter" for a car, but once involved, the self-regulation processes of strategy use and adaptive efficacy beliefs are more important for "steering" and controlling actual performance (cf., Garcia & Pintrich, 1994: Schunk, 1994; Zimmerman, 1994). Similar to this interpretation, results from studies in an expectancy-value framework (see Eccles, 1983; Wigfield, 1994; Wigfield & Eccles, 1992; 1994) consistently reveal that task value is related to the choice of taking additional courses in a subject area, but once actually enrolled in a specific course, task value beliefs do not predict course achievement, while efficacy and competence beliefs do predict actual achievement. Although more microgenetic research is needed to investigate the relations between task value, efficacy and self-regulation processes in "real-time" as students actually learn (see Butler & Winne, 1995), the results seem to be reliable and consistent across a number of different studies from different theoretical frameworks.

Although test anxiety was also an important predictor of both strategy use and performance in similar ways across subject areas, it was related to cognitive strategy use differently than it was to regulation and performance. In particular, students who reported higher levels of test anxiety were more likely to engage in cognitive strategies, but were less likely to use regulatory strategies and tended to receive lower grades. This finding is consistent with previous work in a social cognitive framework (Pintrich & De Groot, 1990). Students who are anxious may use more cognitive strategies in an attempt to do better, but they have difficulties in regulating their learning and often end up performing more poorly (Bandura, 1986; Pintrich & Schunk, 1996).

In summary, these finding provide some evidence that the relation among motivational, strategy use, and performance measures are similar across subject areas. However, the current study did not test the similarity of these relations directly and additional work is needed to replicate these findings. Another caveat to these findings is that the relatively stronger relations between the motivational and strategy use constructs as compared to the relation between motivational and performance measures might be due to the nature in which these different factors were assessed. Both the motivational and strategy use variables were measured using student self-reports, whereas academic performance was collected using school grades. Hence, the strong relations between the motivational and strategy use variables might be inflated somewhat because they are all based on students' self-reports.

Nonetheless, the current findings show that students may report mean level differences in the motivational and cognitive components of self-regulated learning across different academic context, but that the relations among these components are similar across contexts. That is, the level and quality of student motivation or cognition for a subject area may vary, but the pattern of the relations between motivation and cognition seems robust across subject areas. Of course, the generalizability of this study is limited by only including 17 teachers across the three subject areas. Future research will have to examine the reliability of the subject area mean level differences we found by including more teachers within each subject area. In addition, as noted above, actual data on the nature of the classroom context and instructional activities will be important to tease apart subject area differences from general instructional differences. Further, research which employed observational or on-line assessments of motivation and strategy use would provide support for the current conclusions. Nevertheless, our findings on the similarity of the relations between motivation and cognition across subject areas suggest that the general models of self-regulated learning that are being developed are applicable to different academic domains and can be fruitfully used to understand student learning in different classroom contexts.

CHRISTOPHER A. WOLTERS
Department of Educational Psychology and Psychology
University of Houston, Houston TX

PAUL R. PINTRICH
Combined Program in Education and Psychology
University of Michigan, Ann Arbor MI

Footnotes

1. Although students were asked about science, the data for science were not included in the present study because half of the students were not currently enrolled in a specific science class when the questionnaire was administered. In this school eighth graders only took science for one semester out of the two semesters with half the sample taking it first semester and the other half taking it second semester.

Note

1. An earlier version of this chapter was presented at the European Association for Research of Learning and Instruction, Mijmegen, The Netherlands, August 1995. The data reported on in this chapter are part of the Competence and Commitment Project conducted at The Combined Program in Education and Psychology at the University of Michigan. We thank our colleagues on this project including Eric Anderman, Anastasia Danos Elder, Teresa Garcia, Lynley Hicks, Barbara Hofer, Helen Patrick, Allison Ryan, Tim Urdan and Shirley Yu.

Table 1.

Descriptive statistics for the motivational strategy use and performance variables in mathematics, English and social studies for total sample and gender.

Variable	Males M	SD	Females M	SD	Total M	SD
Task Value						
Mathematics	5.51	1.06	5.51	1.10	5.51	1.08
English	5.32	1.08	5.37	1.16	5.34	1.12
Social studies	5.35	1.25	5.11	1.26	5.23	1.26
Self-efficacy						
Mathematics	5.59	1.15	5.36	1.23	5.47	1.20
English	5.64	1.09	5.71	1.03	5.67	1.06
Social studies	5.54	1.21	5.33	1.28	5.43	1.25
Test anxiety						
Mathematics	3.25	1.58	3.67	1.64	3.M	1.62
English	3.13	1.51	3.26	1.41	3.19	1.46
Social studies	3.40	1.65	4.04	1.62	3.73	1.66
Cognitive strategy use						
Mathematics	5.18	1.19	5.38	1.14	5.28	1.17
English	5.22	1.17	5.45	1.12	5.34	1.15
Social studies	5.34	1.13	5.54	1.15	5.44	1.14
Regulatory strategy use						
Mathematics	4.97	1.04	4.94	1.16	4.95	1.10
English	4.96	1.07	4.99	1.14	4.98	1.10
Social studies	5.00	1.08	4.91	1.17	4.95	1.12
Performance						
Mathematics	-.01	.95	.15	.96	.07	.96
English	-.05	.97	.20	.86	.08	.92
Social studies	.01	.92	.16	.94	.08	.93

Note. Total $N = 545$; $n = 265$ for boys; $n = 280$ for girls.

Table 2.
Zero order correlations among the motivational, strategy use and performance variables

	1.	2.	3.	4.	5.	6.	7.	8.	9.	10.	11.	12.	13.	14.	15.	16.	17.
Task Value																	
1. Mathematics																	
2. English	.65																
3. Social studies	.51	.62															
Self-efficacy																	
4. Mathematics	.60	.37	.33														
5. English	.51	.58	.38	.55													
6. Social studies	.42	.38	.57	.58	.59												
Test anxiety																	
7. Mathematics	-.20	-.05	-.05	-.48	-.21	-.22											
8. English	-.13	-.14	-.04	-.23	-.41	-.20	.72										
9. Social studies	-.12	-.07	-.17	-.26	-.24	-.39	.69	.72									
Cognitive strategy use																	
10. Mathematics	.54	.43	.39	.35	.37	.31	-.01	-.01	.03								
11. English	.49	.54	.41	.29	.46	.30	.05	-.02	.04	.87							
12. Social studies	.47	.45	.51	.32	.41	.41	.00	-.03	.00	.85	.85						
Regulatory strategy use																	
13. Mathematics	.57	.40	.37	.46	.39	.35	-.28	-.25	-.24	.66	.58	.61					
14. English	.51	.50	.40	.38	.47	.34	-.24	-.29	-.24	.64	.67	.62	.90				
15. Social studies	.46	.40	.51	.38	.41	.45	-.22	-.25	-.29	.59	.56	.67	.85	.85			
Performance																	
16. Mathematics	.25	.07	.03	.37	.23	.20	-.35	-.26	-.23	.11	.06	.12	.23	.17	.17		
17. English	.27	.19	.06	.28	.38	.25	-.20	-.35	-.24	.13	.14	.19	.23	.23	.21	.68	
18. Social studies	.29	.20	.17	.34	.37	.35	-.30	-.30	-.36	.16	.15	.22	.29	.27	.30	.68	.63

Note. $N = 545$, r's ≥ 0.10, $p < 0.05$.

Table 3
Summary of regression analyses for variables predicting cognitive strategy use, regulatory strategy use, and performance in mathematics. English and social studies (N=545)

	Mathematics			English			Social Studies		
Variable	B	SEB	β	B	SEB	β	B	SEB	β
Cognitive strategy use									
Gender	0.20	0.08	.08*	0.17	0.08	0.07*	0.27	0.02	0.12**
Task value	0.53	0.05	0.49***	0.40	0.04	0.39***	0.36	0.04	0.40***
Self-efficacy	0.13	0.05	0.13**	0.33	.05	0.30***	0.23	0.04	0.25***
Test anxiety	0.10	0.03	0.14***	0.13	0.03	0.16***	0.10	0.03	0.15***
R^2			0.31***			0.36***			0.32***
Regulatory strategy use									
Gender	0.04	0.08	0.02	0.01	0.08	0.00	0.10	0.08	0.04
Task value	0.48	0.04	0.47***	0.36	0.04	0.36***	0.35	0.04	0.39***
Self-efficacy	0.11	0.04	0.11*	0.20	0.05	0.19***	0.14	0.04	0.16***
Test anxiety	-0.09	0.03	-0.13***	-0.12	0.03	-0.16***	-0.12	0.03	-0.17***
R^2			0.36***			0.32***			0.32***
Academic performance									
Gender	0.26	0.07	0.13***	0.24	0.07	0.13***	0.28	0.07	0.15***
Task value	0.04	0.04	0.04	0.02	0.04	0.02	-0.02	0.04	-0.02
Self efficacy	0.18	0.04	0.23***	0.22	0.05	0.25***	0.20	0.04	0.26***
Test anxiety	-0.15	0.03	-0.25***	-0.16	0.03	-0.25***	-0.15	0.02	-0.26***
R^2			0.19***			0.20***			0.18***

Note. *p <0.05; ** p<0.01; *** p< 0.001. For gender, 0=boys, 1:girls. B= unstandardized beta, SEB = standard error of B; β = standardized beta.

REFERENCES

Ames, C. (1992). Classrooms: Goals, structures, and student motivation. *Journal of Educational Psychology*, 84, 261-271.

Bandura, A. (1986). *Social foundations of thought and action: A social cognitive theory.* Englewood Cliffs, NJ: Prentice-Hall.

Brown, A., Bransford, J., Ferrara, R., & Campione, J. (1983). Learning, remembering, and understanding. In P. Mussen (Series Ed.) & J. Flavell & E. Markman (Vol. Eds.), *Handbook of child psychology: Vol. 3. Cognitive development* (pp. 77-166). New York: Wiley.

Butler, D., & Winne, P. (1995). Feedback and self-regulated learning: A theoretical synthesis. *Review of Educational Research*, 65,245-281.

Corno, L. (1989). Self-regulated learning: A volitional analysis. In B. J. Zimmerman & D. H. Schunk (Eds.), *Self-regulated learning and academic achievement: Theory, research, and practice* (pp. 111-141). New York: Springer-Verlag.

Cohen, E. (1994). Restructuring the classroom: Conditions for productive small groups. *Review of Educational Research*, 1-35.

Doyle, W. (1983). Academic work. *Review of Educational Research*, 53, 159-199.

Eccles, J. S. (1983). Expectancies, values, and academic behavior. In J. T. Spence (Ed.), *Achievement and achievement motives* (pp. 75- 146). San Francisco: Freeman.

Eccles, J. S. (1984). Sex differences in achievement patterns. In T. Sonderegger (Ed.), *Nebraska symposium on motivation* (Vol. 32, pp. 97- 132). Lincoln, NE: University of Nebraska Press.

Eccles, J. S., Wigfield, A., Flanagan, C., Miller, C., Reuman, D., & Yee, D. (1989). Self-concepts, domain values, and self-esteem: Relations and changes at early adolescence. *Journal of Personality*, 57, 283-310.

Garcia, T., & Pintrich, P. R. (1994). Regulating motivation and cognition in the classroom: The role of self-schemes and self-regulatory strategies. In D. H. Schunk & B. J. Zimmerman (Eds.), *Self-regulation of learning and performance: Issues and educational applications* (pp. 127-153). Hillsdale, NJ: Lawrence Erlbaum Associates.

Grossman, P., & Stodolsky, S. (1994). Considerations of content and the circumstances of secondary school teaching. In L. Darling-Hammond (Ed.), *Review of Research in Education* (Vol. 20, pp. 179-221), Washington, DC: American Educational Research Association.

Grossman, P., & Stodolsky, S. (1995). Content as context: The role of school subjects in secondary teaching. *Educational Researcher*, (8), 5- 11.

Maehr, M. L., & Midgley, C. (1991). Enhancing student motivation: A school-wide approach. *Educational Psychologist*, 26,399427.

Meece, J., Blumenfeld, P., & Hoyle, R. (1988). Students' goal orientation and cognitive engagement in classroom activities. *Journal of Educational Psychology*, 80, 514-523.

Phillips, D., & Zimmerman, M. (1990). The developmental course of perceived competence and incompetence among competent children. In R. J. Sternberg & J. Kolligian (Eds.), *Competence Considered* (pp. 41-66). New Haven, CT: Yale University Press.

Pintrich, P. R., & De Groot, E. (1990). Motivational and self-regulated learning components of classroom academic performance. *Journal of Educational Psychology*, 82,3340.

Pintrich, P. R., Roeser, R., & De Groot, E. (1994). Classroom and individual differences in early adolescents' motivation and self-regulated learning. *Journal of Early Adolescence*, 14, 139-161.

Pintrich, P. R., & Schrauben, B. (1992). Students' motivational beliefs and their cognitive engagement in classroom tasks. In D. H. Schunk & J. Meece (Eds.), *Student perceptions in the classroom: Causes and consequences* (pp. 149-183). Hillsdale, NJ: Lawrence Erlbaum Associates.

Pintrich, P. R., & Schunk, D. H. (1996). *Motivation in education: Theory, research, and applications.* Englewood Cliffs, NJ: Merrill Prentice-Hall.

Pintrich, P. R., Smith, D. A. .F., Garcia, T., & McKeachie, W. J. (1993). Reliability and predictive validity of the Motivated Strategies for Learning Questionnaire (MSLQ). *Educational and Psychological Measurement*, 53, 801-813.

Schneider, W., & Pressley, M. (1989). *Memory development between 2 and 20.* New York: Springer-Verlag.

Schunk, D. H. (1989). Self-efficacy and achievement behaviors. *Educational Psychology Review*, 1, 173-208.

Schunk, D. H. (1991). Self-efficacy and academic motivation. *Educational Psychologist*, 26, 207-231.

Schunk, D. H. (1994). Self-regulation of self-efficacy and attributions in academic settings. In D. H. Schunk & B. J. Zimmerman (Eds.), *Self-regulation of learning and performance: Issues and educational applications* (pp. 75-99). Hillsdale, NJ: Lawrence Erlbaum Associates.

Siegler, R. S. (1988). Individual differences in strategy choices: Good students, not-so-good students, and perfectionists. *Child Development*, 59, 833-851.

Sternberg, R. J. (1988). *The triarchic mind: A new theory of human intelligence*. New York: Viking.

Sternberg, R. J. (1994). PRSVL: An integrative framework for understanding mind in context. In R. J. Sternberg & R. K. Wagner (Eds.), *Mind in context: Interactionist perspectives on human intelligence* (pp. 218-232). New York: Cambridge University Press.

Stodolsky, S. (1988). *The subject matters: Classroom activity in math and social studies*. Chicago: The University of Chicago Press.

Stodolsky, S., & Grossman, P. (1995). The impact of subject matter on curricular activity: An analysis of five academic subjects. *American Educational Research Journal*, 32, 227-249.

Stodolsky, S., Salk, S., & Glaessner, B. (1991). Student views about learning math and social studies. *American Educational Research Journal*, 28, 89-116.

Weinstein, C. E., & Mayer, R. (1986). The teaching of learning strategies. In M. C. Wittrock (Ed.), *Handbook of Research on Teaching* (pp. 315-327). New York: Macmillan.

Wigfield, A. (1994). Expectancy-value theory of achievement motivation: A developmental perspective. *Educational Psychology Review*, 6, 49-77.

Wigfield, A.. & Eccles, J. S. (1989). Test anxiety in elementary and secondary school students. *Educational Psychologist* 24, 159-183.

Wigfield, A., & Eccles, J. S. (1992). The development of achievement task values: A theoretical analyses. *Developmental Review*, 12, 265-310.

Wigfield, A., & Eccles, J. S. (1994). Children's competence beliefs, achievement values, and general self-esteem change across elementary and middle school. *Journal of Early Adolescence*, 14, 107-138.

Wigfield, A., Eccles, J. S., MacIver, D., Reuman, D., & Midgley, C. (1991). Transitions at early adolescence: Changes in children's domain-specific self-perceptions and general self-esteem across the transition to junior high school. *Developmental Psychology*, 27, 552-565.

Zimmerman, B. J. (1989). Models of self-regulated learning and academic achievement. In B. J. Zimmerman & D.H. Schunk (Eds.), *Self-regulated learning and academic achievement: Theory, research, and practice* (pp. 1-25). New York: Springer-Verlag.

Zimmerman, B. J. (1994). Dimensions of academic self-regulation: A conceptual framework for education. In D. H. Schunk & B. J. Zimmerman (Eds.), *Self-regulation of learning and performance: Issues and educational applications* (pp. 3-21). Hillsdale, NJ: Lawrence Erlbaum Associates.

Zimmerman, B. J., & Martinez-Pons, M. (1990). Student differences in self-regulated Learning: Relating grade, sex, and giftedness to self-efficacy and strategy use. *Journal of Educational Psychology*, 82, 51-59.

PART III METACOGNITION AND TEACHING

The title of this book is strongly influenced by the three chapters in this section. In relationship to the BACEIS model of improving thinking which underlies the organization of this book, the first two parts of the book concentrate on the students' internal supersystem, cognitive and affective components respectively, while the next two parts concentrate on the external supersystem, comprised of the academic and the nonacademic environments Part three represents an interaction between students' internal cognitive subsystem, and a feature of the external supersystem, the academic environment subsystem: the teacher's own metacognition applied to teaching. The model suggests that teachers who use metacognition effectively in their own professional lives are likely to be more successful enhancing their students' metacognition and academic achievement than teachers who do not. All three chapters in this section differ from chapters in the first two sections in that the unit of analysis of metacognition is the teacher rather than the student. Artzt and Armour-Thomas's chapter provides a theoretical framework of teacher metacognition as problem solving, which helps set the stage for many of the teacher metacognition applications presented in the next two chapters. The Artzt and Armour-Thomas framework for metacognition in teaching is similar to those described for metacognition in learning in Chapters 1 and 3 by Schraw and Hartman, respectively.

Artzt and Armour-Thomas's chapter is an exploratory study of teachers' metacognition. It results in their innovative metacognitive framework which uses a "teaching as problem solving" perspective to analyze instructional practices of beginning and experienced high school mathematics teachers. Their methodology involves examining their thoughts before, during and after conducting lessons.

"Teaching Metacognitively" is a chapter I wrote on the use of metacognition in teaching. It examines why teaching metacognitively is important and describes my personal experiences applying metacognitive techniques to my own teaching. In addition it describes methods I use to enhance other teachers' metacognition about their instruction. These methods can be applied or adapted to virtually any subject domain.

In the last chapter in this section I concentrate on metacognition in both science teaching and learning. It draws on my own experiences working with two biology professors: Joseph Griswold and Daniel Lemons, my colleagues at The City College of the City University of New York. It describes: research on students' metacognition in science learning and methods I have used to strengthen science professors' metacognition about their teaching and to develop students' metacognition about their science learning.

CHAPTER 7

MATHEMATICS TEACHING AS PROBLEM SOLVING:
A FRAMEWORK FOR STUDYING TEACHER METACOGNITION UNDERLYING INSTRUCTIONAL PRACTICE IN MATHEMATICS

ALICE F. ARTZT   ELEANOR ARMOUR-THOMAS

ABSTRACT. The purpose of this exploratory study was to use a "teaching as problem solving" perspective to examine the components of metacognition underlying the instructional practice of seven experienced and seven beginning teachers of secondary school mathematics. A metacognitive framework was developed to examine the thoughts of teachers before, during and after lesson enactments. Data were obtained through observations, lesson plans, videotapes, and audiotapes of structured interviews during the course of one semester. Data analysis suggests that the metacognition of teachers plays a well-defined role in classroom practice. These findings provide useful insights for researchers and teacher educators in their preservice and inservice mathematics programs.

Within the last two decades, the perspective on teaching and learning has shifted from one grounded in behavioral psychology to one grounded in cognitive psychology. Researchers have now broadened their lens of inquiry by moving beyond the mere examination of teacher behaviors to studying teacher cognitions (Brown & Baird, 1993; Ernest, 1988; Shavelson, 1986; Shulman, 1986). Our purpose in this exploratory study is to use a "teaching as problem solving" perspective to examine the metacognition underlying instructional practice in mathematics. To this end we developed a metacognitive framework that allowed for a systematic examination of the full range of teacher thoughts. We have conceptualized knowledge, beliefs, and goals as overarching metacognitive components that directly influence teacher thinking across three stages of teaching: preactive (planning), interactive (monitoring and regulating), and postactive (assessing and revising).

In the first section of this paper, we provide a rationale for the development and description of the framework. This is followed by a description of the methodology used to differentiate teacher metacognition associated with fourteen

H.J. Hartman (ed.), Metacognition in Learning and Instruction, 127–148.

mathematics lessons, each taught by a different teacher. This is followed by a discussion of findings that have implications for researchers and teacher educators for conceiving of mathematics teaching as problem solving where metacognition plays a well-defined role.

THEORETICAL BACKGROUND FOR DEVELOPMENT
OF THE FRAMEWORK

Numerous studies conducted within the expert-novice research tradition have yielded consistent findings on the differences in the thoughts and instructional practices of expert and novice teachers (Borko & Livingston, 1989; Leinhardt, 1989; Livingston & Borko, 1990). Some of the components of teacher metacognition as it relates to instructional practice include teacher knowledge (Ball, 1991; Peterson, 1988), beliefs (Dougherty, 1990; Peterson, Fennema, Carpenter & Loef, 1989; Richardson, Anders, Tidwell & Lloyd, 1991), goals (Cobb, Yackel & Wood, 1991; NCTM, 1989), and thought processes (Clark & Peterson, 1986; Fogarty, Wang & Creek, 1983; Wilson, Shulman & Richert, 1987). Although such investigations have called attention to the importance of these mental attributes in the study of teaching, most studied the components of teacher metacognition in isolation of each other. However, it appears that knowledge, beliefs, goals and thinking processes are conceptually intertwined. Thus, studying them in isolation of each other provides an incomplete understanding of the mental life of teachers as it relates to their instructional practice. Some researchers have begun to create frameworks to examine the nature and quality of the interrelationships of different components of teacher metacognition (Fennema, Carpenter & Peterson, 1989; Fennema & Franke, 1992; Shavelson, 1986).

An assumption underlying research in mathematical problem solving is that there is a problem to be solved and the expert problem solver engages in cognitive and metacognitive behaviors as he/she attempts to solve the problem of interest across three stages of problem solving: a) preparation to solve the problem, b) actual problem solving, and c) verification of problem solution (Artzt & Armour-Thomas, 1992; Garofalo & Lester, 1985; Polya, 1945; Silver, 1987). In this study we are applying the problem-solving metaphor in the examination of teacher metacognition in relation to instructional practice. In this case, the problem to be solved is how to teach a lesson that will promote student learning with understanding. This notion about the goal of instruction is widely shared by researchers and teachers (Hiebert & Carpenter, 1992). From this perspective, three questions emerge for study How do teachers prepare to solve the problem of teaching a lesson? How do they solve the problem of teaching a lesson in the classroom? How do they verify that the problem of teaching the lesson was solved?

In our earlier work on student problem solving (Artzt & Armour-Thomas, 1992) we used the term *metacognitive behavior* to describe statements made about the problem or statements made about the problem-solving process. In contrast, *cognitive behaviors* referred to the actual on-line processing of information. With slight modification we use these terms again. Viewing the teacher as problem solver, we consider the "actual on-line processing of information" as the enactment of the lesson in the classroom as the *cognitive* component of the problem-solving endeavor. In contrast, we refer to commentaries *about* the lesson or *about* processes associated with teaching the lesson as the *metacognitive* components of the problem-solving endeavor. These metacognitive components include teachers' commentaries regarding their *goals, beliefs, knowledge, planning, monitoring, regulating, assessing,* and *revising*

Recent research using a conception of teaching as problem solving has begun to shed light on the relationships between metacognition and instructional practice in mathematics (Artzt & Armour-Thomas, 1993; Carpenter, 1989; Fennema, Carpenter & Peterson, 1989). We share the position that metacognition directs and controls the instructional behaviors of teachers in the classroom. (See Figure 1.)

The purpose of this exploratory study is to use a problem-solving perspective to understand the components of metacognition that underlie the instructional practice of teachers of secondary school mathematics. In particular, we wish to characterize the content and focus of teachers' metacognitions and explore how these metacognitions influence their practice in the classroom. In order to systematically examine teacher metacognition we developed a metacognitive framework. A detailed description of the development of this framework follows.

THE TEACHER METACOGNITIVE FRAMEWORK

The Teacher Metacognitive Framework to examine teaching as problem solving (TMF) was developed to examine the mental activities of teachers associated with instructional practice. We used Jackson's (1968) conceptual distinctions of preactive, interactive and postactive stages of teaching to examine teacher thoughts before, during and after teaching a lesson. Over the last two decades a great deal of theoretical and empirical research has been conducted from this perspective on teaching. Based on that work, we have selected eight components of metacognition for study: *knowledge, beliefs, goals, planning, monitoring and regulating, assessing* and *revising*

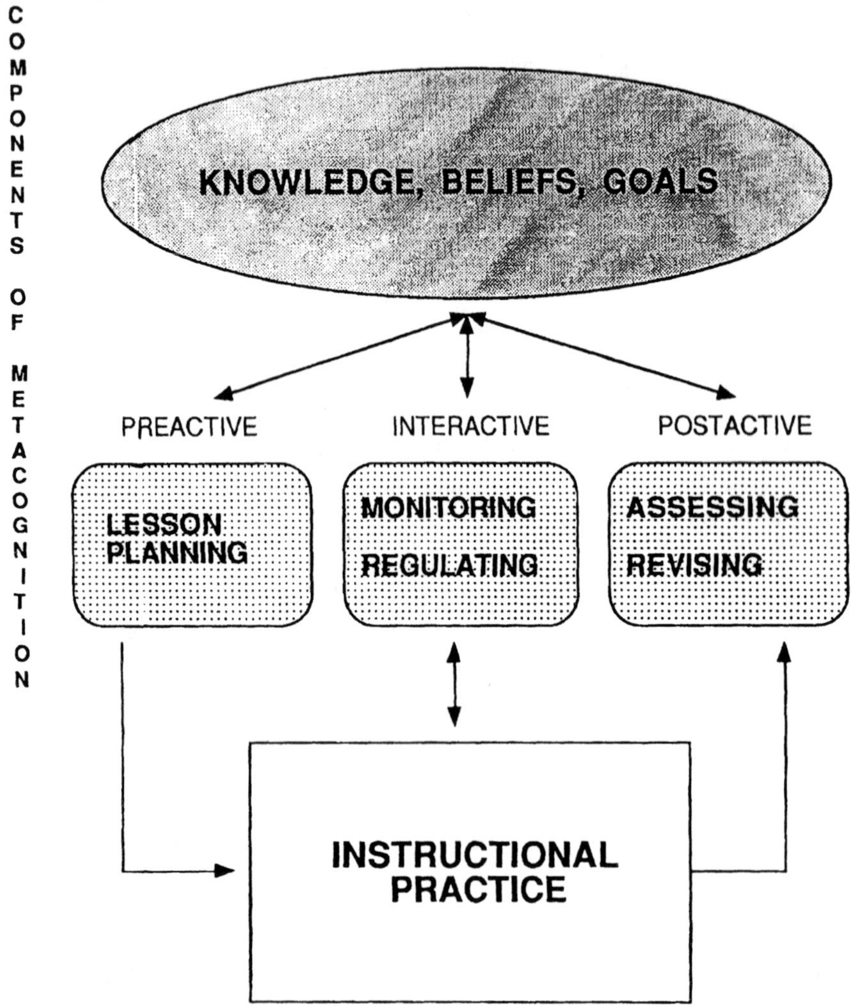

C
O
M
P
O
N
E
N
T
S

O
F

M
E
T
A
C
O
G
N
I
T
I
O
N

KNOWLEDGE, BELIEFS, GOALS

PREACTIVE   INTERACTIVE   POSTACTIVE

LESSON
PLANNING

MONITORING
REGULATING

ASSESSING
REVISING

INSTRUCTIONAL
PRACTICE

Figure 1. **A framework for the examination of teacher metacognition related to instructional practice in mathematics**

We define teacher knowledge as an integrated system of internalized information acquired about pupils, content and pedagogy. This definition is based on Shulman's (1986) conception of leacher knowledge as a multidimensional and interrelated construct that include subject matter knowledge, pedagogical knowledge, and knowledge of students. We concur with the views of other researchers (Fennema & Franke, 1992; Leinhardt, Putnam, Stein, & Baxter, 1991; Peterson, 1988) that these components of teacher knowledge can make a difference in instructional practice and student learning.

Some generalizations regarding *beliefs* have emerged from a synthesis of the existing literature by Ernest (1988), Kagan (1992), Pajares (1992) and Thompson (1992). They include descriptions of beliefs as: a) a personalized form of dynamic knowledge that constrains the teachers' perceptions, judgments and behavior, b) interpretative filters though which new phenomena are interpreted and meanings ascribed to experiences, and c) implicit assumptions about content, students and learning. It would appear from these works that beliefs, though different from knowledge, share attributes similar to knowledge. We define beliefs as an integrated system of personalized assumptions about the nature of a subject, its teaching and learning.

In the *Curriculum and Evaluation Standards,* NCTM (1989) has set forth its vision of mathematical power through the articulation of five general *goals* for all students: that they value mathematics, become confident in their ability to do mathematics, become mathematical problem solvers, learn to communicate mathematically, and learn to reason mathematically (p. 5). The NCTM (1991) expects teachers to reflect these goals in their instructional practice. Furthermore, researchers have begun to give increasing attention to goals that emphasize the importance of teaching for conceptual as well as procedural understanding (Cobb et al., 1991; Hiebert, 1986; Silver, 1986). We define *goals* as expectations about the intellectual, social and emotional outcomes for students as a consequence of their classroom experiences.

Comprehensive reviews of research on teacher thought processes have been done by Clark and Peterson (1986) and Shavelson and Stern (1981). Among the components of metacognition that seem to impact on instructional practice are *planning* during the preactive stage (Clark & Elmore, 1981; Clark & Yinger, 1979); *monitoring* and *regulating* during the interactive stage (Clark & Peterson, 1981; Fogarty et al., 1983); and *assessing* and *revising* during the postactive stage (Ross, 1989; Simmons, Sparks, Starko, Pasch, Colton & Grinberg, 1989). We share Shavelson's (1986) contention that these aspects of thinking are not conceptually distinct, but rather are interconnected components of a process of developing and implementing agendas based on teaching schemata. From this perspective therefore, we define and categorize these thinking processes as mental activities that teachers use in making decisions and judgments before *(planning)*, during *(monitoring* and *regulating)*, and after (assessing and *revising)* a lesson.

THE STUDY

Subjects

Seven experienced teachers and seven beginning teachers of secondary school mathematics voluntarily participated in this study. Teachers were asked to choose any lesson that would allow for an examination of both their classroom practice and their thoughts underlying that practice. The experienced teachers had taught from seven to twenty-five years. The beginning teachers were student teachers teaching in local middle schools and high schools.

Data Collection

Three types of data were obtained: videotapes of the lessons, audiotapes of the interviews, and lesson plans of the teachers. Transcriptions were made of the audiotapes and the videotapes.

Observations and Videotaping

The first author and a research assistant observed and videotaped each of the teachers teaching a mathematics lesson of their own design. Transcriptions were made of the audio part of the videotapes for analysis.

Interviews

Immediately following the lesson each teacher engaged in: a) a postlesson structured interview (Interview 1), followed by b) a stimulated-recall interview as they viewed the videotape of their lesson (Interview 2), followed by c) a debriefing interview (Interview 3). All interviews were conducted by the first author over a period of one semester.

To better understand the components of metacognition during the preactive stage of the lesson, the teachers were asked in Interview 1 to explain their lesson plans and describe their thoughts as they developed the lesson for the class. They were asked the following questions: (a) *Please explain the context in which your plans were made, for example, the type of class, the type of student. (b) What were your areas of concern as you constructed the lesson? © What were your main goals for the lesson?* (d) *What plans or procedures did you intend to use to achieve those goals?*

In Interview 2, a stimulated-recall approach was used to ascertain components of metacognition during the interactive stage of the lesson. As they viewed the videotape of their lesson, they were asked to stop the tape at any point in the lesson where they made a specific decision about what to do next. At each point the tape was stopped, the teachers were asked to describe what they were doing and what they were thinking at that moment.

Finally, to learn about the components of metacognition during the postactive stage, in Interview 3, the teachers engaged in a debriefing session following their viewing of the videotape. They were asked to reflect on their lessons: (a) *Did it go as expected?* (b) *If they were to teach the lesson again, would they do anything differently? Explain.*

Data Analysis

Categorization of Teacher Metacognition

The Teacher Metacognitive Framework (TMF) was used to examine teachers' thoughts through an analysis of the interviews and the lesson plans. For each teacher the thinking processes during the (a) preactive stage (lesson planning) were categorized from the transcription of Interview 1 and the lesson plan; (b) interactive stage (monitoring and regulating) were categorized from the transcriptions of Interview 2; and (c) postactive stage (assessing and revising) were categorized from the transcriptions of Interview 3. Note that the other components of metacognition (knowledge, beliefs, and goals) were categorized from the lesson plans and from the transcriptions of all three interviews. A descriptive analysis was given for each component of metacognition.

We then examined and described the patterns of these components of metacognition and the associated instructional practice.

Examination of Instructional Practice Related to Teacher Metacognition

The two authors used the videotapes and the transcriptions of the lessons to describe the lessons across three broad dimensions of classroom instruction: tasks, learning environment, and discourse. These dimensions were adapted from the

Professional Standards for School Mathematics (NCTM, 1991). A framework was used to examine the nature of these dimensions as they revealed themselves during instructional practice. See Artzt and Armour-Thomas (1996) for more details about the application of this framework.

RESULTS AND ANALYSIS

Emergent Patterns of Metacognition

By applying the TMF to the interview data and the lesson plans we were able to describe and categorize the metacognitive components during three stages of instruction: preactive, interactive and postactive. A descriptive analysis revealed that the metacognitive components of different teachers fell within three groups. That is, specific patterns of metacognition seemed to emerge, falling in two distinct groups, with a third group consisting of teachers whose metacognitive components resembled a combination of the two other groups. For ease of discussion these groups are labeled Group X, Group Y and Group Z respectively. See Table 1 for a summary of the patterns of components of metacognition of Group X and Group Y.

The results are presented according to the three groups of lessons. That is, for each group a description of the metacognitive components along with the characteristics of the lessons are given. Samples of exemplary teacher comments are interspersed throughout the dialogue. To get a clearer understanding of the Group Z lessons, woven through the description will be examples of two lessons from the group and the related commentaries of the teachers of those lessons.

Group X: Metacognition and Related Instructional Practice

Group X consisted of five teachers (four experienced, one beginner). A descriptive analysis revealed that their knowledge, beliefs and goals centered around student learning with understanding, as did their thought processes before, during and after the lesson. The instructional practice seemed to reflect this focus.

Table 1
Summary of Patterns of Metacognition

Metacognition	Components	Group X	Group Y
Overarching	Knowledge Pupils	Revealed specific knowledge of student's prior knowledge, experiences, abilities, attitudes and interests	Revealed a general knowledge of students in relation to the content.
	Knowledge Content	Revealed conceptual and procedural understanding of the content. Viewed content in relation to entire unit and past and future study	Revealed a procedural understanding of the content. Viewed content in isolation of past and future study.
	Knowledge Pedagogy	Revealed understanding of how students learn mathematics. Anticipated specific areas of difficulty and planned suitable teaching strategies.	Focused on time saving management strategies to cover the content.
	Beliefs Student Role	Viewed students as active participants in the lesson who must think, reason, discover, communicate and take responsibility for learning.	Viewed students as passive learners who must pay attention and stay on task.
	Beliefs Teacher Role	Viewed themselves as a facilitator of student learning by selecting problem-solving tasks and asking questions that challenge students to think for themselves and interact with one another	Viewed themselves as dispensers of information and role models for how to do problems.
	Goals	Wanted to help students construct their own meaning so that they will develop conceptual, as well as procedural, understanding and will value the mathematics and feel confident in their abilities	Wanted to cover the content and help students acquire procedural skills.
Preactive	Lesson Planning	Focused on problem solving processes and conceptual meanings and underlying procedures and results. Sequenced the tasks to build on previous student understanding and arouse students' interest and curiosity	Focused on the procedures to be learned and the results to be arrived at. Sequence the tasks illogically where there were large leaps between concepts and confusing examples.
Interactive	Monitoring	Observed, listened to and elicited participation of students to increase participation and assess student learning and disposition toward mathematics for the purpose of adjusting instruction.	Elicited participation of students for the purpose of keeping them on task.
	Regulating	Adapted instruction while teaching based on the information received through monitoring student learning and interest. Excluded examples to save time and added examples to increase student understanding.	Taught the lesson without any deviation from original plans.
Postactive	Assessing	Assessed goal accomplishment in terms of student understanding and content coverage.	Assessed goal accomplishment in terms of content coverage.
	Revising	Gave ideas for better monitoring of students and clearer and more interesting instructional techniques.	Gave ideas for better time management.

Preactive

In their preactive interviews the Group X teachers revealed goals for their students to attain both procedural and conceptual understanding of the content. They also wanted their students to see the value in the mathematics they were learning. They showed knowledge of the content, pedagogical techniques and students in that they were able to: 1) describe the content in relation to the students' past and future study; 2) describe the difficulties they anticipated in students' learning of the content; and 3) describe suitable pedagogical strategies they planned to use. Specific comments follow: *"In general, they have difficulties with proofs. So I thought I'd start with simple diagrams and deal with things they knew and were pretty confident with already. " "I wanted students to really understand the logarithmic rules and understand their important uses. "*

Interactive

The instructional practice of the Group X teachers reflected their concern for and knowledge about students, content and pedagogy. That is, the tasks appeared to be interesting to students, logically sequenced, and at a suitable level of difficulty. The instructional tools they used and the way they organized the tasks contributed towards the clarity of the lesson. There was a relaxed, yet businesslike learning environment in which most of the students appeared to be on task. The instructional routines and pacing seemed to promote active student involvement in the lesson.

During their stimulated-recall interviews, these teachers made specific comments regarding their beliefs about the necessity of a student-centered approach for student learning. *"The idea is I would like them to talk more than I do. Let them listen to each other because that's how you learn." "I didn't want just an answer. I wanted an explanation and I wanted an explanation that everyone would hear."* Furthermore, they gave descriptions of how they used student participation and feedback as a means of monitoring student understanding, which they used for subsequent regulation of instruction. *"I wanted to know how many kids I can actually convince that this was in fact the case* (it wasn't). *Cause if I'm gonna convince a lot of kids of this, then I'm not going on, because they just don't get it."* The discourse during the instructional practice was consistent with these metacognitions. That is, the teachers encouraged the students to think and reason, give full explanations of their thoughts, and listen to and respond to one another's ideas. Some of the questions these teachers asked were: *"Why?" "What do you mean?" "How did you get that?" "Explain it to Maria." "Explain it to the class."* This type of discourse seemed to have been facilitated through the teachers' use of a variety of types and levels of questions with suitable wait times.

Postactive

In their debriefing interviews the Group X teachers showed a consistency with their preactive goals, in that they assessed their lessons primarily in terms of their judgments of how much their students understood. *"By their feedback, I thought they understood what I was talking about."* Finally, they gave detailed suggestions for improving their instructional techniques aimed at increasing clarity and interest for students. *"I didn't get to walk around enough to help. Some students were left confused." "I should have shown that some expressions are really very difficult to handle without logs."*

Group Y: Metacognition and Related Instructional Practice

Group Y consisted of four teachers (all beginners). A descriptive analysis of the metacognitive components of these teachers showed them to be consistently focused on their own practices. That is, their knowledge, beliefs and goals centered around content coverage for skill development and time management, as did their thought processes before, during and after the lesson. The instructional practice seemed to reflect this focus.

Preactive

In their preactive interviews the Group Y teachers expressed only procedural goals for their students and desires to cover the content. *"They have to learn the characteristics of a parabola, mainly the turning point, axis of symmetry, and do the formula for the parabola."* They revealed a vague knowledge of their students, the mathematical content, and related pedagogy. *"It is an average class with good students." "I just wanted to do one example and get right into the graphing."* They spoke about the content in isolation and focused mainly on time-saving strategies to cover the content. *"I wanted to use the projector so I could go over more examples."*

Interactive

The instructional practice of the Group Y teachers was characterized by tasks that were illogically sequenced, and either too easy or too difficult for the students. There was a tense and awkward classroom atmosphere in which many of the students appeared to be off-task.

The teachers asked low-level questions and did not require students to give explanations of their responses. They told students whether they were right or wrong and often resolved questions without student input. There was no evidence of verbal interactions between students.

During the stimulated-recall interviews, unlike the Group X teachers, the Group Y teachers made no statements regarding their beliefs about how students learn best. They gave descriptions of how they monitored student behaviors as a means for improving classroom management but made no mention of monitoring for student understanding. *"When they don 't pay attention to me I call on them."* In fact, some seemed bewildered by students' incorrect responses. "I *think he wasn't thinking." "They don 't think."* None of these teachers described or made any deviations from their original plans, despite feedback from students during the course of the lesson that indicated they were confused.

Postactive

In their postactive interviews, the Group Y teachers showed a consistency with their preactive goals in that their primary focus was on their insufficient content coverage and the student behavior. *"I think we went too slow. I should have done more." "I think the kids were very good today." "Some kids were still not paying as much attention as I 'd like."* Several gave suggestions for improvement of the pacing of their lessons to achieve more efficient content coverage. *"To save time I wouldn't have them organize the data pairs in a table."*

Group Z: Metacognition and Related Instructional Practice

Group Z consisted of five teachers (three experienced and two beginners). A descriptive analysis revealed that the content and focus of their metacognitions in some ways resembled those of Group X and in other ways resembled those of Group Y. In some essential characteristics, to be explained subsequently, the metacognitive components of three of the teachers, two experienced and one beginning (to be referred to as Group Z1) were similar, and the metacognitive components of two of the teachers, one experienced and one beginning (to be referred to as Group Z2) were similar.

The content and focus of the knowledge, goals and planning of the Group Z1 teachers were similar to the teachers in Group X. However, the content and focus of their beliefs, monitoring, regulating, assessing and revising were similar to the teachers in Group Y.

A more detailed description of the results follows with specific examples taken from Betty's lesson and her related commentaries. Betty was in her seventeenth year of teaching secondary school mathematics. She was observed teaching a geometry lesson on proving the properties of isosceles triangles to a class of 22 tenth graders in a suburban high school.

Preactive

In their preactive interviews the three Group Z1 teachers mostly revealed goals for their students similar to those of the Group X teachers. That is, they wanted them to develop conceptual as well as procedural understanding of the content. Also, similar to the Group X teachers, the Group Z 1 teachers exhibited detailed knowledge about their pupils, the content and related pedagogy.

In her preactive interview, Betty stated both procedural and conceptual goals to *"reinforce previous concepts"* and to get the students to *"...realize what does happen in an isosceles triangle."* She revealed knowledge and consideration of the ability level of her students. She stressed the importance of reinforcing previous concepts and proper sequencing of problems.

Interactive

With respect to the tasks and most aspects of the learning environments, the instructional practice of each of the three Group Z1 teachers resembled the instructional practice of the Group X teachers. That is, there was a relaxed, yet businesslike learning environment in which most of the students were on task. Throughout their lessons the tasks were logically sequenced, at a suitable level of difficulty and appeared to be moderately interesting for students.

For example, in Betty's class the students entered the class and immediately attended to their work which was outlined on a handout the teacher distributed. In her interview Betty stated that, "It 's very important to me that at the beginning of each period they settle in quickly. The Do Now (the handout) serves the purpose for me of reviewing constantly and, when I can, leading into the lesson of the day, using parts of *it.* " Her mathematical tasks were carefully prepared and suitably sequenced for the clear development of concepts. With respect to the discourse, however, the instructional practice of the Group Z1 teachers resembled that of the Group Y teachers. Specifically, the verbal interaction was fast-paced (short wait times) with low-level teacher questions requiring one word answers from students. Students were rarely encouraged to interact with one another and the teachers often passed judgment on student responses and resolved questions without student input.

For example, in Betty's class, after a student put his or her work on the board, Betty's overriding questioning technique was to ask the student an easy procedural question, allow a very short wait time, accept a one-word answer from the student, and then give the explanation for the student answer herself. For example, the following verbal interaction took place regarding one proof:

Betty: "OK, now, I'm interested in number 3. AD is perpendicular to BC. Sam, you said that AD is an altitude. Why?"
Sam: "Because, right angles."
Betty: "Um huh. An altitude is a line segment that goes from the vertex and is perpendicular to the opposite side. OK, and AE, I said is the middle. Why is it a median? What is the definition of a median? Scott?"
Sam: "It makes BE = EC."
Betty: "Well, a median is a line segment which goes from the vertex of the triangle to the middle of the opposite side."

During their stimulated-recall interviews, the Group Z1 teachers revealed beliefs quite different from those expressed by the Group X teachers. The Group Z1 teachers stated that in order to cover the content efficiently, it was best to tell students the information rather than spend the time getting them to discover it for themselves. Similar to the Group Y teachers, as they viewed their lessons, all three teachers explained that the primary reason they called on students was to keep them on task.

As Betty watched her lesson on the videotape, she said, *"Sometimes I let students explain their work. But because of time factors, I took charge.... It works well when the teacher stands in front of the room and answers student questions."* While the students did their work, Betty checked attendance, walked around checking homework, and also checked the work they were doing in order to select students to put their work on the board. She stated that her purpose for checking the students' homework at their desks was to ensure they attended to their tasks: *"...they know that there's accountability, that they have to do it."*

Postactive

Similar to the Group Y teachers, in their debriefing interviews, the Group Z 1 teachers assessed their lessons in terms of content coverage and gave suggestions for improvement that focused on ways to accomplish more efficient pacing. This was inconsistent with their preactive commentaries which, similar to the Group X teachers, focused on helping students to attain procedural as well as conceptual understanding.

During her postactive interview, similar to the other Group Z1 teachers, Betty's assessment was focused predominantly on content coverage: *"I accomplished what I wanted to."*

Group Z2

The similarity of the teachers of the two Group Z2 lessons was that their metacognitive components were all similar to those of the teachers in Group X, except for the component, knowledge which was similar to that of the teachers in Group Y

A more detailed description of the results follows with specific examples taken from John's lesson and related commentaries. John was a student teacher in an urban middle school. He was observed teaching a lesson on plotting points on a rectangular coordinate system to a class of 30 seventh grade students.

Preactive

Similar to the Group X teachers, in their preactive interviews the two teachers in this group revealed goals for their students to develop conceptual as well as procedural understanding of the content. They also expressed beliefs about the importance of having students play an active role in their own learning by asking them questions and challenging them to think for themselves and interact with one another. However, unlike the Group X teachers, these teachers either admitted to or demonstrated that they had inadequate or superficial knowledge about some aspects of the content, students, and/or pedagogy.

In his preactive thoughts, John stated procedural and conceptual goals. He wanted his students to learn how to graph a point and, at the same time, review the geometric concepts and enable them to make the relation between the two. However, like the Group Y teachers, he revealed only a general and vague knowledge of his students by anticipating that *"...it would be an easy lesson and [he] wouldn't have any difficulty."* To accomplish his goals, he said, "I plan to help them to do it instead of to do it myself: I 'm going to send them to the board."

Interactive

During the *beginning* of their lessons the tasks, learning environment, and the discourse resembled those of the Group X lessons. That is, the tasks were logically sequenced and at a suitable level of difficulty, the students interacted with one another and with the teacher and there was a relaxed, yet businesslike classroom climate. However, during the *latter part* of their lessons the tasks, and discourse resembled those of the Group Y lessons. That is, the tasks were either too diff~cult or confusing for students, the discourse was fast paced with minimal student input.

As they watched the videotape of the *beginning* of their lessons, similar to the Group X teachers, the Group Z2 teachers claimed that they called on students to check for understanding so as to know how to proceed. However, as they watched the *latter part* of their lessons, they remarked that the tasks they introduced caused confusion which required them to *tell* the students the information.

As John's class began, students received worksheets that concerned the plotting of points on a graph, which they worked on individually at their seats. John circulated around the room checking this work. He said, "*I was trying to see if they are able to do the Do Now, cause if they can 't do it, forget it. And I saw that some of them had some difficulty.*" After all were finished, one student at a time was selected to put his or her work on the board and explain it to the class. The work consisted of plotting one point on the graph. When the students were at the board, the teacher encouraged the seated students to question them about their work. He allowed long wait times and placed the burden of evaluation on the students. While watching the tape of his lesson, he expressed his beliefs about the value of student input: "*If a kid can do it, I prefer if he explains. It helps him.*" He acknowledged that he does this, in spite of the fact that it takes more time from the class than if he would just explain it himself.

During the last ten minutes of class time, John assigned a complex problem, where the students had to plot four points, join the points, and find the perimeter and area of the resulting figure. The students showed a lack of familiarity with the concepts of perimeter and area. Therefore, the teacher was unable to elicit the responses he wanted in the short remaining time. He thus resorted to telling the students how to do the problem and gave them the answers as the bell rang. As he watched this phase of his lesson on the videotape, he said, "I *was thinking how long this part is going to take me, but I have to do it.*" He explained that he made a choice to forego his prepared summary and give this complex problem, since it resembled that evening's homework assignment.

Postactive

In their debriefing interviews, similar to the Group X teachers, both teachers evaluated student understanding and gave appropriate suggestions for how to improve the design of the tasks in their lessons. Both teachers claimed that their inadequate knowledge of the content, students, and/or pedagogy impeded their efforts to teach in a way that was consistent with their goals and beliefs.

During his postactive interview, John recognized that he belabored the point plotting and he noted that his last example was inappropriate: *"I was too ambitious. I'm not sure that many knew what was going on. I should have just focused on plotting points and not include area and perimeter."*

Through the application of our model we were able to discern that components of teacher metacognition played a well-defined role in instructional practice. That is, patterns in the content and focus of metacognition appeared to be related to patterns in the nature of instructional practice.

DISCUSSION AND IMPLICATIONS

The purpose of this study was to apply a problem-solving perspective to examine the components of metacognition underlying instructional practice in mathematics. We developed and used the Teacher Metacognitive Framework to better understand the role of metacognition in teachers' classroom practice in mathematics.

The findings from the application of the Teacher Metacognitive Framework provided some insight into the relationship of specific components of teacher metacognition and instructional practice. The verbal data of five of the teachers revealed that their knowledge with regard to their pupils, the content and pedagogy was detailed and specific. Their beliefs showed that they viewed the role of the student as an active participant in their own learning and their role as teachers as a facilitator of this process. Their goals were to help students value the mathematics they were learning and develop both their conceptual and procedural understandings. Their planning reflected a focus on problem-solving processes and conceptual meaning in addition to procedural techniques. The five teachers having these attributes of metacognition demonstrated instructional practice that was characterized by well-designed tasks and intellectually and socially stimulating learning environments where the discourse fostered interaction in which students shared responsibility for their own learning. These teachers' extensive monitoring of this rich verbal interaction may have accounted for their subsequent accurate postlesson judgments regarding whether they had accomplished their goals of teaching for student understanding. The monitoring behaviors these teachers demonstrated were similar to those of expert teachers (Borko & Shavelson, 1990; Livingston & Borko, 1990; Leinhardt & Greeno, 1986) and good problem solvers (Schoenfeld, 1987; Silver, 1985). Somewhat surprising, though, was the finding that these competencies, usually associated with expertise, were within the repertoire of the skills of a beginning teacher. This has positive implications for preservice teacher educators as well as school-based professionals who employ beginning teachers. That is, although experience plays an important role in the development of a teacher, it is certainly possible for a beginning teacher to think and teach in ways similar to experienced teachers.

In contrast, four of the beginning teachers revealed that their knowledge was fragmented, goals were limited to isolated performance outcomes for students, and no overarching beliefs were articulated. Moreover, these teachers' thoughts before, during and after the lesson revealed minimal attention to students' learning and maximal attention to content coverage. Specifically, it appeared that when there was vague knowledge and an absence of explicit goals for student understanding it was accompanied by instructional practice in which students were minimally involved. The tasks were poorly designed and the learning environments were not conducive to engaging students in rich discourse with one another or with the teacher. The absence of monitoring to gain feedback on student understanding may have accounted for their subsequent inaccurate postlesson judgments that their lesson went well or that their students understood. In some ways, the teachers of these lessons exhibited behaviors similar to those of other novice teachers (Borko & Livingston, 1989; Livingston & Borko, 1990) and naive problem solvers (Hinsley, Hayes & Simon, 1977). These findings have important implications for preservice teacher educators whose primary goal is to empower teachers to teach for student understanding and to reflect on their practice as a means for self improvement.

For some lessons, although the teachers expressed detailed knowledge and goals consistent with teaching for the promotion of student understanding, the nature of the discourse during their instructional practice was not conducive to accomplishing these goals. Contrary to their espoused student-centered goals, these teachers did not monitor for student understanding and subsequently did not regulate their instruction in accordance with student needs. Similarly, their postactive commentaries were not student focused, but rather centered around content coverage and more efficient pacing in subsequent lessons. For these lessons, teachers' beliefs about the value of "teacher telling" may have accounted for the persistent use of teacher-dominated strategies for discourse, which may have resulted in the absence of monitoring for student understanding throughout their lessons. During their stimulated-recall interviews, they expressed the belief that when time is at a premium, covering the content efficiently must take precedence over student learning with understanding. Like the teachers in Lampert's work (1985), these teachers were unable to maintain the "tension" between simultaneously covering the content and attending to student understanding. This tension was not only revealed in their instructional practice but in the conflict of the content and focus of the metacognitions revealed by these teachers.

For other lessons teachers revealed beliefs and goals that suggested the importance of student learning with understanding. However, because of their inadequate knowledge about the content, students and/or pedagogy, in certain phases of their lessons, they were unable to monitor and regulate their classroom teaching in a manner consistent with their preactive commentaries. For teachers of these lessons, regardless of experience, weaknesses in different aspects of their knowledge was the major source of difficulty - a problem that diminishes the quality of teaching (cf., Peterson, 1988; Shulman, 1986). Specifically, at the point in their lessons when they realized that they had (a) introduced tasks that were causing confusion for themselves or for their students, and (b) did not know how to adjust the tasks, they resorted to teacher telling.

Among the critical metacognitive components of teaching is the monitoring and regulating that takes place during instruction. The absence of these metacognitive components was a common weakness in many of the lessons. Equally troubling, though, was teachers' apparent unawareness of the importance of monitoring for student understanding as a means towards accurate postlesson judgment of student understanding. Since accurate postlesson assessment of student understanding is an important means of increasing one's knowledge that can be used for subsequent planning and classroom practice, monitoring and regulation of student understanding play a central role in influencing instruction. This notion is consistent with the research on problem solving which shows that monitoring and subsequent regulation play a pivotal role, not only in the efficacy of the problem solving process, but in the ultimate solution of the problem. (Artzt & Armour-Thomas, 1992; Garofalo & Lester, 1985; Schoenfeld, 1987).

Despite the promising nature of these results, there are some limitations to this exploratory study. First, there was no formal assessment of student learning in the sample of lessons observed. Observations of the teaching-learning transaction should be used in conjunction with other procedures to ascertain what and how much students have learned from their classroom experiences. Second, a larger number of observations of lessons and interviews would contribute to greater validity of the findings. Finally, although the Teacher Metacognitive Framework yielded valuable information on the thoughts of teachers, they were derived only from the comments that the teachers volunteered. For example, given the importance of teachers' beliefs about mathematics, it was disappointing that no comments were made on this issue. These results would need to be complemented with other data sources to tap teacher metacognition, such as questionnaires or experimental tasks as well as data indicating student understanding.

Through the application of the framework, we were able to examine the content and focus of teachers' metacognitions and how they influence instructional practice in mathematics. With further refinement, this framework may prove useful to researchers and teacher educators in their preservice and inservice mathematics programs. They may now approach teaching as an integrated whole, where metacognition plays a well-defined role in instruction.

ALICE F. ARTZT AND ELEANOR ARMOUR-THOMAS
Department of Secondary Education and Youth Services
Queens College of the City University of New York,
Flushing, NY

REFERENCES

Artzt, A.F., & Armour-Thomas, E. (1992). Development of a cognitive-metacognitive framework for protocol analysis of mathematical problem solving in small groups. *Cognition and Instruction, 9,* 137- 175.

Artzt, A.F., & Armour-Thomas, E. (1996, April). *Evaluation of instructional practice in the secondary school mathematics classroom.* Paper presented at the annual meeting of the American Educational Research Association, New York.

Artzt, A.F., & Armour-Thomas, E. (1993.April). *Mathematics teaching as problem solving: A framework for studying the relationship between instructional practice and teachers' cognitive and metacognitive thoughts and behaviors.* Paper presented at the annual meeting of the American Education Research Association, Atlanta.

Ball, D.L. (1991). Research on teaching mathematics: Making subject matter knowledge part of the equation. In J..E. .Brophy (Ed.), *Advances in research on teaching: Teachers' subject matter knowledge and classroom instruction* (pp. 1-48) (Vol. 2). Greenwich, CT: JAI Press.

Borko, H. & Livingston, C. (1989). Cognition and improvisation: Differences in mathematics instruction by expert and novice teachers. *American Educational Research Journal, 26*(4), 473-498.

Brown, C.A. & Baird, J. (1993). Inside the teacher: Knowledge, beliefs, and attitudes. In P. S. Wilson (Ed.), Research ideas for the classroom: High school mathematics (pp. 245-259).

Carpenter, T.P. (1989). Teaching as problem solving. In R. Charles & Silver (Eds.), *The teaching and assessing of mathematical problem solving* (pp. 187-202). Reston, VA: NCTM.

Clark, C.M. & Elmore, J. L. (1981). *Transforming curriculum in mathematics, science and writing: A case study of teacher yearly planning* (Research Series 99). East Lansing: Michigan State University, Institute for Research on Teaching.

Clark, C.M. & Peterson, P. L. (1981). Stimulated-recall. In B..R.. Joyce, C..C. Brown, & L. Peck (Eds.), *Flexibility in teaching: An excursion into the nature of teaching and training* New York: Longman

Clark, C.M. & Peterson, P..L.(1986). Teachers' thought processes. In M. C. Wittrock (Ed.), *Handbook of research on teaching* (3rd., pp. 255-296). New York, NY: Macmillan.

Clark, C.M. & Yinger, R.J. (1979). Teachers' thinking. In P. L. Peterson & H. .A Walberg (Eds.), *Research on teaching* (pp. 231-263). Berkeley, CA:McCutchan.

Cobb, P., Yackel, E., & Wood, T. (1991). Curriculum and teacher development: psychological and anthropological perspectives. In E. Fennema, T. Carpenter, & S. J. Lamon (Eds.), *Integrating research on teaching and learning mathematics* (pp. 55-82). Albany, NY: State University of New York Press.

Dougherty, B.J. (1990). Influence of teacher cognitive/conceptual levels on problem solving instruction. In G. Booker, et al. (Eds.), *Proceedings of the fourteenth international conference for the psychology of mathematics education* (pp. 119 126). Oaxtepec, Mexico: International Group for the Psychology of Mathematics Education.

Ernest, P. (1988, *July). The impact of beliefs on the teaching of mathematics.* Paper prepared for ICME VI, Budapest, Hungary.

Fennema, E., Carpenter, T.P., & Peterson, P. L. (1989). Teachers' decision making and cognitively guided instruction: A new paradigm for curriculum development. In N.F. Ellerton & M. A. (Ken) Clements (Eds.), *School mathematics: The challenge to change* (pp. 174-187). Geelong, Victoria, Australia: Deakin University Press.

Fennema, E. & Franke, M. L. (1992). Teachers' knowledge and its impact. In D. Grouws (Ed.), *Handbook of research on mathematics teaching and learning* (pp. 147164). New York: Macmillan Publishing Company.

Fogarty, J., Wang, M., & Creek, R. (1983). A descriptive study of experienced and novice teachers' interactive instructional thoughts and actions. *Journal of Educational Research, 77,* 22-32.

Garofalo, J., & Lester, F. K. (1985). Metacognition, cognitive monitoring, and mathematical performance. *Journal for Research in Mathematics Education, 16,* 163-176.

Hiebert, J., (Ed.). (1986). *Conceptual knowledge and procedural knowledge: The case of mathematics.* Hillsdale, NJ: Lawrence Erlbaum Associates.

Hiebert, J., & Carpenter, T. P. (1992). Learning and teaching with understanding. In D. Grouws (Ed.), *Handbook of research on mathematics teaching and learning* (pp. 65-97). New York, NY: Macmillan.

Hinsley, D.A., Hayes, J. R. & Simon, H. A. (1977). From words to equation: Meaning and representation in algebra word problems. In M.A. Just & P. A. Carpenter (Eds.), *Cognitive processes in comprehension* (pp. 89-106). Hillsdale, NJ: Lawrence Erlbaum.

Jackson, P. W. (1968). *Life in classrooms.* New York: Holt, Rinehart & Winston.

Kagan, D. M. (1992). Implications of research on teacher belief. *Educational Psychologist,* 27(1), 65-90.

Lampert, M. L. (1985). How teachers teach. *Harvard Educational Review, 55,* 229-246.

Leinhardt, G. (1989). Math lessons: A contrast of novice and expert competence. *Journal for Research in Mathematics Education,* 20(1), 52-75.

Leinhardt, G., Putnam, R..T, Stein, M.. K., & Baxter, J. (1991). Where subject knowledge matters. In J. EW. Brophy (Ed.), *Advances in research on teaching: Teachers' subject matter knowledge and classroom instruction.* (Vol. 2,. pp. 87-113). Greenwich, CT: JAI Press.

Livingston, C. & Borko, H. (1990). High school mathematics review lessons: Expert-novice distinction. *Journal for Research in Mathematics Education,* 21, 372-387.

National Council of Teachers of Mathematics. (1989). *Curriculum and evaluation standards for school mathematics.* Reston, VA: The Council.

National Council of Teachers of Mathematics. (1991). *Professional standards for teaching mathematics.* Reston, VA: The Council.

Pajares, F. (1992). Teacher's beliefs and educational research: Cleaning up a messy concept. *Review in Educational Research, 62: 307-332.*

Peterson, P. L. (1988). Teachers' and students' cognitional knowledge for classroom teaching and learning. *Educational Researcher,* 17(5), 5-14.

Peterson, P. L., Fennema, E., Carpenter, T. P., & Loef, M. (1989). Teachers' pedagogical content beliefs In mathematics. *Cognition and Instruction, 6,* 1-40.

Polya, G. (1945). *How to solve it.* Garden City, NY: Doubleday.

Richardson, V., Anders, P., Tidwell, D. & Lloyd, C. (1991). The relationship between teachers' beliefs and practices in reading comprehension instruction. *American Educational Research Journal,* 28(3), 559-586.

Ross, D. D. (1989). First steps in developing a reflective approach. *Journal of Teacher Education,* 40(2), 22-30.

Schoenfeld, A. H. (1987). What's all the fuss about metacognition? In A. H. Schoenfeld (Ed.), *Cognitive science and mathematics education* (pp. 189-215). Hillsdale, NJ: Lawrence Erlbaum Associates.

Shavelson, R. J. (1986). *Interactive decision making: Some thoughts on teacher cognition.* Invited address, I. Congreso Internacional, "Pensamientos de los Profesores Y Toma de Decisions," Seville, Spain.

Shavelson, R. J. & Stern, P. (1981). Research on teachers' pedagogical thoughts, judgments, decisions and beliefs. *Review of Educational Research,* 51,455-498.

Shulman, L. S. (1986). Those who understand: Knowledge growth in teaching. *Educational Researcher, 15,* 4-14.

Silver, E. A. (1987). Foundations of cognitive theory and research for mathematics problem-solving instruction. In A. H. Schoenfeld (Ed.), *Cognitive science and mathematics education* (pp. 33-60). Hillsdale, NJ: Lawrence Erlbaum Associates, Inc.

Silver, E. A. (1986). Using conceptual and procedural knowledge: A focus on relationships. In J. Hiebert (Ed.), *Conceptual and procedural knowledge: The case of mathematics* (pp. 181-198). Hillsdale, NJ: Lawrence Erlbaum Associates.

Simmons, J. M., Sparks, G. M., Starko, A., Pasch, M., Colton, A., & Grinberg, J. (1989 March). *Exploring the structure of reflective pedagogical thinking in novice and expert teachers: The birth of a developmental taxonomy.* Paper presented at the annual meeting of the American Educational Research Association, San Francisco.

Thompson, A. G. (1992). Teachers beliefs and conceptions: A synthesis of the research. In D. Grouws (Ed.), *Handbook on research on teaching mathematics and learning* (pp. 127-146). New York: Macmillan Publishing Company.

Wilson, S. M., Shulman, L. S., & Richert, A. E. (1987). 150 different ways of knowing: Representations of knowledge in teaching. In J. Calderhead (Ed.), *Exploring teachers' thinking* (pp. 104 124). London: Cassell Educational Limited.

CHAPTER 8

TEACHING METACOGNITIVELY

HOPE J. HARTMAN

ABSTRACT. A growing body of research and theory highlights teachers' use of their metacognitive knowledge and skills before, during and after instruction. This chapter describes what is involved in teaching metacognitively, it explains why teaching metacognitively is important, it describes and illustrates metacognitive techniques used in my own teaching, and it explains procedures for developing other teachers' metacognition about their own instruction.

Teaching metacognitively involves teaching *with and for* metacognition. Teaching *with* metacognition means teachers think about their own thinking regarding their teaching. It includes reflecting on: instructional goals, students' characteristics and needs, content level and sequence, teaching strategies, materials, and other issues related to curriculum, instruction and assessment. Such thinking occurs before, during and after lessons in order to maximize instructional effectiveness. Teaching *for* metacognition means teachers think about how their instruction will activate and develop their students' metacognition, or thinking about their own thinking as learners. This chapter focuses primarily on the former, teachers' use of metacognition in their instruction. First it examines some of the components of teaching metacognitively. Next it explains why teaching metacognitively is important. Then it reviews the literature on metacognitive aspects of instruction. Next the chapter describes some of the metacognitive teaching strategies I use in my undergraduate educational psychology course, and finally it describes some of my approaches to helping other teachers instruct metacognitively. Specific examples of some of the approaches are included in appendices at the end of the chapter.

The metacognitive strategies included in this chapter transcend content domains and can be used in virtually all subjects. The goal of this chapter is to increase understanding of the role of metacognition in teaching and to suggest practical techniques teachers can use to think metacognitively about instruction. Some readers of this and/or the following chapter will notice that a constructivist perspective permeates my views of the role of the teacher and how to best construct and organize instructional material for use in a course.

H.J. Hartman (ed.), Metacognition in Learning and Instruction, 149–172.

WHAT IS TEACHING METACOGNITIVELY?

Ms. Carlson, a high school science teacher and director of the State Council on Educational Opportunity, was at the school to address a group of parents. An electric speaker had been placed on the wall of the auditorium. After she had been talking for only fifteen minutes a number of people started to walk out. As they were leaving one could hear them muttering something about the speaker. Why did the people leave?

One strategy I use to introduce teachers to metacognition is to have them read an ambiguous short passage and answer a question about it (as above), and then ask them to reflect on how they arrived at their answer. In the passage above, the word "speaker" can either refer to the electronic device on the wall of the auditorium, or to the person making the speech. How did you as a reader interpret what happened, and therefore the meaning of the word speaker in the second to last sentence?

Next I ask questions to elicit a definition of metacognition and try to guide them (through questioning) to the central components. Important aspects of metacognition that are not generated by teachers are provided to them. I emphasize the following points:
1.   Metacognition is thinking about thinking or knowing about knowing.
2.   It enables *awareness and control* over how teachers think about their thinking and therefore affects their teaching.
3.   It enables them to self-regulate their teaching activities, depending upon the specific students, goals and situation.
4.   Some metacognition is domain-specific and some is domain-general (See Wolters & Pintrich, Chapter 6).
5.   Two general types of metacognition are: executive management strategies that help you plan, monitor and evaluate/revise your thinking processes and products, and strategic knowledge about *what* information/strategies/skills you have, *when and why* to use them, and *how* to use them.

Executive management metacognition in teaching includes planning what and how you are going to teach, checking up on or monitoring how the lesson is going as you are teaching, making adjustments as needed, and evaluating how a lesson went after it is finished. Based on internal and external feedback, the last phase of evaluating is planning how to improve your future performance in similar situations, thereby completing an executive management cycle (Sternberg, 1985).

Metacognition in teaching also includes knowing what instructional strategies are in your repertoire, what they entail, when and why to use them, and how to apply them. This type of metacognition is needed for effective planning of a lesson, for switching gears during or after a lesson upon awareness that a teaching approach isn't working as expected, and selecting alternative approaches. Research suggests preservice teachers need such explicit information about teaching strategies, because they may not know how to implement teaching strategies they learn in their undergraduate courses. A study of beginning teachers found that although they were taught to use phonics for teaching letter sounds, they could not explicitly describe the procedures necessary to use phonics to teach beginning readers (Moore & Harris, 1986). Illustrations of strategic metacognitive knowledge about teaching strategies are included in the appendix

These general types of metacognition help teachers teach intelligently across subject areas and help them maximize their impacts on students by systematic reflection on and improvement of instruction.

WHY TEACH METACOGNITIVELY?

Teachers need to self-regulate their instruction before, during and after conducting lessons in order to maximize their effectiveness with students. Many teachers conduct lessons without adequate advance planning and without adequately checking to see how a lesson is going while it is underway. Teachers often teach the way they were taught rather than consider the advantages and disadvantages of alternative approaches and how to use them most effectively. When observing classroom teachers, Brophy (1986) found that many were so eager to begin a lesson that they skipped over communicating the lesson's objectives Only five percent explicitly described the purpose of the assignments given to students and only 15% mentioned the explicit cognitive strategies students needed to use when doing the assignment, thereby impeding students' mastery of them. While research shows that low-achieving students need explicit information on how to perform academic tasks (Doyle, 1983), research by Winne and Marx (1982) suggests most teachers are least successful in providing that guidance and structure for students. They interviewed teachers and students to study their views of thinking processes for classroom learning and to examine the degree of consistency between teachers' goals for students' thinking processes and the extent to which they are elicited successfully. The results indicated there were serious problems in classroom communication. Teachers were relatively unsuccessful in setting objectives, defining tasks, and engaging students. Consequently, many teachers need to think more carefully about what they present during a lesson and how they provide students with important information.

Teaching metacognitively can improve classroom communication and facilitate effective academic performance. Research on expert versus novice teachers shows that experts, or more experienced teachers, are better able to monitor, interpret and evaluate what occurs in a classroom during instruction than novices, or inexperienced teachers. Whereas novices were only able to describe classroom behavior, experts were able to explain it (Sabers, Cushing and Berliner, 1991). According to Borko and Livingston (1989), expert teachers characteristically spend much more time in long-range planning than novices, can monitor the effectiveness of a lesson in progress, and change approaches as needed and are generally comparable to experts in other areas in their superior metacognitive skills. Their research indicated that expert teachers were also more effective than novices in managing students' questions, comprehension problems, and wrong answers.

Teachers also need a "bag of tricks" or repertoire of teaching strategies at their disposal in order to meet the needs of different students, as well as to meet the needs of the same student at different times and/or situations. Even the "best" teaching technique is not effective all the time and is likely to become tiresome if overused. Teachers need information on alternative, acceptable approaches and then should experiment with the various techniques to evaluate their effectiveness. Because they are dealing with real people, their students, teachers have an obligation to provide assistance that is consistent with modern research, theory, and practice. Choice of an instructional technique will vary to some extent on the background of the student, the particular subject matter, and the goals of the lesson. For example, students who cannot effectively think about the material at an abstract level may need to have concrete examples or experiences first.

What do teachers consider when selecting teaching strategies and while using them in class? To what extent do teachers know how to manage their instruction and do they carefully plan a lesson before conducting it, monitor its implementation while the lesson is in progress and evaluate its success in achieving target objectives after a lesson is over? To what degree have they been explicitly taught to used such reflective practices? To what extent is reflective, metacognitive teaching a form of tacit knowledge which teachers may or may not acquire on their own? There is a growing body of research on teachers' thinking, including the chapter on metacognition in teaching by Artzt and Armour-Thomas in this book. This chapter is intended is to stimulate theory, research and practice in teachers' thinking about their teaching processes and products so that teachers use their metacognition to become more effective.

Research on teachers' thinking addresses some aspects of teaching metacognitively. There is an extensive literature on teacher planning, which Clark (1983) characterizes as addressing three major issues: models used to describe teacher planning, the types and functions of teachers' plans, and the relationship between teachers' plans and their classroom implementation.

Preparation for teaching not only benefits students, but also increases the instructor's own learning and motivation (Medway, 1991). Planning benefits those delivering instruction because by actively thinking about what to teach and how to teach it, teachers' knowledge broadens and deepens (Annis, 1983). Planning can help ensure use of effective techniques, such as alternating between listening and summarizing, that are likely to enhance both learning and motivation (McKeachie, 1994). In their comprehensive review of the literature on teacher thinking, Clark and Peterson (1986) found that many teachers err in planning by concentrating too much on how the content is presented and too little on whether or not students understand it. Such teachers suffer from the fallacious assumption that "teaching = learning" and need to think more metacognitively about the effectiveness of their methods and possible alternative approaches.

In a review of research on college teaching and critical thinking, three aspects of instruction were found to make a difference: explicit emphasis on problem solving, student discussion, and modeling and verbalizing thinking strategies to encourage the development of metacognition (McKeachie, Pintrich, Lin, and Smith, 1986). Consequently teachers should plan lessons with explicit emphasis on problem solving, verbalization of thinking strategies, use of discussion and modeling techniques. The Madeline Hunter approach to effective teaching is based on teachers considering several factors when planning a lesson. They include: objectives, standards, anticipatory set, teaching (input, modeling, and comprehension monitoring), guided practice, closure and independent practice (Kennedy, 1998). Teachers need to be taught to plan lessons because research indicates that often teachers plan based on their own, unconscious implicit theories rather than the "rational model" provided in their teacher education programs (Clark and Yinger, 1978). Another reason to help teachers think about how they plan lessons is that planning lessons in advance helps teachers feel more secure about conducting a lesson and helps them anticipate problems that might arise and how to overcome them (Haigh, 1981). One method of helping teachers plan their lessons is "Micro teaching", in which mini-lessons are planned and implemented, thereby making teaching simpler and less stressful than when teachers have to plan and conduct an entire lesson (McKeachie, 1994). Sometimes lessons are videotaped, played back and evaluated until each of several, individually addressed teaching components has been mastered.

When monitoring and evaluating student performance, how do teachers decide what feedback they should provide to students? Many teachers provide students with feedback impulsively, without careful consideration of alternative approaches and their consequences. Research on feedback shows the benefits of "constructive failure". It is more helpful to tell students when they are wrong than when they are right. Students need to understand WHY they are wrong so they can learn better strategies and/or concepts and avoid repeating the same mistakes. Feedback, or providing knowledge of the results and/or evaluative information about performance, is an important part of teaching.

Many psychological theories emphasize the importance of feedback in learning. Research shows that learning occurs more rapidly when feedback is provided (Lhyle & Kulhavy, 1987).   While research on the timing of feedback, immediate or delayed, does not show a clear and consistent pattern of results, immediate feedback generally seems to promote learning more than delayed feedback (Pressley & McCormick, 1995). Effective feedback often involves stimulating students' self-awareness or providing explanations to students about the reasonableness of the correct responses in comparison to their own, mistaken responses (Bangert-Drowns, Kulik, Kulik & Morgan, 1991). Feedback (oral or written) on patterns of errors is even more useful than feedback on individual errors. Sometimes feedback that a current conception is wrong can trigger reformulation of that concept at a new and higher level.   Bruner (1966) identifies several considerations to take into account when providing students with feedback, such as its form and timing. Teaching metacognitively includes teachers assessing what feedback they provided to students, how they presented it, how students received it, and its ultimate effects on improving students' performance in the areas targeted by the feedback.

Some educational models explicitly incorporate teachers' thinking into them. For example, Novak's (1998) comprehensive educational theory emphasizes how teachers structure and use knowledge to foster meaningful learning.   He recommends the use of theory-based graphic organizers such as concept maps to help teachers plan and conduct lessons.

There are some practice-oriented resources in the literature to help teachers teach more metacognitively. Posner's (1985) book for preservice teachers doing fieldwork emphasizes reflective teaching and includes questions, exercises and places for trainees to record their reactions to ideas, thereby stimulating them to think reflectively. He characterizes nonreflective teachers as being guided by tradition, impulse and authority and relying on established routines while "...reflective teachers actively, persistently, and carefully consider and reconsider beliefs and practices" (p. 20, 21) in the context of consequences and supporting evidence.   My book for college tutors also has an interactive structure, and is designed to promote tutoring with and for metacognition (Hartman, 1993). It includes general principles, strategies and activities for college tutors to help them plan, monitor and evaluate their tutoring regardless of the subject area. Perhaps the most comprehensive resource for teaching metacognitively is Manning & Payne's (1996) *Self-Talk for Teachers and Students*. This book systematically applies teachers' metacognition to educational psychology content. Osborne (1999) developed a "teacher-friendly" behavioral measure of metacognition for teachers to use to assess the metacognitive abilities of their students.   Knowledge about students' existing metacognition can benefit teachers' metacognition by giving them information that helps aids in planning, monitoring and evaluating instruction designed to improve students' metacognition.

MY EXPERIENCES TEACHING METACOGNITIVELY

For over twenty years I have worked with inservice and preservice teachers on applying their metacognition to their curriculum and instruction. Teachers range from pre-kindergarten through graduate school and include subjects of history, chemistry, physics, biology, mathematics, engineering, nursing, psychology, English and college skills. In addition to public and private school teachers and college professors, I have trained college tutors in virtually all subject areas to tutor metacognitively. The remainder of the chapter focuses on materials and activities I have used to facilitate metacognitive instruction. It is divided into two sections: teaching metacognitively in my own course, and conducting faculty development on teaching metacognitively.

The theoretical framework underlying all my work is the BACEIS model of improving thinking (Hartman & Sternberg, 1993), which identifies components internal and external to students that affect their intellectual performance. In the BACEIS acronym, B stands for behavior, A for affect, C for cognition, E for environments, and IS for interacting systems. Cognition and affect are the overarching system factors that are internal to students, while academic and nonacademic environments are the overarching system factors that are external to students. All of these factors are in reciprocal interaction with each other and with the behavioral consequences of their interactions. See the Preface and Chapter 3 for more details. Teachers' metacognition, which is part of their background knowledge, is an important aspect of the academic contextual system. The next section describes specific activities I use for teaching preservice teachers (undergraduates) metacognitively.

Personal Experiences Teaching Metacognitively

I systematically model both executive management and strategic knowledge metacognition about teaching, which includes explaining what I am doing (or have done), why and how. Frequently I think out loud so preservice teachers can observe me, as an expert model: 1) reflecting on why and how I am using particular teaching strategies, 2) observing and responding to students who appear to be confused during the lesson, 3) deciding whether and how to reword an explanation for greater clarity, to ask a student to provide an explanation, 4) why I keep questioning the same student about a concept of problem instead of moving on to a different student and 5) evaluating how I allocated class time. I put advance organizer outlines on the blackboard so they can see an overview of my lesson plan and use graphic organizers to visually represent course concepts and their relationships. Other metacognitively-oriented techniques I use include a pretest, homework, student journals, exams, and a teaching strategy project. First I'll describe techniques I use to manage (plan, monitor and evaluate) my teaching. Then I'll describe a teaching strategy project through which preservice teachers begin learning to teach metacognitively.

Executive Management Techniques

The first day of the semester of the undergraduate course Human Learning and Instruction (Educational Psychology 2) I generally administer a short, multiple choice test on educational psychology, focusing on content usually covered during the semester. Students are told that the test doesn't affect their grade, but is used by me to assess their prior knowledge of key concepts in the course so I can plan instruction to meet the needs of the individual class. The results are analyzed to identify concepts for which students have 1) no or limited prior knowledge, 2) moderate to substantial valid prior knowledge, and 3) misconceptions. The pretest helps me identify concepts that need extra attention due to no, limited or invalid prior knowledge and helps me identify concepts that need less attention due to moderate or substantial prior knowledge. In addition to the pretest informing my own planning for the course, it is used to introduce preservice teachers to the concepts of prior knowledge and misconceptions. It also helps me model a strategy for eliciting, analyzing and applying prior knowledge for my preservice teachers so that they can understand how to use a similar technique with their future students.

Course Requirements

Homework assignments and student journals provide me with invaluable feedback for monitoring, revising and evaluating several components of the course. Homework assignments are given virtually every week of the semester, and generally require students to apply concepts and skills they are learning. I carefully examine and comment on all students' homework every week, which provides both me and the students with valuable feedback for monitoring progress, identifying difficulties, and planning followup instruction. Whereas homework assignments are most useful for monitoring students' cognitive performance, journal entries are most useful for reflecting on students' affective reactions to the course.

Students are required to write journal entries on the following topics: class activities, homework, the text, their fieldwork assignments, the midterm, and their teaching strategy research project. Journal entries are structured around three issues: describing the topic of the entry; discussing their reflections on the value and applications of what they have learned, both from the perspectives of a learner and teacher; and evaluating their own performance. Journals allow me to individualize attention to developing students' attitudes and motivation to learn and teach. Journals also help me assess students' ability to transfer what they have learned, to evaluate their own performance and their ability to use this awareness for improving their future performance. Students use the feedback I provide them on their homework and journals to assess their own comprehension and progress and to improve cognitive and affective aspects of their performance, which facilitates their planning and monitoring when preparing for exams.

Exams allow me to assess preservice teachers' understanding and ability to apply metacognition to their own teaching. Questions address: what teaching strategy they would use in a particular case study, and why and how they would use it in this case; and how they would plan, monitor, and evaluate implementation of a teaching strategy. Another question asks preservice teachers to reflect on their learning experiences to analyze my teaching techniques, such as how I use to develop their abilities to construct and use graphic organizers. Answer formats for these questions are essays and graphic organizers.

Teaching Strategy Project

Preservice teachers are required to do a library research paper on one of nine teaching strategies that emphasize active learning, including role playing, mental imagery and the Learning Cycle. Their paper emphasizes strategic knowledge metacognition about the teaching strategy they selected to research and implement. The first section of the paper addresses what the teaching strategy is (declarative knowledge) and how it works (procedural knowledge). The second section addresses why the technique is considered useful and what research shows to be the expected outcomes of using this technique (contextual/conditional knowledge). In the final section of the paper students give their assessment of the advantages and disadvantages of the teaching strategy.

After researching the instructional technique, preservice teachers must plan a lesson which includes implementation of this strategy and conduct a mini-lesson in which they actually apply the strategy, as described in their lesson plan. Lesson plans are based on the Rich Instruction Model (RIM), which is derived from the BACEIS model (Hartman & Sternberg, 1993, described earlier in this chapter and in more detail in Chapter 3). It helps teachers think through what they are teaching, why they are teaching it, students' prior knowledge about the topics, how instruction will be conducted and how they will help students transfer what they have learned. The model is designed to promote systematic attention to developing students' internal world (cognition and affect) through utilizing the external world (academic and nonacademic environments). The goal is to help students self-regulate their knowledge, skills and affect. An adapted version of the model is summarized below. To help preservice teachers learn to plan their lessons, I model for them use of the RIM lesson planning approach. They are given several examples of how I apply this to our educational psychology course. The example in Table 1 focuses on the subject of educational psychology and the content objective of teaching them how to summarize text.

When teaching preservice teachers develop RIM lessons only one objective and one transfer activity are required per unit. Preservice teachers are given this sample RIM lesson plan (Table 1), which is based on their own learning experiences in our educational psychology classroom, and are introduced to an abbreviated version of the RIM . In-service teachers planning RIM lessons must develop three objectives (content, thinking and affective) and two transfer activities (selected from: a) within subject across task; b) across subjects; c) everyday life; d) several varied examples of application; e) practice for automaticity) (See Hartman & Sternberg, 1993 for the complete version). Since this is a rather complex lesson planning model even for in-service teachers to use, it is usually developed incrementally.

Pre and inservice teachers are shown how to use self-questions as a tool for planning, monitoring and evaluating their Rich Instruction Model lessons. Sample self questions include: For planning: What prior knowledge might students have that is relevant to this lesson? How will I elicit it? For monitoring: What misconceptions do students appear to have about this topic? How are these misconceptions affecting students' learning? Are students making progress in overcoming their misconceptions? For evaluating: To what extent did I elicit all students' relevant prior knowledge/skills that are needed to master this material? How could I overcome their misconceptions more effectively next time?

In summary, I have described two dimensions of teaching metacognitively from my undergraduate course, "Human Learning and Instruction." First I described course activities and assignments I use in part for management purposes to plan, monitor and evaluate my teaching. Then I described a project in which preservice teachers acquire strategic metacognitive knowledge about a teaching strategy and afterward develop and implement a lesson plan applying this teaching strategy.

Table 1

Sample RIM Lesson Plan Model for Teaching Strategy Project: Summarizing

1. Objectives
A. Content (What is the academic subject material to be taught?)
Students will understand the differences between a reader-based summary and writer-based summary and will be able to write effective reader-based summaries.

2. Lesson Plan Core
A. Benefits (Why am I conducting this lesson?)
1. Immediate Benefit: Students will reflect on their own conceptions of how to summarize text and will become aware of the importance of being able to summarize the main ideas the author is trying to communicate when they read.
2. Long Term Benefit: Students will be able to write effective reader-based summaries. In addition, when they are teachers they will be able to help their students understand the differences between reader and writer-based summaries and will be able to help them write effective reader-based summaries.
B. Prior Knowledge/Experience (What prior knowledge do students have about this content and how will I activate it?)
Most students will have read chapter summaries in textbooks. Some students will have had previous teachers ask them to summarize what they have read. Students will be asked questions to activate this prior knowledge.
C. Instructional Techniques (How will I conduct this lesson? What teaching methods will I use?)
Students will be given models of effective reader-based summaries. When models are put on the blackboard and discussed, there will be an emphasis on: including main ideas, omitting details, and ensuring good writing. They will read in their textbook information on what reader and writer-based summaries are, when and why they are used, and how to write summaries. They will also be given assignments requiring them to write reader and writer-based summaries, and will be given feedback on their reader-based summaries and additional models. Students will also learn the reciprocal teaching method, which requires readers to summarize text using a reader-based approach.

3. Transfer
D. Practice for Automaticity
Students will be given several homework assignments requiring them to write reader-based summaries, and they will be required to write a reader-based summary for the midterm and final exams. This extensive practice should help students overlearn or internalize how to write an effective reader-based summary so they can do so automatically when required.

METACOGNITIVELY-ORIENTED FACULTY DEVELOPMENT

Introducing Teachers to Metacognition

I described one approach to introducing teachers to metacognition at the beginning of this chapter. Another approach I use is administering a questionnaire to stimulate teachers' thinking about the thinking they do in their teaching. The Thinking About College Teaching (TACT) is intended to stimulate teachers' thinking about their executive management of teaching. The TACT focus on planning processes includes: establishing learning objectives, considering students' prior knowledge and experience, reflecting on and evaluating alternative approaches to teaching, selecting and sequencing instructional activities, budgeting time, deciding how to represent material to be learned, and anticipating student questions and problems. The TACT's focus on monitoring processes includes checking up on students' comprehension of the material and their progress mastering it, and assessing whether instruction is leading in the right direction or whether change is needed. Evaluating processes include assessing the strengths and weaknesses of a lesson, judging the pace of instruction, evaluating the extent to which the targeted objectives were achieved, assessing both student and teacher performance during the lesson, and using feedback to improve future teaching.

Teachers respond to a Likert-type scale and derive scores for planning, monitoring and evaluating. When scoring and interpreting the results, emphasis is placed on reflective self-analysis of strengths and weaknesses - not a numerical score. After self-scoring the TACT often there is a structured group activity in which teachers compare their results and discuss their own experiences and thoughts about various aspects of teaching, including planning, monitoring and evaluating lessons, and reflect on their strengths and weaknesses. Next they are given a handout with suggestions for managing their teaching, with sections on planning, monitoring and evaluating instruction. The handout is used to develop an action plan to improve the executive management of their teaching so they are thinking metacognitively about their teaching in a more systematic way.

Another way of introducing or developing teaching metacognition is to videotape teachers while teaching, then have them reflect on and self-assess their own instruction, according to criteria established from research on teaching. Appendix B has a teacher-self assessment instrument I have used for this purpose. As with the TACT, the results of this self-evaluation are used as a source of feedback for teachers to plan how they can teach more effectively.

Strategic Metacognitive Knowledge about Teaching Strategies

Many teachers are likely to have *inert* knowledge about teaching (and learning). Teacher education commonly provides teachers with a variety of classroom methods, but doesn't always ensure teachers understand when, why, and how to use them. As a result, much of what teachers have learned may remain inert or inactive, due to lack of knowledge of the contexts and procedures for using these methods. Another questionnaire, Thinking About Teaching Strategies (TATS) (see Appendix C) asks teachers to think about their typical use of a variety of teaching strategies (e.g. questioning, thinking aloud). After completing the questionnaire, small groups of teachers discuss their experiences with these strategies and when, why and how to use them, they evaluate their advantages and disadvantages and consider applications of new or modified teaching strategies to their classes.

Three basic categories of strategic knowledge metacognition are needed for teachers to effectively remember and use the instructional principles and techniques they have. Declarative knowledge is facts, definitions, or concepts. in a subject area. Declarative information can be elicited by a "What" question, e.g,, What is as a teaching strategy? What is cooperative learning? Contextual or conditional knowledge is information regarding the reason and/or situation in which knowledge or strategies are applied. Contextual or conditional information is often sought by a "When" or "Why" question. This type of knowledge lets teachers identify conditions and situations in which it is appropriate to use specific pedagogical principles and techniques. For example, a teacher must know when it is appropriate to use , and why it is beneficial to use cooperative learning activities.

Procedural knowledge is knowing how to apply information or strategies teachers have learned; it includes procedures and techniques. Often procedural information is activated by a question such as "How can I use to help Tanya solve her math problems?"

Teachers need this type of information to help them decide which techniques to use in particular contexts and helps them think through how to implement the teaching. Appendix A contains examples of the types of strategic metacognitive knowledge I give preservice and inservice teachers about two of the teaching strategies they are studying (cooperative learning and scaffolding) in order to help them learn to use these strategies more effectively.

CONCLUSION

Teachers need to have a repertoire of teaching strategies to allow them to be flexible and shift as the situation requires. Even the most effective instructional technique does not work in all situations and variety is necessary to prevent boredom. Strategic metacognitive knowledge about teaching strategies can help teachers compare various methods that might be used to achieve the same academic objectives and evaluate the advantages and disadvantages of each. While planning a lesson it can help teachers select the best technique for the situation as well as consider alternative strategies that might be used as back-ups if, when monitoring a lesson, it appears that change is needed. To teach intelligently, teachers should think metacognitively about instruction so they effectively manage their teaching and use instructional techniques strategically. Brown and Day (1983) focused on combining *informed* strategy training (strategic metacognitive knowledge) with *self-control* training (executive management), and suggest that the combination promotes acquisition and transfer of learning strategies. Does the same combination promote more effective use of teaching strategies? It would be worthwhile to study the effects of informed and self-control strategy training on teaching.

Research has yet to begin to investigate relationships between teaching metacognitively and culture. How and to what extent may the practice of teaching metacognitively be affected by the teacher's cultural background? How can teaching metacognitively affect an instructor's ability to effectively choose and use instructional techniques that are most effective for classrooms with culturally diverse students?

HOPE HARTMAN
Department of Education
City College of the City University of New York
Department of Educational Psychology
Graduate School and University Center
City University of New York

REFERENCES

Annis, L.F. (1983). The processes and effects of peer tutoring. Paper presented at the Annual Meeting of the American Educational Research Association. Montreal.

Aronson, E., Blaney, N., Stephan, C., Sikes, J. & Snapp, M. (1978) *The jigsaw classroom.* Beverly Hills, CA: Sage

Bangert-Drowns, R. L., Kulik, C. C. Kulik, J .A, & Morgan, M. (1991). The instructional effect of feedback in test-like events. *Review of Educational Research.* 61, 213-238

Berliner, D. 1988?(1987) Ways of thinking about students and classrooms by more and less experienced teachers. In: Calderhead, J. (Ed.) *Exploring Teachers' Thinking.* 60-83 . London: Cassell Educational Limited .

Borko, H. & Livingston, C. (1989) Cognition and improvisation: Differences in mathematics instruction by expert and novice teachers. *American Educational Research Journal.* 26. 473-498.

Brophy, J. (1986). Socializing students motivation to learn. Michigan State University, Institute for Research on Teaching. ED 269 384.

Brown, A. L., & Day, J. D. (1983). Macrorules for summarizing texts. The development of expertise. *Journal of Verbal Learning and Verbal Behavior.* 22, 1-14 .

Bruner, J. (1966). *Toward a Theory of Instruction.* New York: Norton.

Burns, M. (1990). Using groups of four. In. Davidson, N. (Ed.) Cooperative Learning in Mathematics. Menlo Park, CA: Addison-Wesley.

Clark, C. (1983). Research on Teacher Planning: An Inventory of the Knowledge Base. In: Smith, D. (Ed.) *Essential Knowledge for Beginning Educators.* Washington, D.C.: American Association of Colleges for Teacher Education. 5-15.

Clark, C. & Peterson, P. (1986). Teachers' thought processes. In Wittroch, M. C. (ed.)*Handbook of Research on Teaching.* 3rd edition. New York: Macmillan.

Clark, C. M. & Yinger, R. (1987). Teacher Planning. In: Calderhead, J. (Ed.) *Exploring Teachers' Thinking.* 84-103 . Cassell Educational Limited: London.

Clark, C. M. & Yinger, R. (1978). Research on Teacher Thinking. Research Series No. 12. ED160592. East Lansing, MI: Institute for Research on Teaching, Michigan State University.

Doyle, W. (1983) Academic Work. *Review of Educational Research*, 53, 159-199.

Haigh, N. (1981). Research on Teacher Thinking. Paper presented at the National Conference of the New Zealand Association for Research in Education. ED213657.

Hartman, H. (1993) *Intelligent Tutoring.* H & H Publishing Co. Cleawater, FL.

Hartman, H. & Sternberg, R. J. (1993) A Broad BACEIS for Improving Thinking. *Instructional Science.* 21(5). 401-425.

Johnson, D. W. & Johnson, R (1975). *Learning together and alone: Cooperation, competition, & individualization.* Englewood Cliffs: Prentice Hall.

Kennedy, M. M. (1998) The relevance of content in inservice teacher education. Paper presented at the annual meeting of the American Educational Research Association. San Diego, CA.

Lhyle, K. G. &Kulhavy, R. W. (1987). Feedback processing and error correction. *Journal of Educational Psychology*, 79, 320-322.

Manning, B. & Payne, B. (1996). *Self Talk for Teachers and Students.* Allyn & Bacon: Needham,

McKeachie, W. (1994). Teaching Tips. 9th edition. Lexington, MA: D.C. Heath & Co.

McKeachie, W., Pintrich, P., Lin, Y. G.& Smith, D.A. (1986). *Teaching and learning in the college classroom.* National Center for Research on Improving Post Secondary Teaching and Learning: Ann Arbor, MI.

Medway, F. J. (1991). A social psychological analysis of peer tutoring. *Journal of Developmental Education,* 15(1), 20-32.

Meichenbaum, D. (1977). *Cognitive Behavior Modification.* New York: Plenum.

Meichenbaum, D. & Biemiller, A. (1998). *Nurturing Independent Learners.* Cambridge: Brookline Books.

Moore, B.,& Harris, B.(1986). An assessment of prospective teachers' cognitive knowledge of appropriate instructional strategies for teaching letter sound to first grade children. Paper presented at the Annual Convention of the Northern Rocky Mountain Educational Research Association. Missoula, MT. ED313371.

Novak, J. (1998). *Learning, Creating and Using Knowledge.* Mahwah, NJ: Lawrence Erlbaum Associates.

Osborne, J. W. (1999). A behavioral measure of metacognition for teachers. Paper presented at the annual meeting of the American Educational Research Association. Montreal.

Palincsar, A. & Brown, A. (1984). Reciprocal teaching of comprehension fostering and monitoring activities. *Cognition and Instruction.* 1(2) 117-175.

Posner, G. J.(1985). *Field Experience: A Guide to Reflective Teaching.* Longman: New York Pressley, M. & McCormick, C. (1995). *Advanced Educational Psychology for Educators, Researchers and Policymakers.* New York: Harper Collins College Publishers.

Rosenshine, B. & Meister, C. (1992). The use of scaffolds for teaching higher-level cognitive strategies. *Educational Leadership.* April. 26-33.

Sabers, D. S. , Cushing, K. S., & Berliner, D.C. (1991) Differences among teachers in a task characterized by simultaneity, multidimensionality, and immediacy. *American Educational Research Journal*, 28, 63-88.

Sharan, Y. & Sharan, S. (1989/1990) Group Investigation expands learning. *Educational Leadership.* 47(4). 17-21.

Slavin, R. (1995). *Cooperative learning: Theory, research & practice.* Englewood Cliffs: Prentice Hall

Sternberg, R. (1985). *Beyond I.Q.: A Triarchic Theory.* New York: Cambridge University Press.

Vygotsky, L. (1978). *Mind in Society.* Cambridge, MA: Harvard University Press.

Winne, P. H. & Marx, R.W. (1982). Students' and teachers' views of thinking processes for classroom learning. *Elementary School Journal.* 82 (2) 494-518.

Zeichner, K. Tabachnick, B. R. & Densmore, K.(1987). Individual, institutional, and cultural influences on the development of teachers' craft knowledge. In J. Calderhead (ed.) *Exploring Teachers' Thinking.* London: Cassell Educational Limited.

APPENDIX A

Illustrations of Strategic Metacognitive Knowledge for Teaching Strategies

I. Strategic Metacognitive Knowledge about Cooperative Learning.

A. What is Cooperative Learning?

Cooperative learning involves students working together towards a common goal in a teaching-learning situation. There are three basic forms of cooperative learning: tutoring (peer or cross-age), in which one student teaches another; pairs, who work and learn with each other; and small groups of students teaching and learning together. **Not all groupwork is cooperative learning.** Johnson and Johnson (1975) define cooperative learning by criteria including positive interdependence, so that students "sink or swim together".

B. Why Is Cooperative Learning a Useful Teaching Strategy?

Cooperative learning increases students' motivation to learn. Academic work is usually much more fun and exciting to students when they work together cooperatively. Research has shown that cooperative learning increases confidence in students' abilities. It improves self-esteem as well as feelings of competence in specific subjects. There are good reasons for the old saying, "The best way to learn something is to teach it." Teaching requires considerable depth of knowledge, understanding, organization and memory of important concepts and skills. Cooperative learning provides situations for students to teach each other. When students explain and teach concepts to each other, retention of these concepts improves. Explaining also helps students connect their prior knowledge with new information. Research has also documented the positive effects of cooperative learning on improving social relations with students of different ethnicities and cultural backgrounds (Hartman, 1996).

Cooperative learning can be used as a strategy for instruction from other (teacher) direction and control to student self-regulation. Cooperative learning has also been found to activate metacognition (Artzt & Armour-Thomas 1992). There is an increasing amount of ethnic and linguistic diversity in classrooms in the U.S.A. Cooperative learning has been demonstrated to be an especially effective method of teaching in settings characterized by such diversity. Cooperative learning can be done at almost any age and often with teachers' existing instructional materials. It helps improve achievement from elementary grades through graduate school.

C. How Is Cooperative Learning Conducted?

The teacher's role in cooperative learning is different from whole class instruction. In cooperative learning, the teacher is more of a manager and facilitator of learning, or a coach, than a transmitter of knowledge. Major teacher responsibilities include: training students for cooperation, structuring groups, deciding whether/how to assign roles, selecting and preparing instructional materials (planning) and monitoring and evaluating student performance. Teachers can develop personal action plans to design learning lessons that meet the needs of their specific students and curriculum. Resources are available for cooperative learning lessons in many subjects. There are numerous approaches to conducting cooperative learning lessons. Some, such as Learning Together (Johnson & Johnson, 1975) and Jigsaw (Aronson, Blaney, Stephan, Sikes & Snapp, 1978) can be used across subject areas. Other methods are more subject-specific, such as Group Investigation (social studies, Sharan & Sharan 1989/90), Groups of Four (Burns 1990 and Team -Assisted Instruction (Math, Slavin 1995), and Reciprocal Teaching (reading, Palincsar & Brown 1984. Think-Pair-Share is a method of cooperative learning that involves pairs of students working together, sharing their thoughts about a problem or task (Meichenbaum & Biemiller, 1998).

Most forms of cooperative learning involve groups of four to eight students. Many proponents of cooperative learning emphasize the importance of setting up heterogeneous groups. Variables to use in heterogeneous grouping include achievement level, gender, and ethnicity. To set up such groups and effective cooperative learning lessons requires careful management by the teacher.

II. Strategic Metacognitive Knowledge About Scaffolding

A. What Is Scaffolding in Teaching?

Scaffolding is based on Vygotsky's (1978) concept of the **zone of proximal development**. The zone of proximal development (ZPD) " is the distance between the actual developmental level as determined by independent problem solving and the level of potential development as determined through problem solving under adult guidance or in collaboration with more capable peers...The zone of proximal development defines those functions that have not yet matured but are in the process of maturation, functions that will mature tomorrow but are currently in an embryonic state" (Vygotsky, 1978 p. 86). More competent others (teachers, parents, peers) help students by providing them with information and temporary support which is gradually decreased as the students' competence increases.

B. Why Use Scaffolding in Teaching?

Teachers can aid intellectual development in students by providing them with information and **temporary support** which can be gradually decreased as the students' competence increases. The goal of providing scaffolds is for students to become independent, self-regulated thinkers who are more self-sufficient and less teacher dependent. in teaching is comparable to the of a building which is gradually removed as its structure becomes better able to support its own weight. Scaffolds are like training wheels on a bicycle which provide temporary support while the rider learns to maintain balance. Once the bike rider is secure about maintaining balance, the training wheels are removed and the rider self-balances. Through teachers and others can help students perform at higher levels than they could if they were completely on their own, without the benefit from social interactions with others who are more competent. Teachers use as a strategy for shifting instruction from others' (teacher's) control to student self-regulation. The teacher's role shifts from being a model or an instructor to being a manager, who gives prompts and corrective feedback. Reciprocal Teaching, discussed more in Chapter 3, Developing Students' Metacognitive Skills, is a reading comprehension method based on scaffolding.

C. How is Scaffolding Used in Teaching?

Scaffolding involves providing support (models, cues, prompts, hints, or partial solutions) to students to bridge the gap between what students can do on their own and what they can do with guidance from others. When beginning to teach students to perform a new task, often the teacher (expert) completely guides the student's activity, modeling how to perform the task. The student observes the teacher and does little independent thinking at this point, other than reading relevant material and observing the teacher's behavior. Once internalized, the student can copy the expert's thinking/learning strategies and apply them to his/her own academic work. Next, the student attempts to do the task with the teacher providing supportive cuing, assistance, and additional modeling, as needed. If the student has trouble using the strategies, then sometimes the teacher has to model or demonstrate again how to think about and use them. This gives the student another opportunity to observe the thinking and behavior that is appropriate for the situation. Gradually the student plays a greater teaching role and assumes more responsibility for self-instruction and for teaching peers.

Rosenshine & Meister (1992) identify the following six basic components or guidelines for teachers to use when: 1. Present the new cognitive strategies, 2. Regulate difficulty during guided practice, 3. Provide varying contexts for student practice, 4. Provide feedback, 5. Increase student responsibility, and 6. Provide independent practice Eventually the student learns to do all the thinking-- applying the content, skills, and strategies without the teacher-expert's assistance. The teacher plays only a supportive role at this point.

Cognitive Behavior Modification (Meichenbaum, 1977) is a method of gradually changing behavior based on instruction through five stages, 1) Cognitive Modeling; *2) Overt, External Guidance*; 3) *Overt, Self Guidance; 4) Faded Overt Self-Guidance;* and *5) Covert Self Instruction.* The following example shows cognitive behavior modification for the use of self-questions while reading in order to monitor comprehension and clarify misunderstanding. The procedure starts with teacher direction and leads to student self-direction.

1. *Cognitive Modeling:* The teacher reads a section of the text aloud. While reading aloud the teacher asks and answers comprehension monitoring and clarifying self-questions aloud. For example, the teacher says, "Does this all make sense to me? Well, some of it does and some doesn't. Maybe I should reread the parts that are unclear." Then the teacher rereads the unclear parts aloud and says, "That makes more sense now. I skipped over some key words when I read it the first time."

2. *Overt, External Guidance*: This time the student reads a different portion of the text aloud. The teacher says to the student, "What question will you ask yourself to check up on your understanding?" Then the student asks and answers a self-question such as, "Is there anything in here I don't fully understand?" If the student finds there is something unclear, the teacher says, "What can you do to clarify your understanding?" The student then uses a clarification strategy, such as looking at context clues.

3. *Overt, Self-Guidance*: The student reads another section of text aloud, asks a comprehension monitoring self-question aloud, and seeks clarifying information as needed. At this stage, the teacher listens actively to make sure the student asks a comprehension monitoring self-question and clarifies, if needed. If the student forgets to ask a comprehension monitoring question, or has trouble doing it, the teacher prompts or assists the student.

4. *Faded, Overt Self-Guidance:* The student repeats the procedure in step three, but this time **whispers** while reading aloud and self-questioning. The teacher listens to the whispering and tries to tell if the student asks and answers self-questions. If the teacher isn't sure because the whispering made it hard to hear what the student was saying, the teacher asks the student about it when the student has finished the section of text.

5. *Covert Self-Instruction*: The student reads a section of text silently and silently asks and answers self-questions to monitor comprehension and clarify as needed. The teacher watches the student, and when the student is finished, asks what self-question was asked and what, if any, clarification occurred and how. At this point

the student has become self-directed in the use of self-questions to monitor comprehension and clarify confusion.

Having this strategic metacognitive knowledge about cooperative learning or scaffolding - knowing what it is, when and why to use it, and how to implement it - can help teachers effectively use this teaching strategy to promote higher-level thinking in their students.

APPENDIX B

Video Self-Assessment of Instruction

Classroom Behavior	Weakness				Strength	
	1	2	3	4	5	Does Not Apply

Clearly state objectives
Effectively organize material (structure/sequence)
Appropriate scope
Consider student background knowledge/skills
Activate relevant background knowledge/skills
Communicate short and long term objectives
Deliver instruction enthusiastically
Use variety of instructional approaches
Actively engage students with material
Stimulate student motivation to learn
Elaborate on abstract/difficult ideas
Monitor students' comprehension
Identify misconceptions
Clarify areas of confusion
Connect material within the course
Connect material to other courses, with and across subjects
Apply material to careers or a professional context
Apply material to everyday life
Develop students' intellectual skills
Monitor/evaluate effectiveness of teaching strategies
Change teaching strategies as needed
Monitor/evaluate students' communication, both verbal and nonverbal
Monitor/evaluate own communication, both verbal and nonverbal

APPENDIX C

THINKING ABOUT TEACHING STRATEGIES

Please mark the items below in terms of your typical teaching practices: **V**=very typical of you, **N**=not very typical, **S**=somewhat typical **NA**=not apply **DK**=don't know

1.   Ask students questions.___
2.   Demonstrate to students how they should approach tasks.___
3.   Think out loud as I demonstrate to students how they should approach tasks.__
4.   Teach students what types of questions to ask themselves about ideas or problems.___
5.   Ask questions that require yes/no or relatively simple answers. __
6.   Ask questions that require relatively complex answers.__
7.   Give lectures on topics to be learned. __
8.   Write important words, concepts, diagrams on the board.__
9.   Develop ideas gradually, building from the simple to the complex__
10. Focus content coverage on abstract ideas.__
11. Focus content coverage on concrete ideas.__
12. Sequence content coverage from concrete to abstract ideas. __
13. Sequence content coverage from abstract to concrete ideas.__
14. Sequence ideas inductively, from specific to general. __
15. Sequence ideas deductively, from general to specific. __
16. Structure lessons so that students work with other students in pairs or groups.__
17. Serve as a coach or learning facilitator__
18. Consider students' prior knowledge about what they are learning__
19. Identify specific misconceptions students have about content or procedures___
20. Have students give their own examples of concepts__
21. Help students develop good social skills for interacting with others__
22. Help students connect their efforts and strategies in learning to their academic outcomes___
23. Teach students to explain their successes and failures in ways that increase their chances of improving their future performance__
24. Have students relate what they are learning to their own prior knowledge and experience.__
25. Have students discover concepts through their own experiences.__
26. Inform students at the beginning how they should organize the material to be learned.__

27.   Present material in different modalities (e.g. verbal, visual, auditory, tactile-kinesthetic)__
28.   Have students identify specific kinds of relationships between concepts__
29.   Help students think about how they acquire information.__
30.   Help students think about how they remember information__
31.   Have students apply what they learn to new situations__
32.   Have students memorize ideas, even if they don't understand them __
33.   Make sure students have prerequisite knowledge and skills before giving them complex concepts to master or tasks to perform.__
34.   Encourage students to take responsibility and control over their own learning.__
35.   Allow students make some of their own choices when learning.__
36.   Allow students to have more than one opportunity to master material__
37.   Provide students with hints, cues and prompts to help them complete work on their own instead of giving them answers.__
38.   Help students connect concepts across subjects areas. __
39.   Help students connect course material to everyday life experience.__
40.   Gradually shift from my guidance of students' approach to their control over and responsibility for their own performance __

CHAPTER 9

METACOGNITION IN SCIENCE TEACHING
AND LEARNING

HOPE J. HARTMAN

ABSTRACT. Recent research on science teaching and learning emphasizes the importance of active, meaningful learning, with metacognitive processing by both teachers and learners. This chapter describes research on students' reading metacognition and misconceptions in biology and instructional methods I have used to enhance students' metacognition about their science learning and to enhance science professors' metacognition about their teaching.

Students often consider science to be one of the most difficult subjects they take, whether in high school or college. Because of its perceived difficulty, many students even develop science phobias, much like they tend to do with mathematics. Science teachers often reflect on the content they are going to teach, but to what extent do science teachers think reflectively about the pedagogy they use to teach specific scientific concepts and skills? To teach science successfully, teachers can use their metacognitive or high-level thinking about what, why and how they teach in order to manage and regulate their teaching so that it meets the needs of their students. In addition, to help students learn science effectively, teachers can develop their students' use of metacognition so they gain awareness and control over themselves as learners, both intellectually and emotionally. This chapter reviews some of the literature on science teaching that relates to metacognition in teaching and learning science. Then the chapter describes some of my experiences with metacognition in science teaching and learning.

RESEARCH ON SCIENCE TEACHING & LEARNING

In a review of the literature on the implications of cognitive science for teaching physics, Redish (1994) identified four broad principles, each with corollaries, which are useful for physics teachers to help them think about their teaching. First is The Construction Principle, which states that people organize their knowledge and experience into mental models and that people must build

173

H.J. Hartman (ed.), Metacognition in Learning and Instruction, 173–201.

their own mental models. Second is The Assimilation Principle, which says that mental models control how we incorporate experiences and new information into our minds. Related prior knowledge and experience form mental models into which new knowledge and experience are incorporated. Third is the Accommodation Principle, which emphasizes that sometimes existing mental models must be changed for learning to occur. Fourth is the Individuality Principle, which highlights individual differences in students' mental models as a result of their personal constructions. Students have different mental models for learning and different mental models for physical phenomena. These four principles provide a metacognitive framework for physics and other science teachers to help them plan, monitor and evaluate their instruction, classroom activities, and learning assessments so they can maximize students' understanding of science. For example, Redish suggests that looking at the curriculum from the mental models perspective helps teachers establish the goals of identifying the mental models they want students to develop. Additionally, it stimulates teachers to consider the character and implications of students' pre-existing mental models, and helps teachers realize the benefit of using touchstone problems to analyze and identify critical aspects of the curriculum. According to Redish, one of the implications of the individuality principle is that teachers need to think about how students may arrive at the same answer but for very different reasons. To determine how students reason, teachers should listen to them thinking aloud without interrupting their train of thought or guiding them.

Walberg (1991) suggests that in science it is especially useful for students to struggle with interesting, meaningful problems that can stimulate discussion about competing approaches. He recommends using what he calls "comprehension teaching," more commonly called scaffolding, which involves providing students with temporary support until they can perform tasks on their own. Based on Vygotsky's (1978) concept of the zone of proximal development, scaffolding is recommended for teachers to build from what students can do only with temporary guidance from a more competent person, gradually reducing and eventually removing this support as students become independent thinkers and learners who can perform the task or use the skill or knowledge on their own. Scaffolding has been found to be an excellent method of developing students' higher level thinking skills (Rosenshine & Meister, 1992). However, metacognition is needed for teachers to use scaffolding effectively, as they consider issues such as what types of support to provide, what order to sequence them in, and how to decide when it is time to reduce or withdraw support from students.

Activity-based teaching has been found to be especially beneficial for students with lower achievement records, ability and socioeconomic status. Walberg says the following effective teaching methods are particularly-cost effective: cooperative learning, mastery learning, direct instruction and comprehension teaching (scaffolding). Recent research indicates that extensive knowledge is required for excellent teaching (Walberg, 1991). Extensive knowledge needed for effective teaching includes both subject-area knowledge and pedagogical information, such as strategic metacognitive knowledge about teaching strategies. For example, strategic metacognitive knowledge about the teaching strategy of cooperative learning includes knowing what cooperative learning is, knowing when and why it is useful, and knowing how procedures for implementing cooperative learning (See Chapter 8 for details.) Having this kind of information about teaching strategies helps teachers decide among alternative approaches to use in various situations.

How do science teachers decide which teaching methods to use? For over 20 years now the Learning Cycle (Karplus, 1974) has been used to structure science instruction in order to help students move from concrete experience and thinking to formal, abstract thinking about science. This constructivist approach is based on Piaget's theory of intellectual development. Development is structured by three teaching phases: Exploration, Concept Invention/Introduction and Application. Through this sequence students' thinking is expected to progress from concrete thinking about science concepts to being able to deal with these concepts on a formal, abstract level. Application often involves tasks or problems that relate to students' everyday lives (Barman, Benz, Haywood & Houk 1992).

However, the learning cycle might not always be the best approach for teachers to use. A study comparing the learning cycle model to modeling in urban, middle school science students found that although both the modeling and learning cycle groups outperformed the control students in their use of integrated science process skills, students who were taught by modeling developed better integrated science process skills than students who were taught by the learning cycle approach. (Rubin and Norman, 1989). Consequently, rather than just automatically using a commonly accepted approach, such as the learning cycle, teachers should use their metacognition to carefully reflect on the implications of what research has shown about the advantages and disadvantages of a variety instructional methods for their specific students and subject matter. Perhaps a combination of the learning cycle and modeling approaches might be tested to see if it leads to even higher levels of integrated science process skills development than either alone.

Increasingly new technologies are supplementing and enhancing the learning process. These technologies can support new views of science teaching. A high school biology course characterized by "model-based reasoning" emphasized both the development of conceptual and strategic knowledge of classical genetics, as well as the development of insights regarding science as an intellectual activity. This nine-week course for seniors involved *model revising* problem solving in contrast with more common *model using* problem solving. In the model revising approach, students work in research groups sharing their observations of phenomena, building models, and defending models to groups of students who critique each other's models. The critiques lead to model revising. The emergence of competing models increases student awareness of the need for models to explain existing data and predict additional observations. Students also get increased awareness that more than one model may be consistent with the data, and may predict and explain. The computer played an important role in the development of this course. Use of computers was guided by the ..."view that science education should allow students to be engaged in many of the activities of science"... "and science teaching as problem posing, problem probing, and persuasion of peers." (p. 334). Software supplemented work with real organisms, and enabled students to learn genetics by engaging in activities like those of geneticists (Stewart, Hafner, Johnson & Finkel, 1992). Thinking metacognitively about teaching includes exploring such alternative approaches to instruction, monitoring their implementation, evaluating their effectiveness, and using feedback to plan future lessons.

Tobias (1986) characterized introductory college science courses by negative features such as failure to motivate student interest, passive learning, emphasis on competitive rather than cooperative learning, and reliance on algorithms rather than understanding. These features sometimes steer students away from careers in the sciences. Recent research suggests that the mismatch between teaching practices and students' learning styles may account for many of these problems. Felder's (1993) model of learning styles is especially appealing because it conceptualizes the dimensions sensing/intuiting, visual/verbal, inductive/ deductive, active/reflective, and global/sequential as being a variables on a continuum rather than dichotomous variables. He cites research to guide instruction for each of these styles. Felder also recommends systematic use of a few additional teaching methods which overlap learning styles and help meet the needs of all students. These include: give students experience with problems before giving them tools for solving them, balance concrete with conceptual information, liberally use graphic representations, physical analogies and demonstrations, and show students how concepts are connected within and between subjects and to everyday life experience. Teaching science metacognitively can help teachers improve the alignment between their teaching practices and students' learning styles.

Science educators (e. g., Baird & White, 1984) suggest that self-questioning and think- aloud processes are effective strategies to promote scientific thinking. Baird and White conducted a study designed to improve metacognition in ninth grade students learning science and eleventh graders learning biology. They identified seven learner objectives:1) increased knowledge of metacognition, 2) enhanced awareness of their learning styles, 3) greater awareness of tasks' purposes and natures, 4) more control over learning through better decision-making, 5) more positive attitudes toward learning, 6) higher standards for understanding and performance set by the students themselves, with more precise self-evaluation of their achievements, and 7) greater effectiveness as independent learners, planning thoughtfully, diagnosing learning difficulties and overcoming them, and using time more productively. Instructional materials included a question-asking checklist, an evaluation of learning behaviors, an outcomes notebook, and a techniques workbook, where students tried out concept mapping. This extensive study went through four phases and involved 15 methods of collecting data, including video and audiotapes, classroom observations, questionnaires and tests. The results showed increased student control over learning and understanding of science.

Stress on Analytical Reasoning (SOAR) is a program at Xavier University in New Orleans with a record of success teaching science to minority students interested in health sciences, physics, engineering or mathematics (Carmichael, Ryan, Jones, Hunter & Vincent, 1981). One of the teaching strategies it has found especially useful is Pair Problem Solving. Whimbey and Lochhead (1982) describe this technique as a thinker and listener pair working on problems and rotating roles. Students take turns serving as thinkers (problem solvers), who externalize their thought processes by thinking aloud while analytical listeners track and guide the problem solving process as needed. This method makes problems more engaging and promotes self-monitoring and self-evaluating, giving students feedback on what is understood and what is still unclear. It encourages skills of reflecting on beginning and later thoughts. It also teaches communication skills, fosters cooperation, and encourages the formation of study and support groups. Finally, pair problem solving exposes teachers and students to various solution approaches (Heiman, Narode, Slomianko, & Lochhead, J. 1987). By listening to one's own thoughts, the student gains awareness and control over problem solving. Externalizing thoughts enables them to be seen from a fresh perspective. Together, the students can discover errors, misconceptions, organizational problems, and other impediments to academic performance. The teacher needs to observe each pair, monitor progress, and provide feedback on the process. This approach has been demonstrated to be an effective approach for helping students learn science and math (Whimbey & Lochhead, 1982). The findings about pair-problem solving provide strategic metacognitive knowledge science teachers can use to decide when and how to use the pair problem-solving method in their classes.

To what extent do teachers think about their assessment techniques and how well they measure important instructional goals? Research on assessing hands-on science suggests that there should be symmetry between curriculum and assessment, that assessment should be continuous, and that performance measures are needed to supplement traditional multiple choice-type assessments in order to get a comprehensive picture of student achievement. Performance measures should emphasize science process skills, such as observing and inferring, not just getting the right answer. Four performance assessments that can be used to assess science achievement are: 1) lab notebooks recording students' procedures and conclusions; 2) computer simulations of hands-on investigations; 3) short answer paper-and-pencil problems in planning, analyzing and/or interpreting experiments; and 4) multiple choice items developed from observations of students conducting hands-on investigations. Effective science performance assessment requires multiple iterations to revise assessments based on students' experiences and feedback. To shortcut this process often leads to poor assessment and low quality classroom instruction (Shavelson & Baxter, 1992).

Feedback is important for students in several ways: it helps them assess their mastery of course material, helps them assess their use of thinking and learning strategies, and helps them to connect their efforts and strategies to their academic outcomes, which can overcome learned helplessness by increasing self- awareness and control. The primary benefit of feedback is the identification of errors of knowledge and understanding and assistance with correcting those errors. Feedback generally improves subsequent performance on similar items. Research suggests that feedback can guide students in their use of learning strategies, and that adults who try different strategies and are tested on their learning can generally identify effective strategies (Crooks, 1988). Mestre (1994) found that problem posing, when followed by an interview, is a powerful assessment strategy for evaluating the development and understanding of physics concepts in high-performing university physics students. Mestre found that these "good novices" were able to pose appropriate, solvable problems when responding to a problem situation or concept scenario, but they also had major flaws in their conceptual understanding. The flaws suggested that students were deficient in how their knowledge was organized in memory and how it was connected with procedures and problems. Most teachers could benefit from having such information about assessment and feedback and using it metacognitively to improve their teaching and evaluation practices as well as to improve students' performance.

REPRESENTATION STRATEGIES IN SCIENCE LEARNING

Mental representations of information to be learned or used in problem solving are important determinants of whether and how learning will occur. Representations can be internal, like mental images, or external, like charts or tables, as metacognitive aids. McIntosh (1986) found that teaching ninth grade physical science students to generate visual images helped them remember rules in science (e.g., Boyle's Law).   Sternberg (1985) characterized intelligent performance by the use of multiple representations. Similarly, in his review of the learning strategies literature, Dansereau (1978) reported that multiple encodings have a more facilitative effect on retrieval than do single encodings. For example, it is better to use both visual imagery and mnemonics to remember than to use either encoding strategy alone.

In a review of research on using concrete, visual models to facilitate understanding of scientific information, Mayer, (1989) found that such models consistently helped lower aptitude learners think systematically about scientific material. According to Mayer, concrete models, which consist of words and/or diagrams, help students construct representations of the major objects, actions and their causal relations in the scientific content being studied. He identified seven characteristics of effective models in this review. The good models he found were: complete, concise, coherent, concrete, conceptual, correct and "considerate" (i.e. using vocabulary and organization appropriate for the learner). In short, models are "good" with respect to certain learners and certain instructional goals. He also identified some guidelines for application of concrete models, including when and where they should be used, why to use them.

Concept Maps and Vee Diagrams

Concept maps and Vee diagrams help people learn how to learn. Procedures for creating them are in appendices of Novak's (1998) *Learning, Creating and Using Knowledge,* which describes his human constructivist theory Concept maps, developed by Novak in 1972, are graphic representations of knowledge with the most general concept at the top, hierarchically leading to more specific concepts. Concepts are in boxes or circles, with labeled connecting lines identifying relationships. The labels are words that link one concept to another, and the label is placed in the middle of the linking line. For example, .as shown in Figure 1, the concept "body fluid compartments" is in a box, with a line drawn from it to linking words, such as "are" which has a line drawn from it to the more specific concepts "intracellular fluid" and "extracellular fluid" which are also in a box. The linking line coming from intracellular fluid, with the word "has", leads to a more specific box containing the concepts "low concentration of sodium ions" and "high concentration of potassium ions" and so forth. According to Novak, concept maps help students become empowered, and reduce the need for rote learning, and they help teachers negotiate meaning with students and design better instruction. See Figure 1, next page.

HOPE J. HARTMAN

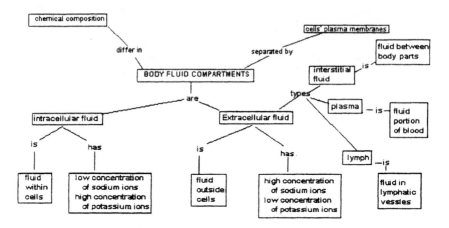

Figure 1 Sample Concept Map: Body Fluid Compartments

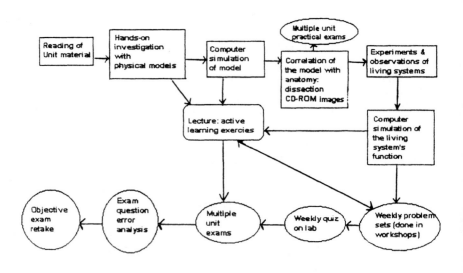

Figure 2   Modified Learning Cycle Model Used to Design the New Anatomy & Physiology Curriculum

Griswold, Lemons & Hartman (1995)

Concept mapping can be used successfully individually and in teams; with concepts, events, and social relationships; with young children and adults; in schools and corporations with researchers, teachers/managers and students/ workers; and in everyday life. They are used in teacher education, curriculum development, and assessment (Hartman, 1999). One example is from a handbook for college chemistry workshop leaders illustrating the integrated components of their Workshop Model (Roth, Strozak, Cracolice & Gosser, 1997). The concept map consists of four circled concepts arranged in a diamond. The concepts are students (top circle), learning specialists (bottom circle), workshop leaders (left circle), and faculty (right circle). The circles are connected by four diagonal lines labeled Workshop, connecting circles of workshop leaders and students; Lectures & Laboratory, connecting circles of students and faculty; Program Direction, connecting circles of faculty and learning specialists; and Leader Training, connecting circles of Learning Specialists and Workshop Leaders. The leadership training includes intensive experience learning how to construct and use concept maps, so the workshop leaders can teach the chemistry students how to construct and use them.

Extensive work has been done using concept maps in schools and corporations. Many benefits of concept maps cited include promoting meaningful learning (especially in science), understanding superordinate and subordinate relationships, improving peer relationships and trust, resolving conflicts, and improving understanding of one's role in and contributions to team projects. They also help students and teachers differentiate misconceptions from valid conceptions, decrease anxiety, improve self-confidence, and more. Junior high school science students taught to use concept maps and Vee diagrams outperformed students who were not taught these strategies on tests of novel problem solving (Novak, Gowin, & Johansen 1983). Research by Okebukola on using concept maps with high school biology students in Nigeria showed that students using concept maps had significantly better content mastery, better attitudes toward biology and less anxiety than students who did not use concept maps (Novak, 1990). Chemistry students, ages 16-18 in a technical school, were taught concept mapping to aid their visualization of knowledge structures and to document and explore changes in their knowledge structures as a result of learning (Regis & Albertazzi, 1996). After four years of experience Regis and Albertazzi found, "...we have grown more and more impressed by the potential of this metacognitive tool to help chemistry teachers and learners to improve teaching and learning" (p. 1088). They found that concept maps help teachers know what students know and how they relate concepts in their knowledge base, as well as highlight what misconceptions students have and let teachers see how students reorganize their cognitive structures after a specific learning activity. They found that concept maps benefit learners by making learning of new subject matter meaningful. Support was also found for using a concept map to design an artificial intelligence training program for diagnosing coronary problems (Ford, Canas, Jones , Stahl, Novak, & Adams-Weber 1991).

Vee diagrams (The Knowledge Vee) were developed by Novak's retired colleague Gowin in 1977 to help students understand research. They are Vee-shaped graphic organizers that help learners systematically observe and measure all the relevant variables by focusing on the specific principles and concepts that are involved in the event and the focus question. They consist of four basic sections: top center - focus question, bottom center - event, left side - thinking, conceptual/theoretical, and right side - doing, methodological . The left side consists of the learner's world view, philosophy/epistemology, theory, principles, constructs and concepts. The right side consists of value and knowledge claims, transformations and records.   All Vee components interact to create new knowledge.

Thinking metacognitively about conducting science lessons often includes selecting which representations or models to present to a class (e.g, flow charts, diagrams, concept maps), determining when to present them (e.g. order in the instructional sequence), and deciding how to present them (e.g. blackboard, transparency, CD-ROM). It also includes the teacher's self-assessment of the effectiveness of the representations selected, the timing of their implementation, the method of presentation, and a lesson improvement plan for more effective use of representations.

READING SCIENTIFIC TEXTS

Students often complain about reading their science texts. Even otherwise competent readers aren't aware of the top-level structures underlying scientific texts (Cook and Mayer, 1988). Top-down structures are important because they trigger higher-order ideas that activate schemata which allow details to be inferred and attention to be allocated effectively (Pressley and McCormick, 1995). Research by Cook and Mayer suggests that college students who don't understand the structure of scientific texts have problems representing the material, thereby impeding comprehension and retention. One study found that students had difficulty sorting text into the text-structure categories of classification, comparison/contrast, enumeration, sequence and generalization. In another study, after receiving eight hours of training in analyzing, recognizing, and organizing relevant information in scientific texts, experimental junior college chemistry students outperformed controls on measures of comprehension. Text structure instruction included modeling reading strategies, explicitly explaining how to identify a sequence (for example, how to put a sequence into one's own words), how to identify the key words signaling a sequence, and how to identify supporting evidence. Thus developing students' metacognition about how to read scientific texts can improve their comprehension by helping them focus on relevant information and use it to create internal connections and representations.

In a related study, Speigel and Barufaldi (1994) focused on four of the same common science text structures as Cook and Mayer, classification, enumeration, sequence and generalization, and one different one, cause and effect. Community college students in anatomy and physiology were taught to recognize these text structures and to construct graphic organizers of them after reading (postorganizers). Students who constructed postorganizers demonstrated superior memory on immediate and delayed posttests when compared to students who used rereading, highlighting or underlining. Spiegel (1996) emphasizes the importance of providing students with strategic metacognitive information (what, when, why and how) on the use of learning strategies such as graphic organizers. To what extent do science teachers regularly provide students with the metacognitive knowledge needed to effectively and efficiently learn to use graphic organizers and other text digestion strategies?

When reading scientific texts students often try to rotely learn big words, facts and details instead of trying to understand ideas. They learn so that they can "report back" information but not apply it (Roth, 1991). Roth reported that some students, "conceptual change readers", tried to understand and accommodate their beliefs to the information in the text. They activated their prior knowledge and recognized when it was somewhat inconsistent with the meaning described in the text. Conceptual change readers thought about the meaning and worked to resolve the discrepancy to refine their own thinking. This effort to clarify the misconception was described as a "conceptual change strategy." These students exhibited the self-awareness and self-regulation that are the essence of metacognition in learning. How did the conceptual change readers learn to use these strategies?

Scientific textbooks sometimes contain misconceptions and alternative conceptions about science, so reading them can interfere with learning unless the teacher filters conceptual problems before students read them and treat them as valid knowledge (Abimbola and Baba 1996). Abimbola and Baba developed a procedure for teachers to use to analyze textbooks and identify misconceptions. In their analysis of one textbook, STAN Biology, they found 117 misconceptions and 37 alternative conceptions which were distributed in 18 of the 22 chapters. One type of misconception is using wrong or out-of-date words to represent concepts: e.g. "semi-permeable membrane" has been replaced with "selectively permeable" or "differentially permeable," so it is not misunderstood as partially permeable or partially impermeable. Another type of misconception is statements that are wrong: e.g., "Oxygen is produced as a waste product", is erroneous because in the context of nutrition and photosynthesis, where it appeared in the text, oxygen is really a useful end product of photosynthesis because it oxidizes food to release energy. An example of an alternative conception they found is defining dentition by teeth, without including that dentition also includes the arrangement of teeth. Abibola and Baba recommend that teachers consider the number of misconceptions and alternative conceptions when selecting among science textbooks and select the one with the fewest. This research suggests that effective science teaching metacognition includes awareness of how commonplace misconceptions are in standard science texts, and control over textbook selection and use in order to avoid or at least address those with false statements.

MISCONCEPTIONS

Students are far from "*tabula rasa*" who simply acquire information teachers and books provide. They usually come to courses with at least some prior knowledge, beliefs, values, attitudes and experiences that influence what and how they think and learn. Background information provides a foundation to build upon. Some of what students bring is an emerging foundation, parts of which can be built on, parts of which must be revised, and parts of which must be discarded. Some of what they bring creates obstacles to, inhibits or prevents learning. Finally, some of their misconceptions don't really matter.   What are misconceptions? Misconceptions are faulty ideas that are based on false or incomplete information, limited experience, incorrect generalizations or misinterpretations and are consistent with the student's basic understanding. Some misconceptions result from cultural myths or scientifically out-of-date information. Others may arise from vague, ambiguous, or discrepant information. Some researchers view and refer to misconceptions as "alternative frameworks" or "preconceptions" which emphasize the emergent nature of structures of knowledge. Anderson, Sheldon & Dubay's (1990) study of college biology students looked at concepts of respiration and photosynthesis. Sample misconceptions include the simplistic definition that respiration is exhaling CO_2 , and not understanding that plants manufacture their own food but thinking that plants get their food from nutrients in the soil. Textbooks are not the only source of students' misconceptions. Teaching science metacognitively includes teacher awareness of the sources and characteristics of students' misconceptions, selection of strategies to overcome students' misconceptions, and monitoring/evaluating the extent to which important misconceptions have been replaced with accurate conceptions.

Research shows that misconceptions are deeply entrenched and enduring, even after students learn new information that is inconsistent with their prior knowledge. Learners must have extensive and deep, meaningful learning for the new, correct knowledge to come to mind and be applied instead of the old misconceptions

(Pressley & McCormick , 1995). According to Duit (1991), prior knowledge affects students' observations, guiding them to information that is consistent with their own perspectives. Students selectively attend to information, seeking to confirm what they already "know." Sometimes students' prior knowledge is so strong that they won't even believe what they see. A videotape "A Perfect Universe" (Schneps, 1994) shows that even students and professors at Harvard suffer from deeply entrenched scientific misconceptions.

Research suggests that usually multiple knowledge levels (or domains) of misunderstandings are involved in any given misconception. Teachers should pay attention to each level and the relationships between them. Each domain or level contains a variety of kinds of knowledge. According to Perkins and Simmons' (1988) integrative model of misconceptions, deep understanding involves four interlocked levels of knowledge and teachers need to address all four: 1) *Content*: e.g. recalling facts, using vocabulary; 2). Problem Solving: e.g. strategies, self-regulation; 3) *Epistemic*: e.g. explaining rationales, providing evidence; and 4) *Inquiry*: critical thinking - extending and challenging domain-specific knowledge. To apply teaching metacognition to this problem, science teachers could develop plans to identify the types of misconceptions their students have and select or develop procedures to overcome them.

Many researchers believe that students overcome misconceptions by recognizing and replacing them. Nussbaum & Novick (1982) proposed that awareness of beliefs is necessary before students can overcome misconceptions. Awareness creates cognitive conflict which motivates conflict resolution to accommodate current beliefs or cognitive structures. Accommodation may lead to modifying existing structures and/or creating new ones. Minstrell (1989) claims that earlier ideas are seldom pulled out and replaced. He believes it is more effective for teachers to help students differentiate between their present ideas and those of scientists and to help them integrate their ideas into conceptual beliefs more like those of scientists.

Research on teaching for conceptual change suggests that students can be taught active processing strategies (e.g. predict, explain) to help them notice and correct their misconceptions, thereby deepening scientific understanding. Students can learn to distinguish similar concepts from each other (e.g., force, impulse, work) and from properties of systems or objects (McDermott, 1984). Direct hands-on experiences can be used to help students develop a model of a concept based on their own observations, thereby enabling them to make more accurate predictions and explanations (McDermott, 1991). Posner, Strike, Hewson and Gertzog (1982) highlight conditions for conceptual change: dissatisfaction with a current concept, perceived plausibility of a new concept, and perceived usefulness of a new concept. They also emphasize some aspects of the learner's "conceptual ecology," e.g. epistemological commitments about the nature of evidence, the importance of parsimony, and metaphysical beliefs, such as faith in nature's orderliness. Their conceptual change model emphasizes confronting existing concepts and facts, pointing out contradictions, asking for consistency, and making theory intelligible, plausible and fruitful.

Several aspects of this literature have been applied to my work with science teachers and learners. The next section describes some of this work.

EXPERIENCES WITH METACOGNITION IN COLLEGE BIOLOGY TEACHING AND LEARNING

Fortune smiled upon me in 1987 when Professor Joseph Griswold, of CCNY's biology department wanted to work with me on Introductory Biology, a high risk course primarily taken by Nursing, physician assistant and physical education majors. Through funding from the Aaron Diamond Foundation we restructured the course and provided out-of-class academic support using the Supplemental Instruction model (Blanc, De Buhr, & Martin, 1983). Additional support from CUNY Exemplary Programs allowed us to integrate multimedia technology - laser videodiscs and video microscopes- into classroom instruction to motivate both faculty and students. We began working on Anatomy and Physiology in 1989, with a Title 111 grant. These experiences, like all of my work were guided by the BACEIS model of improving thinking (Hartman & Sternberg, 1993) which emphasizes the internal world of the student (cognition and affect) and the environmental context (academic and nonacademic) as interacting systems affecting students' academic performance (See the Preface and Chapter 3 for more details).

Eylon and Linn (1988) report that cognitively, students respond better to systematic in-depth treatment of a few topics than they do to conventional "in-breath" treatment of many topics. Increasingly it is recommended that science teachers streamline the curriculum and focus more on a limited set of ideas. Students' misconceptions and lack of understanding of science basics reflect limitations of mental processing and memory. Thinking metacognitively about teaching led first to Professor Griswold streamlining the curriculum of the introductory biology course after examining the knowledge required for the advanced courses in anatomy and physiology these same students would take. This comparative analysis enabled him to identify fundamental concepts that students needed to learn well in the introductory course so they could be built upon in the advanced courses. Selecting critical content enabled the professor to identify less fundamental concepts that could be cut from the course so that the critical concepts could be treated in greater depth. Teaching metacognitively included creating advance organizer outlines to be put on the blackboard at the beginning of each lecture and structuring more active student involvement in the lecture through different types and levels of questioning. In addition, Professor Griswold started incorporating vocabulary building skills (e.g. recognizing prefixes, suffixes and root words) into the beginning of the course. The first lecture exam was changed to include assessment of critical vocabulary and word attack skills.

Professor Griswold used several metacognitive teaching techniques, including graphic organizers such as flow charts and concept maps, to help his students organize, understand and remember what they had learned. Lectures and laboratories were designed to begin with the concrete and lead to the practice of formal operational functions such as problem solving, using symbols and verbal reasoning based on a Learning Cycle type approach. For example, initially small groups of students brainstorm together about how smoking could interfere with gas exchange in the lungs. Sharing ideas activates prior knowledge, reveals misconceptions, and identifies information gaps that need to be filled. This exploratory phase is followed by a dissection of the respiratory system and a study of function using demonstrations and videomicroscopy. Next, students analyze the issue of smoking using their new knowledge. Finally they apply what they have learned to explaining new situations such as a change in function with physical exertion or pathology (Griswold & Hartman, 1991). During application, students return to the original question on the impact of smoking, with a new understanding of the mechanics of interference.

Developing Scientific Thinking Skills

One of our goals for the Supplemental Instruction component of our program was to help students develop the thinking and reasoning skills they needed to master science. This goal is based on the assumption that students will master science content more effectively if they use well- developed intellectual processes when thinking and learning about science. Research has indicated that if we want students to be able to apply their knowledge and skills to academic and professional tasks on a long term basis, then instruction should address both cognitive and metacognitive aspects of students' performance. We targeted cognitive skills from Sternberg's (1985) triarchic theory of intelligence (e.g., comparing, applying, justifying) and provided them with strategic metacognitive knowledge about each skill (Hartman & Griswold, 1991) to facilitate their effective use, long-term retention and transfer. Metacognitive knowledge includes what the skills are (declarative), when/why to use them (contextual or conditional) and how to use them (procedural). There are several teaching strategies that can be used to develop intellectual skills, such as activation of prior knowledge, self-questioning, imagery, and graphic organizers such as concept maps, flow charts and, matrices (Narode, Heiman, Lochhead and Slomianko, 1987; Hartman, 1993). We used scaffolding strategies to help students develop their cognitive skills so that they could ultimately self-regulate their use of these skills; this meant providing students with models, guided practice with feedback in groups, guided individual practice with feedback, and unguided individual practice with feedback. Many activities during Supplemental Instruction were designed to develop students' metacognitive strategies for mastering biology. These included: comprehension monitoring, graphic organizers, self- questioning, imagery, thinking aloud, time management, testwiseness, and error analysis. Table 1 is an example of the strategic metacognitive knowledge we gave students about the cognitive skill of justifying.

Another way we tried to improve students' scientific thinking skills was to teach them the "I DREAM of A"(Hartman, 1996a) method to help them think systematically about how they plan, monitor and evaluate their approaches to solving problems, thereby using their metacognition for self-management or self-regulation. I DREAM of A is an approach to developing metacognitive aspects of scientific and mathematical problem solving skills by using thinking aloud and questioning stratgies, and is derived from Bransford and Stein's (1984) IDEAL problem solver. Each capitalized letter stands for a component of the problem solving process, so the acronym represents a systematic guide to problem solving. These components involve executive management skills for planning, monitoring and evaluating the problem solving process. The first four letters are all planning steps (identify and define, diagram, recall, explore alternatives) which may be performed in different sequences. The next two letters (AM) focus on applying and monitoring the plan, and the final A stands for assessment, where students evaluate their solutions to the problem, both before and after getting someone's feedback.

The I DREAM of A approach is **not** a rigid, cookbook, rote formula; rather it is a method of remembering to plan, monitor and evaluate one's problem solving. For example, problem solving often begins with "D", diagraming the problem, which sets the stage for "I," identifying the problem. The method addresses both cognitive and affective aspects of students' performance and it must be personally adapted by the problem solver to fit the specific needs of each problem-solving situation.

Table 1
Strategic Knowledge about Justifying

KNOWING WHAT: Justifying is explaining reasoning, providing evidence underlying conclusions/reasoning; comparing obtained outcome with achieved outcome and evaluating degree of difference. For example, if a professor asks" What makes you think that the small intestine is involved in protein digestion?", the student must provide supporting factual knowledge, such as "You can see from the professor's concept map that the small intestine has intestinal glands which produce peptidase. Peptidase acts on polypeptides, which are broken into amino acids. The small intestine receives acid chyme, which includes proteins, which are broken into polypetides, which are broken into amino acids. Amino acids are the final products of protein digestion."

KNOWING WHEN/WHY: Use justifying to establish a sound basis of support for beliefs, decisions, and/or actions.

KNOWING HOW: To justify one must understand the concept of evidence or support and its value in making decisions about what one does, knows, or believes. Procedures include finding evidence, weighing and comparing evidence to a standard or set of criteria, evaluating its strengths, weaknesses and degrees of difference from the criteria, and looking at all possibilities. When there is strong support for one answer, interpretation, approach etc., and weak support for all the others, justifying includes judging that one to be the best explanation, approach, answer-choice, etc. under the circumstances.

The teacher can serve as an expert model, demonstrating how to use I DREAM of A by playing the role of questioner, who guides the problem-solving process by questioning the other student and by having the problem solver think aloud periodically while problem solving. The problem solver answers questions thinking aloud and self-questions while solving problems. Then two work together, as in the pair-problem solving method described in Chapter 3. Questions are asked for each of seven components of " I DREAM of A." For example, "What do I know about this type of problem?" "Am I going in the right direction?" Although most questions focus on knowledge and strategies needed to solve a problem, the questioner occasionally asks about the problem solver's feelings to establish and maintain a positive attitude. The questioner decides what questions to ask, when to ask the problem solver to think aloud, and when to ask about the problem solver's attitudes. Finally, the student can use the model alone to stimulate self-management of problem solving, asking self-questions and thinking aloud, always adapting it to the specific context.

Restructuring introductory biology involved multidimensional aspects of teaching and learning metacognition. Restructuring involved modifying both the curriculum and instruction, implementing new teaching strategies, and developing students' scientific thinking and learning skills and attitudes. .In Spring 1986, 34.7% of the class earned grades of C or above. By Spring 1989, 64.6% of the class earned grades of C or above. In Spring 1986, 40.3% of the class failed or withdrew from the course; in Spring 1989, only 17% failed or withdrew from the course (Hartman & Griswold, 1994). The results suggest that the restructuring efforts were beneficial: student achievement increased and course failure and attrition decreased over seven semesters.

Anatomy and Physiology

In 1994 NSF grants with Daniel Lemons and Joseph Griswold focused on revising curriculum, instruction and assessment in two advanced anatomy and physiology courses taken by the same set of students whose introductory biology we had worked on previously. Students taking these two courses were primarily ethnic minorities whose native language was not English. Most of these students (75%) were nursing majors who were required to take these courses . For many years students had a history of a high failure rate (defined as D or below) in both courses. This project was based on the assumption that there is a substantial discrepancy between how traditional Anatomy and Physiology courses are taught and how non-traditional students learn. Traditionally, learning in anatomy and physiology courses has emphasized extensive memorization of facts about human systems rather than understanding how they work. Thinking metacognitively about what, why and how to teach anatomy and physiology to nontraditional students led the biologists to the following curriculum innovations: 1) in the context of a broad, organizing theme, sequence instruction so that function is presented first, followed by the anatomical and physiological details which explain that function; 2) start with explorations using hands-on physical models, then progress to higher-level activities, such as applications of models to new situations; 3) to help students learn to solve problems, place the highest priority on critical thinking; 4) use computer-based activities (e.g., simulations , CD-ROM images) to support learning at all phases; 5) provide students with structured, out-of-class academic support; and 6) use assessment not just as an endpoint, but as a integral component of the learning process (Griswold, Lemons & Hartman, 1995).

Using their teaching metacognition to revise the curriculum for the two anatomy and physiology course led Lemons and Griswold to develop a curriculum planning model to serve as a framework for managing the content, pedagogy and assessment of their courses. The curriculum model, a modified learning cycle, is summarized in Figure 2.

Another example of their teaching metacognition was their awareness that their students tended to think concretely instead of abstractly (confirmed by students' pretest scores on the Group Abstract Logical Thinking (Roadrangka, Yoany, & Padilla,(1983). Therefore, a learning cycle model framework is appropriate because it is specifically designed to help students progress from concrete to abstract thinking about content. However, again using their teaching metacognition, Lemons and Griswold determined that the original learning cycle model needed to be adapted for the needs of their students, goals and activities. Hence, they modified the original learning cycle model, systematically integrating into it their computer-based learning activities and simulations and their formative and summative evaluations. Thus their metacognitive awareness of the learners' and learning cycle's characteristics led to their metacognitive control of modifying the model for the specific context.

Another example of their teaching metacognition is their reflection on how to design a curriculum to achieve the targeted objectives. This goal led Lemons and Griswold to design specialized materials and activities to support their curriculum. These include a CD-ROM of computer simulations and instructional activities, physical models and manipulatives, and A Laboratory Guide for Human Anatomy and Physiology (Lemons, 1994), a student workbook of laboratory activities. Each curriculum unit has explicit objectives identified and disseminated to students to establish a shared framework from which to view the material and activities. Explorations introducing students to the concepts to be studied in the unit involved students activating their prior knowledge about a topic and relating their prior knowledge (and/or experience) to the material to be learned. In each unit activities were designed specifically to stimulate students' critical thinking, and therefore required students to think metacognitively about their interpretations, explanations and solutions.

Because learning biology requires extensive reading of technical text, students with limited-English proficiency may encounter more difficulty processing the text than their professors and the text authors realize. Research on the influences on reading achievement of language minority children found oral language proficiency to be the best predictor across eight ethnolinguistic groups (DeAvila & Duncan, 1985). Again illustrating Professor Lemon's metacognition, he realized that his students were reading the textbook incorrectly, if at all, so he decided to model for them how to read the text. Serving as an expert he demonstrated how to use the figures to improve their understanding of the text and their ability to identify important information in the text. Thus he used his teaching metacognition to develop their science reading metacognition. The next section describes two studies on these students' thinking about biology.

Metacognition, Reading Comprehension and Misconceptions in Biology

Two exploratory studies were designed to help us learn about factors affecting students' performance in their biology courses on anatomy and physiology. The first study focused on students' reading of their textbook; the second focused on their misconceptions about biology.

Due to the high failure rate of students in the two course anatomy and physiology sequence, we wanted to identify students likely to have difficulties learning the material so we could both help them and identify variables that predict success. This research examined students' biology reading comprehension and metacognition to identify effective correlates of success in college anatomy and physiology, The *Biology Reading Test* was developed using students' actual text as the source of material in order to assess their comprehension and reading-test metacognition (Hartman , 1996b).[1]

The test consists of four reading selections from the first two chapters of the text, which are reviews of information students are expected to bring to the course. Each passage has four reading comprehension items. Each of the 16 comprehension items is followed by a metacognitive question requiring students to evaluate their answer to the preceding comprehension item, judging whether they thought their answer was right, wrong, or if there were uncertain, comprising a 32- item test.

Metacognition was studied by examining students' evaluations of the accuracy of their answers to biology reading comprehension items. Correct metacognitive assessments (knowing you got the answer right and knowing that you didn't) were expected to positively correlate with achievement; incorrect assessments (thinking you know when you don't and thinking you don't know when you do) were expected to negatively correlate with achievement. Being unsure whether you know the answer was expected to have a small positive correlation with achievement. Comprehension was defined as the total number of items correct on this reading test and achievement was measured by final grades. Data were collected on 75 students enrolled in Anatomy and Physiology 1, for non-science majors, at an ethnically diverse urban college. Most were majoring in nursing (75%) and other health professions; 74% were female and 26% were male. Most students were ethnic minorities: 30% African American, 20% Latino, 13% Asian, 9% Caucasian and 27% Other. Many of these students do not have English as their native language.

The mean number of correct comprehension items was only 10 out of 16 (62.5%). Comprehension showed a low but significant   positive Pearson correlation with achievement $r = .30$, $p < .01$). Students' judgements about the accuracy of their answers were compared to the actual accuracy of their answers, resulting in six metacognitive measures. Two were accurate metacognitions: knowing you know the answer (++) and knowing you don't know the answer (- -), two were inaccurate metacognitions, thinking you know the answer when you don't (+ -) and thinking you don't know the answer when you do (-+), and two were unsure - knowing the answer, but not being sure about it (+?), and not knowing the answer and not being sure about it (-?). These results are summarized in Table 2. The most common form of metacognition was the correct metacognitive assessment of knowing they knew the answer (Meta 1 ++), while the least common form was the incorrect metacognitive variable of knowing the answer, but thinking they didn't (Meta 2 +-) . The other incorrect metacognition, not knowing the answer but thinking that they did (Meta 4 - +) was the second most common occurrence. The other correct metacognition, not knowing the answer and knowing they didn't know it, occurred very infrequently.

Table 2
Summary of Results: Reading Comprehension, Metacognition and Course Achievement

Type of Metacog.	Symbols	1st Symbol Answer to Compre.	2nd Symbol Eval.of Answer	Frequency Rank Order & (means)	Correl. with Achieve.	Correl. with Compre.
accurate	+ +	got right	thought right	1 (8.67)	.37***	.86***
	- -	got wrong	thought wrong	5 (0.11)	- .12	- .01
inaccurate	+ -	got right	thought wrong	6 (0.08)	- .27*	.06
	- +	got wrong	thought right	2 (3.49)	- .03	- .74***
doubtful	+ ?	got right	not sure	4 (1.59)	- .12	.16
	- ?	got wrong	not sure	3 (2.04)	- .35**	- .53***

* $p < .05$

** $p < .01$

*** $p < .001$

Students most commonly thought they had the right answer to the comprehension questions, occasionally were unsure about the accuracy of their answer and rarely thought their answer was wrong. Three of the metacognitive measures showed significant Pearson correlations with comprehension and three correlated significantly with final grades. Knowing that they knew the answer had a high, positive correlation with comprehension $r = .86$, (p <.001), and a positive correlation with achievement $r = .37$, (p <.001). Getting the answer wrong but thinking it was right had a high negative correlation with comprehension $r = - .74$, (p > 001), but no correlation with achievement. Two metacognitive measures that correlated negatively with final grades were: got the answer right but thought it was wrong $r = - .27$, (p < .05) and got the answer wrong and was not sure if it was right/wrong $r = -.35$, (p < .01). Only two of the metacognitive measures correlated significantly with both achievement and comprehension. Getting the answer wrong and not being sure about it (-?) had negative correlations with achievement and comprehension and getting the answer right and knowing it was right (++) had positive correlations with achievement and comprehension.

Metacognition often differentiates successful from unsuccessful readers and students in general. Results of this study partially supported the prediction that correct metacognitive assessments would positively correlate with achievement. However, because some of the n's were small for these different types of metacognition, the results are subject to chance and should be considered exploratory. The important points are that a metacognitive variable (knowing that you know) correlated more highly with achievement than the traditional cognitive reading variable (comprehension) did, and that the direction of the correlations is as predicted, so they suggest a real underlying relationship between reading metacognition and achievement, except for the prediction for the correct metacognitive assessment of "knowing that you don't know." Uncertain metacognition (doubting whether the answer is right or wrong) had stronger negative correlations with achievement than inaccurate metacognition. These variables should be studied with larger numbers of items to verify their stability. Also, reliability and validity studies should be conducted on the *Biology Reading Test*.

Many students in this study had difficulty understanding word/phrase meanings, main ideas and generalizations. It is somewhat astounding that the comprehension mean was only 10 out of 16, considering that students supposedly had learned the material they were reading in a previous, prerequisite course. How and to what extent do misunderstandings of the meaning of specific words or phrases inhibit further learning from text when reading biology? What are the implications of misunderstanding main ideas and generalizations? Reading difficulty appeared to be topic-dependent to some extent. Why? Were selections written at different levels, which Zook and Mayer (1994) might call an *instructional variable*? Were differences related to students' prior knowledge about the material, and/or a function of most these students being ethnic minorities, many of whom are not native speakers of English, which Zook and Mayer might call *learner variables*? Applying Perkins and Simmons' (1988) model, these students appear to have misunderstandings at three levels or in three domains: *content*, such as using vocabulary, *problem solving*, such as self-regulation of their test taking strategies, and *epistemic*, such as explaining the author's main idea.

Because mastery of reading comprehension and other academic objectives often is determined by multiple-choice tests, assessing whether one has selected the right answer is important for maximizing success. Self-regulating students learn with specific goals in mind, observe their performance as they work, evaluate progress in attaining their goals and react by continuing or changing their approach as needed, depending upon the value of the task and upon perceived self-efficacy (Schunk, 1991). How can students detect when they are making errors so they have the opportunity to self-correct before turning in their tests? The metacognitive assessment technique used here forces students to self-evaluate their answers to reading comprehension test items. When taking a test, students who evaluate their performance accurately are more likely to react appropriately by keeping and/or changing their answers to maximize their test score if they feel it is important. Students need to act like scientists, investigating their own learning strategies and their relative effectiveness.

We intended to administer the *Biology Reading Test* to students before they enrolled in the first anatomy and physiology course so we could advise students who might need substantial improvement in their reading comprehension before taking the course. We also planned to implement methods in the course to enhance students' reading and test-taking strategies so that their knowledge, understanding and performance in anatomy and physiology would improve.

Misconceptions in Biology

The second exploratory study identified misconceptions students have about anatomy and physiology and examined whether they were overcome after the two-course sequence in anatomy and physiology. The *Biology Knowledge Test* (Griswold and Lemons, 1995) was developed to assess students' prior knowledge of biology before taking anatomy and physiology. It was administered over a two-semester anatomy and physiology sequence, at the beginning of the first A&P course as a pretest and at the end of the second A&P course as a posttest. Content of the test spanned three levels. We knew that many of our students had reading comprehension problems, especially because many are not native speakers of English, and we wondered about other types of problems that might be interfering with our students' ability to master the material in Anatomy and Physiology 1 and 2. Mindful of the literature on scientific misconceptions we wondered whether these were affecting our students, and if so, how we might help them. This study, funded by a City College of New York President's Fund for Innovation Grant, is a pilot project to identify and examine potential misconceptions and other faulty ideas in anatomy and physiology and see what happens to them over the two-semester sequence of anatomy and physiology courses. Which are overcome and which remain? Why? This pilot study focused on potential misconceptions at the most basic level. The results showed that students had many erroneous conceptions of biology. Of the numerous problematic conceptions and misconceptions identified at the beginning of Anatomy and Physiology 1, some were overcome and some remained by the end of Anatomy and Physiology 2. A few misconceptions were actually more common at posttesting than at pretesting. Problematic conceptions appeared to range from no conception to problematic conception to misconception. In this pilot study two different levels of faulty ideas were classified preliminarily as misconceptions (not all wrong answers are misconceptions): those at the level of the test question itself were called item misconceptions and those at the level of a wrong answer choice were called distractor misconceptions (Hartman, 1996c).

Why were some misconceptions overcome while others were not? The concepts the professors emphasize in course work tended to become clarified so misconceptions were overcome. However, just reading valid conceptions in the text did not appear sufficient for overcoming misconceptions. Some misconceptions remained entrenched and even worsened despite coursework emphasis. The results suggest there are many possible sources of faulty conceptions students have about anatomy and physiology. Some of these are:

1. genuine misconception: wrong idea about something as part of a working system of beliefs.
2. some conception, but incomplete understanding- good guess
3. no conception, lack any idea - pick answer at random - wild guess.
4. confused by wording of question.
5. confused by labeling of diagram.
6. forgot important concepts from other courses that need to be applied to the problem/question.
7. confused by similarity of concepts, diagrams or problems.
8. remember concepts but not sequence.
9. trouble with part/whole relationships, focusing on specific details instead of the general point or big picture or focusing on the big picture/general point and missing important details.
10. problems with both content knowledge & problem solving.
11. problems with whole/whole relations.

What were we to do with the information about students' misconceptions? Teaching science metacognitively includes awareness of such misconceptions as well as planning, implementing, monitoring and evaluating strategies to help students overcome them.   Our grant contained funds to provide one-on-one tutoring for students to help them succeed in the course. After reviewing the literature on conceptual change models, Driver's (1987) model was adapted as follows:

1.   *Orientation*: introduction to the topic and motivation.
2.   *Awareness:* Recognition of misconceptions may occur through:
    a. independent recognition: without feedback from an external source, by the student using her/his own knowledge and reasoning which interacts with the context to discover there is a misunderstanding.
    b. disconfirmational feedback: students are exposed to information from an external source (e.g. lab experiment/ professor/tutor/book/) that directly contradicts their conceptions; change through cognitive conflict.
    c. relational recognition: students are exposed to information that is related to their conceptions, and this information helps them discover that their conceptions are inadequate.
    d. induced recognition: students are directly told their conception is invalid; they are confronted with conflicting concepts and facts (Hartman, 1981).
3.   *Elicitation*: explication of student ideas and misconceptions. dissemble concepts into component parts - deconstruct. (Like Gagne's 1965 task analysis- break component knowledge and skills into a learning hierarchy).
4.   *Restructuring*: students are receptive to changing their conceptions. New and revised conceptions are integrated. Students exchange and clarify ideas after exposure to conflicting meanings, recursively expanding and reworking information.
5.   *Application*: consolidation of new or restructured ideas by using them to solve problems or answer questions.
6.   *Review*: reflection on concepts, what they are, when, why and how they are used; what they are related to - how they fit into the big picture.

The plan was for the tutor to apply this model when working individually with students. However, we were unable to implement it because the School of Nursing was retrenched so at least 75% of our students were gone and science majors, who quickly filled their seats, did not have the same conceptual difficulties (i.e., reading comprehension and misconceptions).   Nevertheless, the course restructuring efforts were not done in vain because the changes led to these Anatomy and Physiology courses becoming popular with science majors for the first time!

This project shows several examples of metacognition in teaching. First, we became aware of the need to consider students' misconceptions about anatomy and physiology, because the high failure rate of students in the courses made us wonder whether misconceptions might be contributing to their difficulties. Second, we developed a strategy for identifying students' misconceptions. Third, we developed a plan to help students overcome their misconceptions. Fourth, we realized that the students' reading problems were even more fundamental than their misconceptions about biology. Finally, we realized that the new students taking Anatomy and Physiology did not have the same types of misconceptions as the original group so Professors Lemons and Griswold adapted instruction to the needs of the new population.

CONCLUSION

Science teaching and learning are complex processes, both because of the content and thinking skills required to understand science at a deep enough level to be meaningful and useful. Metacognition helps science teachers think about how they manage curriculum, instruction and assessment, as well as systematically reflect on what they teach, why and how. Metacognition helps science learners develop and use effective and efficient strategies for acquiring, understanding, applying and retaining extensive and difficult concepts and skills. Good science teaching requires teaching both with own metacognition and for the development of their students' metacognition.

HOPE J. HARTMAN
Department of Education
City College of City University of New York
Department of Educational Psychology
Graduate School and University Center
City University of New York

Notes

Work on restructuring Anatomy and Physiology was supported by NSF grants with Daniel Lemons and Joseph Griswold (DUE-93544477 and DUE-9451852).

I am grateful to Joseph Griswold and Daniel Lemons for their assistance in developing and administering the Biology Reading Test.

REFERENCES

Abimbola, I.O., & Baba, S. Misconceptions and Alternative Conceptions in Science Textbooks: The Role of Teachers as Filters. *The American Biology Teacher*. 58(1). 14-19

Anderson, R. C. and Kuhlavy, R.W. (1972). Imagery and prose learning. *Journal of Educational Psychology*, 63, 242-243.

Anderson, C., Sheldon, T. & Dubay, K. (1990). The effects of instruction on college nonmajors conceptions of respiration and photosynthesis. *Journal of Research in Science Teaching*. 27, 761-776.

Baird, J. & White, R. (1984). Improving Learning through Enhanced Metacognition: A Classroom Study. Paper presented at the Annual Meeting of the American Educational Research Association. New Orleans

Barman, C., Benz, R. Haywood, J. & Houk, G. (1992). Science and the Learning Cycle. *Perspectives in Education and Deafness*. 11(1) 18 Bransford, J. & Stein, B.. (1984) *The IDEAL Problem Solver:* New York: Freeman.

Blanc, R., De Buhr, L., & Martin, D. (1983). Breaking the Attrition Cycle. *Journal of Higher Education*. 54(1). 80-90.

Carmichael, Jr. J., Ryan, M. A., Jones, L., Hunter, K & Vincent, H. (1981). Project SOAR. New Orleans: Xavier University of Louisiana

Cook, L. & Mayer, R. E. (1988). Teaching Readers about the structure of scientific text. *Journal of Educational Psychology*. 80(4), 448-456.

Crooks, T. 1988. Impact of classroom evaluation practices on students. *Review of Educational Research*. 58(4). 438-481

De Avila, E & Duncan, S.. 1985. The language-minority child: A psychological, linguistic, and social analysis. in S. Chipman, J. Segal, and R.Glaser *Thinking and Learning Skills: Vol. 2. Research and Open Questions*. Hillsdale, NJ, Lawrence Erlbaum Associates.

Driver, R. (1987). cited by Skane and Graeber (1993). A conceptual change model implemented with college students: Distributive law misconceptions. *The Proceedings of the Third International Seminar on Misconceptions and Educational Strategies in Science and Mathematics*. Ithaca, NY: Misconceptions Trust

Duit, R. (1991). Students' conceptual frameworks: Consequences for learning science. In S. M. Glynn, R. Yeany, and B. Britton (Eds.) *The Psychology of Learning Science*. (pp. 65-85), Hillsdale, NJ: Erlbaum & Associates.

Eylon, B. & Linn, M. (1988) Learning and Instruction: An examination of four research perspectives in science education. *Review of Educational Research*. 58, 251-301

Felder, R. (1993). Reaching the second tier - Learning and teaching styles in college science education. *Journal of College Science Teaching*. March/April 286-290.

Ford, K., Canas, A., Jones, J., Stahl, H., Novak, J.. & Adams-Weber, J. (1991). ICONKAT: An integrated constructivist knowledge acquisition tool. *Knowledge Acquisition*. 3, 215-236.

Gagne, R. M. (1965). *The Conditions of Learning*. New York: Holt.

Glynn, R. Yeany, and B. Britton (Eds.) *The Psychology of Learning Science*. (pp. 65-85), Hillsdale, NJ: Erlbaum & Associates

Griswold, J. & Hartman, H. (1991).*Restructuring Introductory Biology for Success with Minority Students: A Developmental Approach*. Invited participation in City University of New York Colloquium On Introductory Science Courses: New Approaches to Teaching and Learning. City University of New York, New York

Griswold, J. & Lemons, D. (1995/1996) Biology 332/333 Pretest. City College of City University of New York. NY.

Griswold, J., Lemons, D. & Hartman, H. (1995). Developing critical thinking and content mastery in the Anatomy and Physiology Laboratory: A Workshop. Presented at the Annual Meeting of the National Science Teaching Association: Philadelphia, PA

Hartman, H. (1999). A Blueprint for Reform? Learning, Creating ,and Using Knowledge: Concept Maps as Facilitative Tools in Schools and Corporations. *Contemporary Psychology*: APA Review of Books. 44(1) 111-113.

Hartman, H. (1996a). Cooperative Learning Approaches to Mathematical Problem Solving. In: *The Art of Problem Solving: A Resource for the Mathematics Teacher.* Alfred S. Posamentier & Wolfgang Schulz (Eds.). Corwin Press, Inc. Thousand Oaks CA (1996) pp.401-430

Hartman, H.(1996b) Metacognition and Reading Comprehension in Biology. College Reading and Learning Association, Albuquerque, NM

Hartman, H. (1996c) Misconceptions in Anatomy and Physiology. Human Anatomy and Physiology Society. Portland, OR

Hartman, H. & Griswold, J. (1994). Restructuring Introductory Biology. Paper presented at the Annual Meeting of the American Educational Research Association. New Orleans.

Hartman, H. & Sternberg, R..J. (1993). A broad BACEIS for improving thinking. *Instructional Science.* 21 (5) 400-425

Hartman, H. & Griswold, J. (1991) Metacognition and Cognition in Learning Science. Invited participation in City University of New York Colloquium On Introductory Science Courses: New Approaches to Teaching and Learning. City University of New York, New York

Hartman-Haas, H. (1981). Story Clarification: Comprehension-Directed Problem Solving. *Dissertation Abstracts International* 41 (10)

Herman, J. 1992. What research tells us about good assessment. *Educational Leadership.* 49(8) 74-78.

Hooper, S. & Hannafin, M. 1991. Psychological Perspectives on Emerging Instructional Technologies: A Critical Analysis. *Educational Psychologist* 6(1), 69-95.

Karplus, R. 1974. *The Science Curriculum Improvement Study.* (SCIS) Lawrence Hall of Science, University of California, Berkeley

Lemons, D. (1994). A Laboratory Guide for Human Anatomy and Physiology, New York: City College of City University of New York

Mayer, R. (1989). Models for Understanding. *Review of Educational Research,* 59(1). 43-64.

McIntosh, W. A (1986) The effect of imagery generation on science rule learning. *Journal of Research on Science Teaching.* 23(1) 1-9.

McDermott, L. (1991). Millikan Lecture 1990: What we teach and what is learned - Closing the gap. *American Journal of Physics,* 59 (4) 301-315.

McDermott, L. (1984). Research on conceptual understanding in mechanics. *Physics Today.* 37, 24-32.

McKeachie, W., Pintrich, P., Lin, Y. G., & Smith, D. (1986). Teaching and Learning in the College Classroom: A Review of the Research Literature. Ann Arbor: University of Michigan

Mestre, J. (1994). Problem Posing as a Tool for Probing Conceptual Development and Understanding in Physics. Paper presented at the Annual Meeting of the American Educational Research Association, New Orleans

Minstrell, J. (1989). Teaching science for understanding. In. L. Resnick & L. Klopfer (Eds.) *Toward the Thinking Curriculum: Current Cognitive Research.* Association for Supervision and Curriculum Development, Alexandria, VA.

Narode, R., Heiman, M. Lochhead, J. & Slomianko, J. (1987) Teaching Thinking Skills: Science. Washington, D.C., National Educational Association.

National Research Council (1996). *National Science Education Standards.* Washington D.C.: National Academy Press

Novak, J. (1998). *Learning, Creating and Using Knowledge.* Lawrence Erlbaum Associates: Mahwah NJ

Novak, J. (1990). Concept maps and Vee diagrams: two metacognitive tools to facilitate meaningful learning. *Instructional Science.* 19(1). 29-52.

Novak, J. D., Gowin, D. B., & Johansen, G. T. (1983). The use of concept mapping and knowledge Vee mapping with junior high school science students. *Science Education,* 67(5)625-645.

Nussbaum, J. & Novick, S. (1982). Alternative frameworks, conceptual conflicts and accommodation: Toward a principled teaching strategy. *Instructional Science.* 11, 183- 200.

Perkins, D. and Simmons, R. (1988). An integrative model of misconceptions. *Review of Educational Research.* 58(3) 303-326.

Posner, G., Strike, K., Hewson, P, & Gertzog, W. (1982). Accommodation of a Scientific Conception: Toward a Theory of Conceptual Change. *Science Education,* 66, 211-228.

Pressley, M. and McCormack, C. (1995). *Advanced Educational Psychology.* Harper Collins: NY

Redish, E. F. (1994). The Implications of Cognitive Science for Teaching Physics. American Journal of Physics, 62(6). 796-803.

Regis, A. & Albertazzi, P. G. (1996). Concept Maps in Chemistry Education. Journal of Chemical Education. 73 (11). 1084-1088

Roadrangka, V., Yoany, R., & Padilla, M. (1983). The Construction and Validation of Group Assessment of Logical Thinking (GALT). Paper presented at the annual meeting of the National Association for Research in Science Teaching. Dallas TX

Rosenshine, B. & Meister, C. 1992 The use of scaffolds for teaching higher level cognitive strategies. Educational Leadership. April. 26-33.

Roth, K. (1991). Reading science for conceptual change. In C. M. Santa & D. E. Alvermann (Eds.) Science Learning: Processes and Applications. (pp. 48-63). Newark DE: International Reading Association.

Roth, V., Strozak, C., Cracolice, M. & Gosser, D. (1997). The Workshop Model: Peer Leadership and Learning. A Guidebook. City College of City University of New York

Rubin, R. L. and Norman, J. T. (1989) A comparison of the effect of a systematic modeling approach and the learning cycle approach on the achievement of integrated science process skills. Paper presented at the annual meeting of the National Association for Research in Science Teaching San Francisco CA ED 305268

Schneps, M. (1994). A Private Universe. San Francisco: The Astronomical Society of the Pacific

Schunk, (1991) Self-efficacy and academic motivation. Educational Psychologist, 26(3 & 4), 199-205.

Shavelson R. & Baxter, G. 1992. What we've learned about assessing hands-on science. Educational Leadership 49(8). 20-25

Spiegel, G. (1996). Text structure awareness and graphic postorganizers of reading. Workshop presented at the Tenth Annual Human Anatomy and Physiology. Portland OR

Spiegel, G. and Barufaldi, J. (1994). The effects of a combination of text structure awareness and graphic postorganizers on recall and retention of science knowledge. Journal of Research in Science Teaching. 31(9) 913-932.

Sternberg, R. (1985). Beyond IQ: A Triarchic Theory of Intelligence. New York: Cambridge University Press.

Stewart, J., Hafner, R., Johnson, S. & Finkel, E. (1992). Science as model building: Computers and high-school genetics. Educational Psychologist, 27(3) 317-336.

Tobias, S. (1986). Peer Perspectives on the Teaching of Science. Change. March/April. 36-41

Walberg, H. (1991). Improving School Science in Advanced and Developing Countries. Review of Educational Research. 61(1) 25-69.

Whimbey, A. & Lochhead, J. (1982) Problem Solving and Comprehension Franklin Institute Press: Philadelphia

Zook, K. B. & Mayer, R.E. (1994). Systematic analysis of variables that contribute to the formation of analogical misconceptions. Journal of Educational Psychology, 86(4) 589-600.

PART IV: METACOGNITION AND CULTURE

The dimension of the students' dominant language examined in the chapters here really cut across two components of the BACEIS model's nonacademic environment: culture and family background. Many countries around the world have numerous languages forming a mosaic of cultural linguistics. The culture of my particular college, City College of New York, has 85 different native languages. Within this diverse cultural community, one's dominant language is usually one's native or first language, which is often determined by one's family background. Students' language, and the extent to which it matches that of the classroom, can be an extremely important factor affecting academic performance because reading, writing, speaking and listening in the language of the classroom are vitally important for academic success.

This section of the book has two chapters focusing on cultural-linguistic issues and metacognition The chapter by Ellis and Zimmerman is an empirical study of students whose cultural background emphasizes nonstandard English as the dominant language, while the dominant culture emphasizes standard English.. Their chapter describes an innovative study of the role of metacognition in learning standard English speech. Their research, based on a social-cognitive view of self-regulation, compares the traditional laboratory approach to improving standard spoken English with an approach that emphasizes self-monitoring and self-regulation.

The chapter by Carrell, Gajdusek and Wise concentrates on students whose cultural background has languages other than English and who are in a (standard) English dominant academic environment (sometimes called English as a Second Language students). Their chapter applies metacognitive reading comprehension strategies to second language learners, summarizing recent research and describing their own study in progress in which college English as a second language students receive training in four reading strategies. This chapter emphasizes the importance of complete teacher explanations in strategy training, including instruction in declarative, conditional and procedural metacognitive knowledge about the reading strategies.

CHAPTER 10

ENHANCING SELF-MONITORING DURING SELF-REGULATED LEARNING OF SPEECH

DOROTHY ELLIS   BARRY J. ZIMMERMAN

ABSTRACT. Self-monitoring is a process we use to direct attention to enhance metacognitive awareness of some aspect of our cognitive and behavioral functioning. To study the metacognitive effects of self-monitoring in conjunction with behavioral and motivational influences during learning, researchers have developed models of self-regulation, and this chapter describes a social-cognitive version and its application to speech in second language and second dialect learning. We discuss several key problems in self-directed efforts to learn a second language or dialect and describe the results of an experimental investigation indicating that discrimination training significantly enhances the effects of self-monitoring on the learning of a second language or dialect. A comparison between traditional language laboratory and a self-regulated language learning laboratory is also included.

Self-monitoring is a process we use to direct attention and enhance metacognitive awareness of some aspect of our cognitive and behavioral functioning. Research shows that self-monitoring not only provides us with essential feedback regarding the execution and outcomes of cognitive and behavioral processes, such as strategy choices, it also influences our motivational processes, such as attributions and perceived satisfaction. To study the metacognitive effects of self-monitoring in conjunction with behavioral and motivational influences during learning, researchers have developed models of self-regulation, and we will describe a social cognitive version and its application to speech in second language and second dialect learning. We will also consider several key problems in self-directed efforts to learn a second language or dialect and how language learning laboratories might be redesigned to include self-monitoring when learning a second language or second dialect.

ROLE OF SELF-MONITORING DURING SELF-REGULATED LEARNING

Self-regulated learners can be recognized by their self-awareness, resourcefulness, and confidence. They stand out when they demonstrate their awareness of when they know a fact or possess a skill and when they do not, and

205

H.J. Hartman (ed.), Metacognition in Learning and Instruction, 205–228.
© 2001 *Kluwer Academic Publishers. Printed in the Netherlands.*

this self-knowledge is directly linked to their exceptional self-monitoring. Self-regulated students seek out information when it is needed and take the necessary steps to acquire it. They found a way to surmount obstacles such as poor study conditions, confusing teachers, and abstruse textbooks. They view learning as a systematic and controllable process, and they accept greater responsibility for their achievement (Borkowski, Carr, Rellinger, & Pressley, 1990; Zimmerman & Martinez-Pons, 1986, 1990).

Although this description may readily bring one or more specific students to mind, scientific efforts to study self-regulation require operational definitions of component processes. Self-regulated learners have been defined as "metacognitively, motivationally and behaviorally active participants in their own learning" (Zimmerman, 1989, p. 4). They metacognitively plan, organize, set goals, and self-monitor their performance; they motivationally self-initiate, self-react, and display persistence; they behaviorally arrange or create environments where it is easy to concentrate and to access needed resources.

Researchers distinguish between self-regulatory processes, such as self-monitoring, and strategies designed to optimize these processes, such as self-recording e.g. keeping a physical record of one's functioning in qualitative or quantitative form, such as a performance narrative or frequency count. Self-regulated learning strategies refer to planned sequences of action directed at acquisition of information and skill, such as verbal elaboration to assist recall (Zimmerman & Martinez-Pons, 1986). All learners use self-regulatory processes to some degree, but exemplary learners display awareness of strategic relations between regulatory processes and outcomes and modify their strategies adaptively. These learners have the motivation and competence to improve their skills when learning alone.

During self-regulated learning, self-monitored information is processed cyclically through a self-oriented feedback loop (Carver & Scheier, 1981; Zimmerman, 1989). Humanistic researchers depict this feedback loop in terms of changes in covert perceptual processes (e.g., McCombs, 1989) whereas operant researchers depict it in terms of changes in behavior or environments (Mace, Belfiore, & Shea, 1989). Social cognitive researchers (Zimmerman, 1986, 1989) view self-monitoring as involving three self-oriented feedback loops: personal (cognitive and emotional), behavioral, and environmental. (See Figure 1).

Behavioral self-regulation refers to self-monitoring and adjusting performance processes, such as a method of learning, whereas environmental self-regulation entails monitoring and adjusting environmental conditions or outcomes. Covert self-regulation involves monitoring and adjusting cognitive and affective states, such as imagery for remembering or relaxing. These three feedback and adaptation

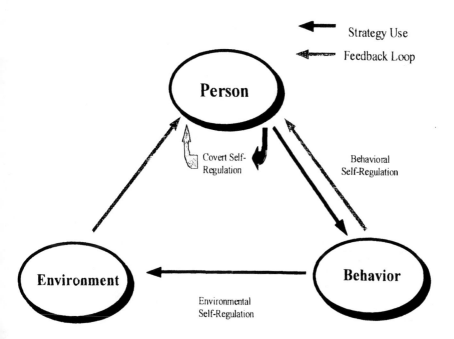

Figure 1 Triadic Forms of Self-Regulation

Adapted with permission from: A social cognitive view of self-regulated academic learning by B.J. Zimmerman, 1989, Journal of Educational Psychology, 81, p. 11. Copyright by the American Psychological Association.

loops operate in conjunction to produce changes in learners' self-beliefs, overt behavior, and environment. The accuracy and constancy of learners' self-monitoring of these three sources of self-control directly influence the effectiveness of their strategic adjustments and the nature of their self-beliefs. Thus, in order to master an academic skill self-regulatively, learners must behaviorally apply personal strategies to an academic task within an environmentally relevant setting. This usually requires repeated attempts to learn (i.e., practice) because mastery involves coordinating personal, behavioral, and environmental processes. Self-regulated learners must constantly reassess their effectiveness because the effectiveness of a learning strategy depends on dynamic personal, behavioral, and environmental conditions.

SELF-REGULATED LEARNING CYCLES

These repeated self-regulatory attempts have been described in terms of three cyclical phases: forethought, performance, and self-reflection (see Table 1). The forethought phase refers to influential processes and beliefs that precede efforts to learn and set the stage for those efforts. Such processes involve task analysis and self-motivational beliefs. The second self-regulatory phase involves processes that occur during performance efforts and affect the control and self-observation phase of selfmonitoring, of those efforts. The third self-regulatory phase involves self-reflective processes that occur after learning efforts and influence a learner's self-judgments of and self-reactions to that experience. Finally, these self-reflections influence forethought regarding subsequent learning efforts, thus completing the self-regulatory cycle. Although self-observation occurs during the second phase, it is affected by forethought phase processes and in turn influences self-reflection processes cyclically, as we will describe below (see Table 1). The term self-monitoring has been defined as "deliberate attention to some aspects of one's behavior" (Schunk, 1996b, p. 342) and thus, distinct from self–judgmental processes. In practice, however, it is very difficult to separate these two subprocesses and often self-monitoring is used to describe their joint use.

One form of forethought phase task analysis is *goal setting*, which refers to focusing on specific outcomes of learning or performance, such as mastering a list of vocabulary words (Locke & Latham, 1990). Highly self-regulated individuals organize their goal systems hierarchically, with process goals linked to more distant outcome goals. This guidance system can provide direction to their learning over long periods of time. Another form of task analysis is *strategic planning* (Weinstein & Mayer, 1986). Learners need methods that are appropriate for the task and setting in order to master or perform a skill optimally. Strategies can enhance performance by aiding cognition, controlling affect, and directing motoric execution (Pressley & Woloshyn, 1995). For example, new vocabulary can be acquired more readily through the use of verbal or imaginal elaboration strategies (Schneider & Pressley, 1997). As we mentioned, cyclical adjustments in the form of strategies are essential because of fluctuations in covert personal, behavioral, and environmental feedback. Self-regulated learners know that the effectiveness of a strategy depends on conditional information. As a skill develops, the effectiveness of an initial acquisition strategy often declines to the point where a different strategy becomes necessary. For example, when self-regulated language learners recognize that a rehearsal strategy is no longer necessary, they may, if necessary, begin to use a different learning strategy based on their current level of skill, knowledge, and/or goals.

Table 1
Phase Structure and Subprocesses of Self-Regulation

Cyclical Self-Regulatory Phases		
Forethought	Performance	Self Reflection
Task Analysis	Self Control	Self-Judgment
Goal Setting	Self Instruction	Self Evaluation
Strategic Planning	Imagery	Causal Attribution
	Attention Focusing	
	Task Strategies	
Self-Motivation Beliefs	Self Observation	Self Reaction
Self Efficacy	Self Monitoring	Self Satisfaction/Affect
Outcome Expectations		Adaptive-Defensive
Goal Orientation		
Intrinsic Interest		

Because forethought is anticipatory, it depends on a number of key self-motivational beliefs: self-efficacy, outcome expectations, intrinsic interest, and goal orientation. *Self-efficacy* refers to personal beliefs about having the means to learn or perform effectively and *outcome expectations* refer to beliefs about the ultimate ends of performance (Bandura, 1997). For example, self-efficacy may involve a student's belief that he or she can use standard American English during a job interview, and outcome expectations would refer to the consequences of using standard English on the job interview, such as being offered the desired position. There is extensive evidence that learners' perceptions of efficacy influence their motivation to engage and sustain self-regulatory efforts, such as self-monitoring (Bouffard-Bouchard, Parent, & Larivee, 1991), self-evaluation, and goal setting (Zimmerman & Bandura, 1994).

Students' self-motivation is also influenced by their *goal orientation.* Those who value learning progress goals rather than performance outcome goals tend to learn more effectively (Ames, 1992). Finally, learners with an *intrinsic interest* orientation will continue their learning efforts even in the absence of tangible rewards (Deci, 1975; Lepper & Hodell, 1989). Having a learning goal orientation and intrinsic interest in a task are especially important when learners must practice or learn on their own and when external rewards are not available or are delayed in time.

Self-observation is a synonym for self-monitoring, which is one of two major types of performance phase control. During high quality self-monitoring, people must track their performance, the conditions that surround that performance, and the effects that the performance produces (Zimmerman & Paulsen, 1995). Often the amount of information involved in complex performances can exceed people's capacity, and this can lead to disorganized or cursory self-monitoring or a complete stoppage of the self-monitoring process. To surmount this problem, self-regulated students learn to *selectively* track themselves when necessary. By setting hierarchical process goals during the forethought phase, these students can selectively self-observe specific processes and proximal events.

The effectiveness of self-monitoring can be influenced by several variables. The first variable is the temporal proximity or the timing of one's self-observations (Bandura, 1986; Kazdin, 1974). For example, self-feedback that is delayed, such as monitoring one's speech from a tape recording, precludes that person from taking immediate corrective action. A second variable is the informativeness of performance feedback. Practicing a skill in a standardized or structured setting can enhance the meaning of the results (Ericsson & Lehman, 1996). For example, if a learner repeatedly videotapes and then observes her speech performance during practice sessions, over time the learner will detect changes in her oral communication skill. A third variable is the accuracy of self-observations. Some language learners misperceive or are unable to accurately discriminate subtle pronunciation sounds and, therefore, cannot correct them appropriately when necessary. For example, some nonstandard speakers of English are not aware that they are substituting the /f/* or /t/* sound for the final <th>* in words such as *death*

Note: when letters are written using the following notation: /skt/, the letters represent sounds based on the International Phonetic Alphabet. However, when letters are written using this type of notation: <ed>, then the letters represent the usual alphabetical letters.

or *birth*. A fourth variable that influences self-monitoring involves the valence of the behavior. Monitoring negative aspects of one's functioning, such as the number of wrong answers, can diminish a person's motivation to self-regulate these activities (Kirschenbaum & Karoly, 1977). Often it is possible to record performance accomplishments rather than deficits thereby focusing on behavior with a positive valence.

Self-recording is a good way to enhance self-monitoring because it can capture personal information at the point it occurs, structure it to be most meaningful, preserve its accuracy without need for intrusive rehearsal, and provide a longer data base for discerning evidence of progress. For example, through self-observation one can classify and self-record covert thought processes, or emotional reactions as well as overt performance; and learners can begin to notice recurrent patterns in their functioning, such as anxiety reactions that consistently precede stammering responses. If any regularities in pattern can be discerned, they can be used to improve subsequent practice efforts. Krashen (1981) has suggested that language learners are better able to monitor their production of the target language when attention is focused on form or structure of the language, i.e. grammar or pronunciation. When the focus is on communicating a message (content), students may not use their knowledge of language as a basis to avoid errors.

Self-monitoring can lead to self-experimentation (Bandura, 1991) when natural variations in behavior do not provide adequate self-diagnostic information. Under these circumstances, people can compensate by systematically varying the aspects of their functioning. For example, a learner might intentionally vary their tongue thrust between the teeth to determine its impact when trying to pronounce the final <th> phoneme. In this way, systematic self-monitoring or self-observation can lead to greater personal understanding and to better control of performance.

The self-reflective process of self-judgment involves self-evaluating one's performance and attributing causal significance to the results. Self-evaluation refers to comparing self-monitored information with a standard or goal such as when learners compare the pronunciation of the nonstandard dialect to the standard dialect and evaluate that performance unfavorably (See Feigenbaum, 1970).

Making complex self-evaluative judgments depends on high levels of discriminatory skill, and a key pedagogical issue is what types of criteria are used. People can evaluate themselves according to four criteria: mastery, previous performance, normative, and collaborative. Mastery criteria involve use of a graduated sequence of tests or test scores ranging from novice to expert performance, such as when asked to rate one's skill in a second language or second dialect. Self criteria involve comparisons of current performance with earlier levels of one's behavior, such as when judging one's growing facility in another language by tracking the frequency of consulting a dictionary to understand conversation in that language. Normative criteria involve social comparisons with the performance of others, such as classmates or competitors. In most competitions, awards are given, such as winning a public speaking contest, to the person who comes in first, regardless of whether he or she gave a flawless performance. Unfortunately, normative criteria for self-evaluative judgments can de-emphasize selective self-monitoring and emphasize negative aspects of functioning instead of the positive ones, such as when a person loses a contest despite greatly improving his or her performance from previous efforts. Finally, collaborative criteria are used primarily during team performances where success is defined in terms of fulfilling a particular role, such as the romantic lead in a play. The criteria of success for the lead role are different than those for other roles, and how well an actor can work cooperatively with other members of the cast is the ultimate criterion of success.

Another type of self-judgment would be causal attributions about the results, such as whether poor performance is due to one's limited ability or to insufficient effort. Attributions of errors to a fixed ability prompt learners to react negatively and discourage efforts to improve (Weiner, 1979). Attributions of errors to learning strategies are highly effective in sustaining motivation during periods of subpar performance because strategy attributions sustain perceptions of efficacy until all possible strategies have been tested (e.g., Zimmerman & Kitsantas, 1997). Attributions depend on cognitive appraisal of such factors as perceptions of personal efficacy or mitigating environmental conditions (Bandura, 1991). For example, if a student felt a speech evaluation occurred during atypical circumstances, such as when that student had a headache, he or she might attribute it to bad luck rather than inability.

Self-evaluative and attributional self-judgments produce several key forms of self-reactions. Self-satisfaction refers to perceptions of satisfaction or dissatisfaction and associated affect regarding one's performance. This is important because people engage in activities that lead to satisfaction and positive affect, and they avoid those activities that produce dissatisfaction and negative affect, such as anxiety (Bandura, 1991). Adaptive inferences are self-reactive conclusions based on performance that direct people to new and potentially better forms of performance self-regulation, such as setting a new goal or changing a strategy (Zimmerman & Martinez-Pons, 1992). Defensive inferences. On the other hand, are self-reactions designed to protect people from future dissatisfaction and aversive affect, but unfortunately they can also undermine successful adaptation. Helplessness, procrastination, task avoidance, cognitive disengagement, and apathy are all forms of defensive inferences. Defensive reactions can often be self-handicapping because, despite their intended protectiveness, they can limit personal growth (Garcia & Pintrich, 1994).

These self-reactions affect forethought processes in a cyclical fashion. Self-satisfaction reactions strengthen one's self-motivation beliefs, such as self-efficacy and intrinsic interest in the task (Schunk, 1996, Zimmerman & Kitsantas, 1997). These enhanced self-motivation beliefs form the basis for peoples' sense of personal agency about continuing their cyclical self-regulatory efforts and eventually attaining their goals. In contrast, self-dissatisfaction reactions reduce one's sense of efficacy and intrinsic interest in pursuing the task further. Research in achievement settings indicates that feelings of self-efficacy can dramatically influence a student's choice of tasks, persistence, effort expenditure, and skill acquisition.

PROBLEMS IN SELF-DIRECTED EFFORTS TO LEARN A SECOND LANGUAGE OR DIALECT

Second language and second dialect learning present important theoretical, experimental and practical challenges in today's classrooms. "Over the last decade, immigrants have been arriving to America at the rate of one million a year, mostly from Hispanic countries." "By the year 2000, one in four Americans will be Black, Hispanic or Asian" (Klein, 1990); "and by the year 2035, we are expected to be Anglo 54%, Black 16%, Latino 22% and Asian 10%" (Riche, 1988). The multicultural, multi-lingual, multi-dialectical classroom is a reality across America and will continue to be so into the 21st Century.

Although the teaching of Standard American English is an implicit and/or explicit goal of almost every school in this country, evidence clearly indicates that "The national performance of American schools in teaching standard American English to nonstandard speakers of English is dismal." "On almost every reported measure at the national or state level, children from nonstandard English-speaking communities achieve lower competency levels in the language of education than children who come from standard English-speaking communities" (Taylor, 1986, p. 156). One of the consequences of a lack of competency in standard American English is that such speakers may be linguistically locked out of the social, political and economic rewards of American society.

Taylor (1986) argues that traditional teaching methodologies have failed primarily because educators and speech clinicians viewed "...nonstandard English dialects—and many foreign accents—as pathological linguistic systems that are to be eradicated." Taylor asserts that such a viewpoint lacks a valid understanding of linguistic differences because sociolinguistic studies, historical facts and research data have demonstrated that "Nonstandard English dialects are linguistically valid, useful to their speakers, and devoid of inherent pathology"(p.187). Most linguists recognize that one does not have to eradicate the nonstandard dialect but rather teach students how to be bidialectical. Just as many bilingual speakers use different languages with different people in different communication contexts (Grosjean, 1982), such versatility in language style can also work for students who speak a nonstandard dialect (Berger, 1988). They can learn to shift their dialect based on the communication context. (See Taylor, 1986; Wiley & Lukes, 1996 for a full discussion of these linguistic issues.)

The authors agree that a language learning curriculum should be grounded in sound, linguistic principles. However, we also argue for the importance of teaching and learning methods that are substantiated by rigorous research grounded in a sound, theoretical model. A self-regulated learning model (SRL) may be especially suited for language learning and bidilectilism because the SRL model perceives learners as active decision-makers, who, once given the appropriate tools, can decide why, when and how to learn effectively and how to monitor their progress.

SECOND LANGUAGE AND METALINGUISTIC AWARENESS

Historically, it has been argued that the acquisition of more than one language in childhood promotes metalinguistic awareness (Vygotsky, 1962). Metalinguistic awareness refers to the ability to reflect on and manipulate the structural features of language independent of meaning (Nagy & Anderson, 1995). Lambert (1981) reports that metalinguistic skills -- such as flexibility in manipulating linguistic codes, auditory reorganization of language items and separations of words from their physical referents -- are more evident in bilinguals than in monolinguals.

Although a number of studies report advantages in favor of bilinguals' word awareness (Oren, 1981; Hakuta, 1987), other studies report no differences in word awareness between bilingual and monolingual children (Bowey, 1987; Nicoladis, 1992). However, Bialystock (1986) reported that bilingual children do show higher levels of syntactic awareness. Bruck and Genesee (1995) examined phonological awareness which refers to "The ability to reflect on and manipulate sublexical phonological units such as syllables, onsets, rimes and phonemes" and reported that schooling "can influence the patterns of development of a young child's phonological awareness skills." "However, that influence is mediated by the child's age, amount of exposure to the second language and introduction to literacy" (p.319). Bruck and Genesee further report that their data suggest that bilinguilism has "selective rather than universal effects on the development of phonological awareness." (p.319). These findings suggest that learning another language or dialect may enhance one's metalinguistic knowledge, which in turn enhances future language learning because it facilitates comparison between L1 and L2 and encourages self-corrections (Gass, 1983).

SELF-MONITORING AND SECOND LANGUAGE AND SECOND DIALECT LEARNING

A number of second language learning researchers have reported that self-monitoring is a metacognitive strategy used primarily by more advanced second language learners (Huang & Van Naerssen, 1987; Naiman, Frolich, Stern & Todesco, 1978; O'Malley, Chamot, Stewner-Manzanares, Russo & Kupper, 1985, Lambert, 1981). The most well-known work on monitoring in second language research is the work of Krashen (1977, 1981). Krashen believes there is a difference between the acquisition and learning of a second language. He views language acquisition as an unconscious process and language learning as a conscious process. Krashen argued that monitoring is a highly deliberate process in which the learner applies grammatical rules to language production and, therefore, can only be used during language learning. He identified three types of monitorers: 1) over monitorers who pay too much attention to rules and are inhibited in conversation; 2) under monitorers who do it by "feel" and not by using conscious rules; and 3) optimal monitorers who monitor effectively so that it does not interfere with natural conversation. Acton (1984) suggested that fossilized speakers (Speakers who may be fluent but highly inaccurate and whose pronunciation may be highly resistant to change [Selinker, 1972]), may find it necessary to do some type of conscious monitoring in order to be able to effect change in everyday conversation.

It should be noted that the majority of the aforementioned studies relied on anecdotal reports and self-report data rather than comprehensive tests based on a formal theoretical model of self-monitoring. Therefore, these studies reveal little about the role of self-monitoring as a mediating variable in the learning of a second language.

In reviewing the literature on pronunciation change and second language and second dialect learning, there are few experimental studies that test the effects of discrimination training on self-monitoring. One of the reasons for this is revealed in a review by Morley (1991) who reported that "....since the 1970's, the field of second language learning, in particular, English as a second language, has been in a quandary as to whether pronunciation should (and can) be taught and how" (p. 481). Second language researchers were at a loss to explain individual differences in performance with respect to rates and ultimate levels of achievement in phonology. The effect was that many ESL programs "gave less and less time and explicit attention to pronunciation; and many programs dropped it entirely." (p. 485).

Some practitioners advocate "the natural approach" wherein speakers learn the appropriate pronunciation through interaction with native speakers or standard speakers of English rather than through formal training. Unfortunately, such a model does not take into consideration that vast numbers of non-native speakers arrive in the United States and live and interact in ethnic enclaves that require little or no knowledge of the host country's language. If they do interact with native speakers, such episodes may be brief and what is learned may be rarely reinforced at home where the first language (or dialect) dominates speech (Wyatt & Seymour, 1988). In addition, "the natural way" does not consider that those non-native speakers who learn English informally or "on the street" may learn a nonstandard pronunciation (or grammar) of English rather than a standard pronunciation because that is what is "natural" in their community.

Although self-monitoring is mentioned as a learning strategy by a number of second dialect researchers (Berger, 1988; Lee, 1971), there are few empirical studies that test its efficacy in learning standard American English. The major emphasis in this literature has been in describing the morphological and phonological structure of Black Vernacular English and Southern Nonstandard English as well as the social, political and educational ideologies surrounding nonstandard American English (Baker, 1993; Dillard, 1972; Fasold & Wolfram, 1976; Hopper & Naremore, 1978; Kachu & Nelson, 1996; Labov, 1972; Labov, 1980; Lee, 1994; Manning, 1996; Roy, 1987; Ruiz, 1995; Sridhar, 1996; Wiley & Lukes, 1996).

A review of the research on self-monitoring and speech (pathology) revealed a number of empirical studies that found self-monitoring to be effective in reducing stuttering (Ingham, Adams & Reynolds, 1978; Ingham, 1982; LaCroix, 1973), verbal disfluencies (Mace & Kratchowill, 1988) and enhancing the maintenance and transfer of speech therapy effects (Koegel, Koegel & Ingham, 1986; Koegel, Koogel, Voy, & Ingham, 1988; Ruscello & Shelton, 1979). Although a critical analysis of these studies revealed limitations in the experimental designs (e.g., confounds with reduction in speaking time, external monitoring, external reinforcement, and the addition of other learning strategies such as planning), the research does suggest that self-monitoring can be useful in enhancing speech habits.

In summary, most of the prior research by second language and second dialect researchers has been predominantly descriptive and/or prescriptive rather than experimental in nature. Although much of the empirical research in self-monitoring and speech pathology suggests that self-monitoring is a useful tool, these studies did not focus on the acquisition phase of learning. The subjects in these studies had the desired pronunciation in their linguistic repertoire (albeit at low levels) before self monitoring was introduced. Therefore, little is known about the role of self-monitoring in facilitating de nova acquisition of a second language or second dialect.

AN INVESTIGATION OF SELF-MONITORING AND SECOND DIALECT LEARNING

One of the most challenging tasks for any learner can be the learning of a second language or second dialect. With the exception of young children, mastery of fluent speech and pronunciation usually requires countless hours of practice and accurate selfmonitoring of one's pronunciation.

Among the most difficult speech pronunciation problems for both native and non-native speakers of English is the triple consonant cluster /skt/ embedded in the word asked . (Berger, 1988; Bianchi, Bond, Kandel, Seidler, 1983) Difficulty arises because instead of saying /aeskt/ as in 'asked' speakers may: (1) reverse the sounds and say /aekst/ as in 'axed'; (2) omit a sound and say /aesk/ as in 'ask'; or (3) substitute another sound such as /aeskId/ as in 'askid'.

The consequences of students' inability to master this key sound have been high. The word asked when pronounced as /aekst/ 'axed', is one of the most noticeable and socially stigmatized forms of nonstandard English (Bianchi, Bond, Kandler, & Seidler, 1983; Smith, 1979). In cases where speakers are aware of the adverse social impact of this triple consonant cluster, they will often try to avoid words, and phrases that contain the cluster. However, the word *asked* is a commonly occurring word, and, therefore, difficult to completely avoid. Because speech acquisition involves considerable self-directed practice, the role of self-monitoring and self-evaluation are especially important to investigate.

According to the cyclical model of self-regulation presented earlier, self-evaluation is a separate self-regulatory subprocess from self-observation (or self-monitoring) of one's performance. Self-evaluation involves a comparison between a self-monitored performance and some standard or criterion. From this perspective, dysfunction in learning new speech patterns may be due to poor self-observation or to failures to compare accurate self-observations with the proper standard. Self-regulation of learning is undermined when students cannot accurately discriminate between the wanted and unwanted pronunciation or grammar. The frustrations of inaccurate self monitoring during practice episodes were dramatically enacted in the musical adaptation of Pygmalian, *My Fair Lady*. As Eliza Doolittle struggled with the line "The rain in Spain falls mainly in the plains", Professor Higgins had to constantly monitor Eliza's speech to keep her from slipping back into her cockney accent. Informal classroom observations reveal that unsuccessful language learners, whether native or non-native speakers of English, encounter the same frustrations as Eliza because they are unable to accurately discriminate between the standard and nonstandard pronunciation of certain sounds.

To investigate this distinction during self-directed pronunciation learning, the role of self-observation was separated experimentally from self-evaluative judgments. The quality of self-observation or self-monitoring was manipulated by asking some students to self-record their utterances during practice efforts in a speech learning laboratory.

The quality of self-evaluation was manipulated by giving some students discrimination training. Discriminating between subtle inflections in speech can be a daunting task, especially if they are absent from one's native language or dialect. Training that assists the individual in distinguishing the desired sound from closely associated ones may be an integral part of the puzzle and has been advocated by a number of practitioners (Gilbert, 1984,1992; Hahner, Sokoloff & Salisch, 1988).

In an initial investigation of this issue, Ellis (1994) studied 80 undergraduate students enrolled in a remedial speech course at an urban community college. Participants in this investigation varied in gender and language status (i.e., 33 males, 47 females; 35 native speakers and 45 non-native speakers of English), and approximately half of them received some form of financial aid. Initially, 151 students were pretested to see if they could pronounce the word *asked* using the standard pronunciation embedded in a story they were told to record. They were then instructed to listen to their own speech recordings and judge whether they had used a nonstandard pronunciation. This provided an index of their self-evaluative accuracy (i.e. ability to discriminate between the standard and nonstandard pronunciation). Only students who could *not* use the standard pronunciation of the word *asked* /aeskt/ and could *not* reliably discriminate whether they had used a nonstandard pronunciation were included in the study. In addition, students were eliminated if they displayed speech pathology, audiology, or learning disability (visual reversal) problems. Over 90% of the students tested met the criteria, but due to time constraints, only 80 were randomly assigned to one of five experimental groups: discrimination plus self-monitoring training, discrimination only training, self-monitoring only training, no discrimination or selfmonitoring training (practice only) and a no treatment control condition.

Students who received *discrimination* training were taught to hear (but not say) the difference between the standard pronunciation of the word *asked*: #1: /aeskt/ and three, common nonstandard varieties #2: /ackst/ as in 'axed', #3: /aesk/ as in 'ask', and #4: /aeskid/ as in 'askid' using aural discrimination. A visual example of the four pronunciations was also displayed on a poster. Each example was segmented into individual phonemes and said aloud five times by a videotaped model. The students then watched and listened to the model saying a list of sentences that varied the four pronunciations of the word *asked*. After listening to each sentence, the students had to indicate whether the speaker used pronunciation #1, 2, 3 or 4. They received immediate feedback on their answer and could review the sentence again. For example, they would listen to the following sentence: *Tanya /aekst/* (as in 'axed') *Ernie to go shopping*. If the student said, "#2", then the experimenter would say "correct". If the student answered any other number, the experimenter would say "incorrect," and they would review the sentence again. The videotaped training also required the students to make a distinction between two pronunciations, such as: /aekst/ as in 'axed' and /aeskt/ as in 'asked'. Subjects listened and were asked whether the two pronunciations were the same or different. Subjects were trained to a 95% level of accuracy. Students who did not receive discrimination training were asked to listen very carefully to the standard pronunciation of the word *asked* only once.

Students given *self-monitoring* training watched a videotape that explained what self-monitoring is and how it can help the student learn standard American English pronunciation. They were instructed to read aloud from a list of sentences containing the target word *asked*. and were told to use the standard pronunciation. After each sentence, they indicated aloud whether they used the standard or nonstandard pronunciation. Each student received immediate feedback on whether he/she monitored correctly or incorrectly but not whether he/she used the standard or nonstandard pronunciation. For example: if a student used a nonstandard pronunciation and said "nonstandard", the experimenter told the student: "You monitored correctly". If a student used a standard pronunciation and monitored his or her pronunciation as nonstandard, the student was told "You monitored incorrectly."

After training was completed, all students, except those in the no treatment control condition, were told to practice alone saying the word *asked* using three, different practice exercises. Students in the self-monitoring groups practiced saying the sentences aloud and indicated whether they had used the standard or nonstandard pronunciation of the word *asked*. When they completed the first trial, they were instructed to rewind the audiotape and listen to themselves. Students who self-monitored recorded the accuracy of their monitoring on a form, but students who did not self-monitor kept no records of their practice efforts.

After the three practice trials, all students were posttested. The students were first allowed to examine the posttest sentences, and then were asked to make a self-efficacy judgment of how sure they were that they *could* say the word *asked* using a standard English pronunciation (on a percentage basis). At the end of the posttest, they self-evaluated how sure they were that they *had* used a standard pronunciation (on a percentage basis). After completing the posttest, subjects were asked to record two, 20 sentence exercises that represented a near and far transfer of the /skt/ sound to other words containing that sound. The near transfer test consisted of 20 sentences (10 each) that contained the words *masked* and *basked*. The far transfer task consisted of sentences that contained the words *risked* and *whisked*. Upon completion of these tests, subjects were asked how sure they were that they could pronounce the word *asked* using a Standard English pronunciation when "giving a speech in front of 30 strangers". Estimated accuracy measures were also taken after the posttest and two transfer tests. Subjects were asked: "How many do you think you said using a standard pronunciation of the word *asked* out of a total of 20?"

The statistical analyses supported a cyclical view of self-regulation. As Table 2 illustrates, discrimination and self-monitoring training had a significant effect on students' learning of the standard English pronunciation of the triple consonant cluster /skt/. This occurred whether the phoneme was embedded in the target word *asked* or in near transfer words such as *masked, basked* or far transfer words such as *risked* or *whisked* when compared to students who merely practiced or who did not receive any treatment. Of special importance is the fact that the students who received discrimination training plus self-monitoring training significantly outperformed those students who received only one type of training (either discrimination or selfmonitoring) and their self-evaluations of their performance were more accurate. Although self-observation and self-recording improves students' pronunciation to some degree, discrimination training designed to help learners form a clear self-evaluative standard significantly enhances the accuracy of their self-monitoring and the quality of their pronunciation.

Perhaps the most interesting findings were that students who received only self-monitoring training reported significantly lower ratings of self-efficacy and self-evaluation than those in the practice only and control group; whereas students who received both discrimination and self-monitoring training reported significantly higher ratings of self-efficacy and self-evaluation. There is an explanation for these complex findings. During self-monitoring training, the pronunciations of students were never corrected by the experimenter, nor were the students given further models of the standard American English pronunciation, but they were taught to self-observe their pronunciation in order to increase their metacognitive awareness of its accuracy. Subjects in the practice only and control group received no training in self-monitoring and as a result, remained relatively unaware of their ineffectiveness, according to self efficacy and self-evaluation measures. Students who self-monitored without receiving discrimination training were aware of their deficiency in pronunciation but could not adapt their speech sufficiently, and this led to low levels of self-efficacy and self-evaluation. In contrast, students given self-monitoring and discrimination training were not only aware of but could adapt their pronunciation, and this led to high levels of self-efficacy and self-evaluation. These findings indicate that asking students to observe their behavior without showing them how to accurately discriminate specific subcomponents of standard pronunciation (which obviously aids self-correction) can have an adverse effect on students' self-evaluations and self-efficacy beliefs. (For a more complete discussion of the statistical analyses and results of this study, see Ellis, 1994.)

Table 2
Group Means and Standard Deviations of Pronunciation

Pretest and Posttest Scores

	Pretest		**Posttest**	
	Group Mean	Std.	Group Mean	Std.
Discrimination +				
Self Monitoring	.06	.25	35.88	5.71
Discrimination Only	.00	.00	14.63	17.20
Self-Monitoring Only	.06	.25	13.06	16.28
Practice Only	.06	.25	1.38	2.75
No Treatment Control	.06	.25	.98	1.18

Note 1: 2 points for /aeskt/ as in 'asked' and 1 point for /asst/ as in 'assted' (a degraded but acceptable version of the standard).

Note 2: no significant differences on pretest scores, but significant differences on posttest scores at the p < .01 level for the treatment groups.

In summary, self-monitoring led to improvements in students' language pronunciations, and to be optimally effective, the students also needed discrimination training. It was found that even college students did not possess sufficient self-regulatory skill to acquire language and speech very well on their own. The idea that nonstandard speakers of English will learn standard pronunciation "the natural way" through interaction (or exposure) to the standard is not substantiated by this study. The practice only and no treatment control groups were "exposed" to the standard yet displayed significantly lower levels of change in pronunciation. This study suggests that just pointing out a pronunciation issue, or having the student practice on their own is insufficient. Teachers need to intervene and help students to accurately discriminate between the standard and nonstandard pronunciation.

REDESIGNING LANGUAGE LABORATORIES TO ENHANCE
SELF-REGULATION OF LEARNING

This study indicates the value of an alternative model for teaching standard English pronunciation to both native and non-native speakers of nonstandard English and poses the question: How should we conceptualize second language and second dialect learning laboratories in light of this research on self-regulated learning? What follows is a comparison of a traditional audio-lingual language lab and a self-regulated lab.

Both the self-regulated learning and the traditional audio-lingual speech laboratories provide audio or videotaped (CD-ROM) models and provide an opportunity for practice alone. However, the traditional model assumes that students will repeat what the model is saying and that students will self-correct (self-repair). However, Ellis (1994) has shown that students cannot always discriminate language properties that are the goal of instruction, and even when they can, they may not be able to incorporate those properties into their speech. Although traditional language laboratories may now include some form of computer-assisted modeling and practice, they have largely ignored the metacognitive role of self-monitoring. This omission appears to be costly and in need of urgent redress given the high current levels of failure in learning Standard American English, especially among ethnic minorities. In the Ellis study, subjects who practiced without discrimination or self-monitoring training (the practice only group) did not perform any better than students in the no treatment control group. Such a finding suggests that the optimal language laboratory experience needs to include in-depth discrimination training and self-monitoring training, guided practice, and opportunities to practice alone using self-monitoring. Just having students practice their pronunciation without being able to accurately self-evaluate their performance rarely results in change. Unless students can accurately discriminate between the wanted and unwanted performance, practice time may become a frustrating waste of time and can lower students' motivation, feelings of self-efficacy and persistence on task.

As Table 3 illustrates, the first phase of a Self-Regulatory Language Learning Laboratory involves *Orientation and Goal Clarification* of each student's use of nonstandard pronunciation (and grammar). Students arrive at the lab with a diagnostic assessment administered by the instructor. The lab tutor orients the students to the use of the equipment, and students begin working on their individual learning goal(s). The self-regulated learning (SRL) laboratory curriculum is sufficiently flexible to permit different students to work on different goals during the same laboratory period. Such flexibility is dependent on the technology available and the instructors' goals.

The second phase in the SRL model is *discrimination training* and is designed to enhance students' self-evaluative skills. Students are taught to discriminate between the standard and nonstandard forms by watching and listening to a CD-ROM (or videotape) similar to the in-depth discrimination training explained in the Ellis study. This proposed model assumes the use of an interactive, computer-assisted instruction program. The program allows students to respond on the computer, and for the computer to provide immediate feedback. In the SRL laboratory, a student must reach 95% mastery level in each training phase in order to move to the next phase. Some traditional laboratories may include cursory discrimination training, but students usually do not receive much feedback on the accuracy of their discriminations. Phase Three of the SRL laboratory is *modeling with guided practice*. This phase requires each student to meet briefly with the laboratory tutor who guides the student in the appropriate pronunciation. The student then practices and receives feedback from a voice recognition computer program. In a traditional laboratory, students also listen to a model on audio or video (CD-ROM) and then repeat what they hear. However, the amount of feedback they receive is dependent on the availability of the tutor and/or the sophistication of the laboratory equipment. (This modeling phase was not included in the Ellis study because of the nature of the experiment.) Phase Four, *self-monitoring training,* represents the most significant difference between the SRL laboratory and the traditional laboratory. During this phase, students learn (on CD-ROM or video monitors) how self-monitoring can assist in language learning and how to accurately self-monitor their pronunciation. Each student then meets briefly with the laboratory tutor for, *guided practice* to ensure that the student is (1) using the standard pronunciation and (2) self-monitoring accurately. Each student then practices aloud both the standard pronunciation and self-monitoring and receives feedback from a voice recognition computer telling the student whether he/she is monitoring accurately. Once students achieve 95% mastery in accurate self-monitoring, they can move to Phase Five, *self-directed practice*, where they practice accurate self-monitoring of their pronunciation during three, increasingly complex, practice trials. Students self-evaluate their own performance without any assistance from a computer or tutor. Upon completion of the practice trials phase, the computer provides a *posttest* that is a combination of the posttest and the two transfer tests described in the aforementioned Ellis (1994) study. This is the Sixth and final phase of the SRL laboratory model. The results of the test are checked by the computer and discussed with the tutor. The classroom instructor is informed of the results for each student. As Table 2 indicates, the traditional laboratory may or may not assess a student's performance at the end of the laboratory hour, and the instructor rarely receives feedback from the lab on each student's progress. One of the proposed benefits of the inclusion of self-monitoring is that the maintenance of this learning will be enhanced because a speaker now has the knowledge and skill necessary to self-repair his/her own speech without assistance.

Table 3

Comparison of Self-Regulated and Traditional Language Learning Laboratories

	Self-Regulated Model	Traditional Model
Phase One	Orientation and Goal Clarification	Orientation only
Phase Two	In-Depth Discrimination Training Mastery level must be reached.	Cursory Discrimination Training
Phase Three	Modeling with Guided Practice Mastery level must be reached.	Modeling with Practice Feedback
Phase Four	Self-Monitoring Training Mastery level must be reached.	
Phase Five	Self-Directed Practice	
Phase Six	Posttest Mastery level must be achieved. Feedback to student and instructor.	

Note 1: Both laboratories are based on a one hour lab period.
Note 2: Whether or not students receive feedback on their lab work depends on the sophistication of equipment and software programs. Most traditional laboratories only have students repeat what they hear without any feedback.

CONCLUSION

Acquiring a new language or dialect is a daunting task. Although such learning can occur during "naturalistic" episodes, many people avoid exposure to different language communities and don't profit greatly from such experiences when they do occur. There is a growing body of research indicating that linguistic novices are handicapped by their inability to self-monitor accurately and make appropriate linguistic corrections in the new language and dialect. These self-regulatory deficiencies have implications for the design of language laboratories as we enter the 215' Century. Self-regulatory processes need to be incorporated more systematically, and a model of such a self-regulated language laboratory was described. With the acquisition of speech, as with other vital human skills, students depend on their capability to learn on their own. Teaching students to accurately self-observe, self-evaluate, and self-repair enhances not only their metacognitive awareness but also their sense of self-efficacy about their acquisition and their usage of Standard American English.

DOROTHY ELLIS
Humanities Department
LaGuardia College
City University of New York

BARRY J. ZIMMERMAN
Department of Educational
Psychology
Graduate School and University
Center
City University of New York

Footnote
We would like to thank Eleanor Hanlon and Carol Montgomery for their helpful comments on an earlier draft of this chapter.

REFERENCES

Acton, W. (1984). Changing fossilized pronunciation. *TESOL Quarterly*, 18, 71 -85.

Ames, C. (1992). Achievement goals and the classroom motivational climate. In D. H. Schunk & J. L. Meece (Eds.), *Student perceptions in the classroom* (pp. 327-348). Hillsdale, NJ: Lawrence Erlbaum Associates.

Baker, C. (1993). *Foundations of bilingual education and bilingualism*. Clevedon, England: Multilingual Matters

Bandura, A. (1986). *Social foundations of thought and action: A social cognitive view*. Englewood

Bandura, A. (1991). Self-regulation of motivation through anticipatory and self-reactive mechanisms. In R.A. Dienstbier (Ed.), *Perspectives on motivation: Nebraska symposium on motivation* (vol. 38, pp. 69-194. Lincoln: University of Nebraska Press.

Bandura, A. (1997). *Self-efficacy: The exercise of control*. New York: Freeman.

Berger, M. I. (1988). *Speaking Standard Too*. Chicago, IL.: Orchard.

Bialystok, E. (1986). Children's concept of word. *Journal of Psycholinguistic Research*, 15, 13-32.

Bianchi, D. B., Bond, W., Kandel, G. & Seidler, A. (1983). *Easily Understood: A basic speech text*. Wayne, NJ: Avery.

Borkowski, J. G., Carr, M., Rellinger, E. & Pressley, M. (1990). Self-regulated cognition: Interdependence of metacognition, attributions, and self-esteem. In B. F. Jones & L. Idol (Eds.) *Dimensions of thinking, and cognitive instruction* (pp.53-92). Hillsdale, NJ: Erlbaum.

Bouffard-Bouchard, T., Parent, S., & Larivee, S. (1991). Influence of self-efficacy and performance among junior and senior high school age students. *International Journal of Behavioural Development*, 14, 153-164.

Bowey, J. A. (1987). *The development of metalinguistic ability*. Sydney: Deacon Press.

Bruck, M. & Genesee, F. (1995). Phonological awareness in young second language learners. *Journal of Child Language*, 22, 307-324.

Carver, C. & Scheier, M. (1981). *Attention and self-regulation: A control theory approach to human behavior*. New York: Springer-Verlag.

Deci, E. L.(1975). *Intrinsic motivation*. New York: Plenum Press.

Dillard, J. (1972). *Black English*. New York: Vintage Books

Ellis, D. (1994). Effects of self-monitoring and discrimination training on pronunciation change by nonstandard speakers of English. Ann Arbor, MI: UMI Dissertation Services.

Ericsson, A. K., Lehman, A. C. (1996). Expert and exceptional performance: Evidence of maximal adaptation to task constraints. *Annual Review of Psychology*, 47, 273-305.

Fasold, R. W & Wolfram, L. R. (1976). Some linguistic features of Negro dialect. In R. Fasold & R. Shuy (Eds.) *Teaching standard English in the inner city* (pp.41-86), Washington, D. C: Center for Applied Linguistics.

Feigenbaum, I. (1970). The use of nonstandard English in teaching standard: contrast and comparison. In R. Fasold & R. Shuy (Eds.) *Teaching standard English in the inner city* (pp.87-104), Washington, D.C.: Center for Applied Linguistics

Garcia, T. & Pintrich, P. R. (1994). Regulating motivation and cognition in the classroom: The role of self-schemes and self-regulation. In D.H. Schunk & Zimmerman, B.J. (Eds.), *Self-regulation of reaming and performance: Issues and educational applications* (pp.127-53). Hillsdale, NJ: Erlbaum.

Gass. S. (1983). The development of L2 intuitions. *TESOL Quarterly*, 17, 273291.

Gilbert, J. B.(1984). *Clear speech*. New York: Cambridge University Press.

Grosjean, F. (1982). *Life with two languages: An introduction to bilingualism*. Cambridge, MA.: Harvard University Press.

Hahner, J., Sokoloff, M. A., & Salisch, S. (1988). *Speaking clearly: Improving voice and diction*. New York, NY: McGraw Hill.

Hakuta, K. (1987). Degree of bilingualism and cognitive ability in mainland Puerto Rican children. *Child Development*, 58~1372-1388.

Hopper, R. & Naremore, R. (1978).*Children's speech: A practical introduction to communication development*. New York: Harper & Row.

Huang, X. H. & Van Naerssen, M. (1987). Learning strategies for oral communication. *Applied Linguistics*, 8, 286-303.

Ingham, R. J. (1982). The effects of self-evaluation training on maintenance and generalization during stuttering treatment. *Journal of Speech and Hearing Disorders*, 47, 271-280.

Ingham, R. J., Adams, S. & Reynolds, G. (1978). The effects on stuttering of self-recording the frequency of stuttering or the word "the". *Journal of Speech and Hearing Research, 21*, 459-469.

Kachu, B. B. & Nelson, C. L. (1996). World Englishes. In S. L. McKay & N. H. Hornberger (Eds.), *Sociolinguistics and language teaching* (pp.71-102). Cambridge: Cambridge University Press.

Kazdin, A. (1974). Self-monitoring and behavior changed. In M. J. Mahoney & C. E. Thoresen (Eds.), *Self-control: Power to the person* (pp. 218-246). Monterey, CA: Brooks/Cole.

Kirschenbaum, D. S. & Karoly, P. (1977). When self-regulation fails: Tests of some preliminary hypotheses. *Journal of Consulting and Clinical Psychology, 42*, 1116-1125.

Klein, E. (1990, Jan.-Feb.). Tomorrow's work force. *D&B Reports*, pp. 30-35.

Koegel, R. L., Koegel, L. K. & Ingham, J. C. (1986). Programming rapid generalization of correct articulation through self-monitoring procedures. *Journal of Speech and Hearing Disorders*, 51, 24-32.

Koegel, R. L., Koegel, L. K., Voy, K. V., & Ingham, J. C. (1988). *Journal of Speech and Hearing Disorders*, 53, 392-399.

Krashen, S. (1977). The monitor model for second language performance. In M. Burt, H. Dulay and M. Finochhairo (Eds.). *Viewpoints on English as a second language*. New York: Regents.

Krashen, S. (1981). *Second language acquisition and second language learning*. Oxford: Pergamon Press.

Labov, W (1972). *Language in the inner city*. Philadelphia, PA: University of Pennsylvania Press.

Labov, W. (1980). "Allow Black English in schools? Yes--the most important thing is to encourage children to speak freely," *U.S. News and World Report.* (March 31), pp. 63-64.

LaCroix, Z. (1973). Management of disfluent speech through self-recording procedures. *Journal of Speech and Hearing Disorders, 38,* 272-274.

Lambert, W. E. (1981). Bilingualism and language acquisition. In H. Winitz (Ed.). Native language and foreign language acquisition. *Annals of the New York Academy of Sciences, 379,* 9-22.

Lee, F. R. (1994, January 5). Lingering conflict in the schools: Black dialect vs. standard speech. *The New York Times,* Al, 22-23.

Lee, R. (1971). Linguistics, communication, and behavioral objectives. *The Speech Teacher, 20,* 1-9.

Lepper, M. R., & Hodell, M. (1989). Intrinsic motivation in the classroom. In C. Ames & R. Ames (Eds.), *Research on motivation in education* (Vol. E, pp. 255296). Hillsdale, NJ

Locke, E. & Latham, G. P. (1990). *A theory of goal setting and task performance.* Englewood Cliffs, NJ: Prentice Hall.

Mace, F. C., Belfiore, P. J., & Shea, M. C. (1989). Operant theory and research on self-regulation. In B. J. Zimmerman & D. H. Schunk (Eds.), *Self-regulated learning and academic achievement: Theory. research and practice.* New York: Springer-Verlag.

Mace, F. C., & Kratchowill, T. (1988). Self-monitoring: Applications and issues. In J .Witt, S. Elliott, F. Gresham (Eds.), *Handbook of behavior therapy in education* (pp. 489-502). New York: Pergamon.

Manning, A. (1996, December 20). Schools to recognize Black 'Ebonics'. *USA Today,* p. 3A.

McCombs, B. M. (1989). Self-regulated learning and academic achievement: A phenomenological view. In B. J. Zimmerman & D. H. Schunk (Eds.), *Self-regulated learning and academic achievement: Theory. research. and practice,* (pp. 51-82). New York: Springer.

Morley, J. (1991). The pronunciation component in teaching English to speakers of other languages. *TESOL Quarterly, 25,* 481-519.

Nagy, W. & R. Anderson, (1995). Metalinguistic awareness and literacy acquisition in different languages. *Technical Report No., 618,* Urbana, IL: Center for the Study of Reading.

Naiman, N., Frohlich, M., Stern, H. H., and Todesco, A., (1978). *The good language learner.* Toronto: Ontario Institute for Studies in Education.

Nicoladis, E.(1992). Word and phonological awareness in preliterate children: the effect of a second language. M.A. thesis, Psychology Department, McGill University.

O'Malley, J. M., Chamot, A. U., Stewner-Manzanares, G., Russo, R. & Kupper, L. (1985). Learning strategies used by beginning and intermediate ESL students. *Language Learning, 35,* 21-36

Oren, D. L.(1981). Cognitive advantages of a bilingual child related to labeling ability. *Journal of Educational Research, 74,* 163- 169.

Pressley, M. & Woloshyn, V. (1995). *Cognitive strategy instruction that really improves children's academic performance.* Cambridge, MA: Brookline Books.

Riche, M. (1988, February). America's new workers. *American Demographics,* pp. 33-41.

Roy, J. D. (1987). The linguistic and sociolinguistic position of Black English and the issue of bidilectilism in education. In P. Homel, M. Palij, & D. Aaronson (Eds.), *Childhood bilingualism: Aspects of linguistic. cognitive and social development* (pp. 231-242). Hillsdale, NJ: Erlbaum.

Ruiz, R.(1995). Language planning considerations in indigenous communities. *Bilingual Research Journal,* 19, 71-81.

Ruscello, D. M., & Shelton, R..L. (1979). Planning and self-assessment in articulatory training. *Journal of Speech and Hearing Disorders, 27,* 504-512.

Schneider, W., & Pressley, M. (1997). *Memory development between two and twenty (*2nd ed.). Mahwah, NJ: Lawrence Erlbaum Associates.

Schunk, D. H. (1996). Goal and self-evaluative influences during children§s cognitive skill learning. *American Educational Research Journal, 33,* 359-382.

Schunk, D.H. (1996b). *Learning theories: An educational perspective.* New York: Merrill/Macmillan

Selinker, L. (1972). Interlanguage. *International Review of Applied Linguistics,* 0, 209-232.

Smith, B. (1979). It ain't what you say, it's the way you say it. *Journal of Black Studies,* 2(4), 480-493

Sridhar, S. L. (1996). Societal multilingualism. In S. L. McKay & N. H. Hornberger (Eds.), *Sociolinguistics and language teaching,* pp. 47-70. Cambridge: Cambridge University Press.

Taylor, O. L. (1986). A cultural and communicative approach to teaching Standard English as a second dialect. In O. Taylor (Ed.) *Treatment of communication disorders in culturally and linguistically diverse populations.* San Diego, CA: College Hill Press.

Vygotsky, L. (1962). *Thought and language.* Cambridge, MA: MIT Press

Weiner, B. (1979). A Theory of motivation for some classroom experiences. *Journal of Educational Psychology*, 71, 3-25.

Weinstein, C. E. & Mayer, R. (1986). The teaching of learning strategies. In M. Wittrock (Ed.) *Handbook of research on teaching and learning* (pp. 315-327). New York: Macmillan.

Wiley, T. G. & Lukes, M. (1996). English only and Standard English ideologies in the U.S.. *TESOL Quarterly*, 30, 511-535.

Wyatt, T. A. & Seymour, H. M. (1988). *The pragmatics of code switching in Black English speakers.* Paper presented at the American Speech-Language-Hearing Association Convention, Boston, MA.

Zimmerman, B. J. (1986). Development of self-regulated learning: Which are the key subprocesses *Contemporary Educational Psychology, 11,* 307-313.

Zimmerman, B. J. (1989). A social cognitive view of self regulated learning. *Journal of Educational Psychology, 81,* 329-339.

Zimmerman, B. J. & Bandura, A. (1994). Impact of self regulatory influences on writing course attainment. *American Educational Research Journal, 31,* 845-862.

Zimmerman, B. J. & Kitsantas, A. (1997). Developmental phases in self regulation: Shifting from process to outcome goals. *Journal of Educational Psychology.*

Zimmerman, B. J. & Martinez-Pons, M. (1986) Development of a structured interview for assessing students use of self regulated learning strategies. *American Educational Research Journal, 23,* 614-628.

Zimmerman, B. J. & Martinez-Pons, M. (1986) Student differences in self regulated learning: Relating grade, sex, giftedness to self efficacy and strategy use. *Journal of Educational Psychology, 82,* 51-59.

Zimmerman, B. J. & Martinez-Pons, M. (1986) Perceptions of efficacy and strategy use in the self regulation of learning. In D.H. Schunk & J. Meece (Eds.) *Student perceptions in the classroom: Causes and consequences* (pp. 185-207), Hillsdale, NJ: Erlbaum.

Zimmerman, B. J. & Paulson, A.S. (1995). Self monitoring during collegiate studying: An invaluable tool for academic self-regulation. In P. Pintrich (Ed.), *New directions in college teaching and learning: Understanding self regulated learning,* (No. 63, pp. 13-27). San Francisco, CA: Josey-Bass, Inc.

CHAPTER 11

METACOGNITION AND EFL/ESL READING

PATRICIA L. CARRELL   ⁄   LINDA GAJDUSEK   TERESA WISE

ABSTRACT. Several distinct research streams are converging in the field of foreign or second language reading in the U.S. Separate research streams in metacognition, in reading strategies, and in the training of reading strategies are converging in the field of English as a foreign or second language. This confluence of research is dramatically impacting the teaching of English to adult non-native speakers for academic purposes. In this chapter we will briefly review these distinct research streams for their relevance to the population in question, and will then describe the research design for an empirical study we are currently conducting to further investigate the efficacy of metacognitive strategy training for adult EFL/ESL reading.

READING STRATEGIES

Both first and second language reading research has recently begun to focus on reading strategies. Reading strategies are of interest not only for what they reveal about the ways readers manage interactions with written text but also for how the use of strategies is related to effective reading comprehension. The term "strategies" is used deliberately, rather than the more traditional term "skills," to refer to actions that readers select and control to achieve desired goals or objectives (Johnston & Byrd, 1983; Paris, Lipson & Wixson, 1983; van Dijk & Kintsch, 1983). Although there is no clear agreement (cf. Paris, Wasik & Turner, 1991) on the "deliberate" aspect of using strategies (cf. Wellman, 1988, on the one hand who says: "To be a strategy, the means must be employed deliberately, with some awareness, in order to produce or influence the goal" (p. 5), and on the other hand Pressley, Forrest-Pressley, and Elliot-Faust, 1988, who say: "It is now recognized that strategy functioning at its best occurs without deliberation. It is more reflexive than voluntary" (p. 102), overall, the emphasis with the term "strategies" is on "deliberative actions." The term "strategies" emphasizes the reader's active participation and actual way of doing something, or the reader's performance, whereas the term "skills" may suggest the reader's competence or only passive abilities which are not necessarily activated.

A similar perspective on the relationship of "strategies" to "skills" has been provided by Paris et al. (1991): *Skills* refer to information-processing techniques that are automatic, whether at the level of recognizing grapheme-phoneme

229

H.J. Hartman (ed.), Metacognition in Learning and Instruction, 229–243.
© 2001 *Kluwer Academic Publishers. Printed in the Netherlands.*

correspondence or summarizing a story. Skills are applied to a text unconsciously for many reasons including expertise, repeated practice, compliance with directions, luck, and naive use. In contrast *strategies* are actions selected deliberately to achieve particular goals. An emerging skill can become a strategy when it is used intentionally. Likewise, a strategy can "go underground" (cf. Vygotsky, 1978) and become a skill. Indeed strategies are more efficient and developmentally advanced when they become generated and applied automatically as skills. Thus, strategies are "skills under consideration" (see Paris, Lipson & Wixson, 1983). (p. 611).

As reading research has progressed, researchers have sought to identify the surprisingly wide variety of strategies used by both native and non-native language readers. Reading strategies run the gamut from such traditionally recognized reading behaviors as skimming and scanning, to rereading, contextual guessing or skipping unknown words, tolerating ambiguity, making predictions, confirming or disconfirming inferences, and using cognates to comprehend, to more recently recognized strategies such as activating background knowledge or schemata (Zvetina, 1987) and recognizing text structure (Block, 1986; Carrell, 1985, 1992; Carrell, Pharis & Liberto, 1989).

In exploratory, descriptive investigations with small numbers of individual learners using think-aloud techniques, studies have identified relations between certain types of reading strategies and successful and unsuccessful foreign or second language reading. In Hosenfeld's 1977 study of U.S. high school students reading in a foreign language (French, German, or Spanish) but thinking aloud in English, her example of a 'successful' French reader did the following things: (1) kept the meaning of the passage in mind during reading, (2) read in what she termed 'broad phrases', (3) skipped words viewed as unimportant to total phrase meaning, and (4) had a positive self-concept as a reader. By contrast, Hosenfeld's 'unsuccessful' French reader: (1) lost the meaning of sentences as soon as they were decoded, (2) read in short phrases, (3) seldom skipped words as unimportant and viewed words as equal in their contribution to total phrase meaning, and (4) had a negative self-concept as a reader.

Block (1986), in a study of generally nonproficient readers -- specifically entering university freshmen, both native and nonnative English speakers, enrolled in remedial reading courses in the U.S. -- found that four characteristics seem to differentiate the more successful from the less successful of these nonproficient readers: (1) integration, (2) recognition of aspects of text structure, (3) use of general knowledge, personal experiences, and associations, and (4) response in extensive versus reflexive modes. In the reflexive mode, readers relate affectively and personally, directing their attention away from the text and toward themselves, and focusing on their own thoughts and feelings rather than on the information in the text. In the extensive mode, readers attempt to deal with the message conveyed by the author, focus on understanding the author's ideas, and do not relate the text to themselves affectively or personally. Among the nonproficient readers Block investigated, one subgroup, which she labeled 'integrators' integrated information, were generally aware of text structure, responded in an extensive mode, and monitored their understanding consistently and effectively. They also made greater progress in developing their reading skills and demonstrated greater success after one semester in college. The other subgroup, which Block labeled 'nonintegrators', failed to integrate, tended not to recognize text structure, and seemed to rely much more on personal experiences, responding in a reflexive mode. They also made less progress in developing their reading skills and demonstrated less success after one semester in college.

Several additional case studies have similarly shown relationships between various reading strategies and successful or unsuccessful second language reading (Devine, 1984; Hauptman, 1979; Knight, Padron & Waxman, 1985; Sarig, 1987).

Yet, the picture is more complex than suggested by these early case studies. Unfortunately, the relationships between strategies and comprehension are not simple and straightforward; use of certain reading strategies does not always lead to successful reading comprehension, while use of other strategies does not always result in unsuccessful reading comprehension. Research reported by Anderson (1991) shows that there are no simple correlations or one-to-one relationships between particular strategies and successful or unsuccessful reading comprehension. His research, with native Spanish-speaking university level intensive ESL students reading in English as their second language and self-reporting their strategy use, suggests wide individual variation in successful or unsuccessful use of the exact same reading strategies. Rather than a single set of processing strategies that significantly contributed to successful reading comprehension, the same kinds of strategies were used by both high and low comprehending readers. However, those readers reporting the use of a higher number of different strategies tended to score higher on the comprehension measures. Anderson concludes from his data that successful second language reading comprehension is "not simply a matter of knowing what strategy to use, but the reader must also know how to use it successfully and [to] orchestrate its use with other strategies. It is not sufficient to know about strategies, but a reader must also be able to apply them strategically" (1991, p. 19).

Within EFL/ESL, much of the recent work on reading strategies is part of a larger focus on the general learning strategies of second language learners:

> ... second language learners are not mere sponges acquiring the new language by osmosis alone. They are thinking, reflective beings who

consciously apply mental strategies to learning situations both in the classroom and outside of it (Chamot, 1987, p. 82).

METACOGNITION

What is metacognition? In contrasting metacognitive and cognitive strategies, O'Malley, Chamot, Stewner-Mazanares, Russo and Kupper (1985) posit that metacognitive strategies involve thinking about the learning process, planning for learning, monitoring of comprehension or production while it is taking place, and self-evaluation of learning after the language activity is completed. Cognitive strategies are more directly related to individual learning tasks and entail direct manipulation or transformation of the learning materials. (p. 560)

One reason metacognition is significant is that if learners are not aware of when comprehension is breaking down and what they can do about it, strategies introduced by the teacher will fail. As O'Malley et al. (1985) have said: "Students without metacognitive approaches are essentially learners without direction or opportunity to review their progress, accomplishments, and future directions" (p. 561). Pressley, Snyder and Cariglia-Bull (1987) suggest that metacognition helps students to be consciously aware of what they have learned, recognize situations in which it would be useful, and processes involved in using it.

As early as 1978, Flavell defined metacognition as "knowledge that takes as its object or regulates any aspect of any cognitive behavior" (p. 8). Two dimensions of metacognitive ability have been recognized: (1) knowledge of cognition, and (2) regulation of cognition (Flavell, 1978). The first, knowledge of cognition, includes the reader's knowledge about his or her own cognitive resources and the compatibility between the reader and the reading situation. If a reader is aware of what is needed to perform efficiently, then it is possible to take steps to meet the demands of a reading situation more effectively. If, however, the reader is not aware of his or her own limitations as a reader or of the complexity of the task at hand, then the reader can hardly be expected to take preventative or corrective actions to anticipate or recover from problems.

The first aspect of metacognition, "knowledge about cognition," includes three components which have been labeled "declarative," "procedural," and "conditional" knowledge (Paris et al., 1983). Declarative knowledge is propositional knowledge, referring to "knowing what." A learner may know what a given reading strategy is, for example, s/he may know what summarization is and what summaries are. Procedural knowledge is "knowing how" to perform various actions, for example, "how to study, how to deal with analogies, or how to write summaries" (Winograd & Hare, 1988, p. 134). Conditional knowledge refers to "knowing why", and includes the learner's understanding the value or rationale for acquiring and using a strategy, and when to use it. Conditional knowledge is necessary if a reader is to know whether or not a certain strategy is appropriate, and whether or not it is working effectively for that learner.

The second aspect of metacognition, the executive or regulatory function refers to when a "higher order process orchestrates and directs other cognitive skills" (Paris, Cross & Lipson, 1984, p. 1241). This notion of an executive skill is based on an information-processing model of human cognition (Brown, Bransford, Ferrara & Campione, 1982). In reading, these skills relate to the planning, monitoring, testing, revising, and evaluating of the strategies employed during reading (Baker & Brown, 1984).

As Carrell (1987) has maintained, these self-regulatory metacognitive skills are used in reading for: (a) clarifying the purposes of reading, that is, understanding both the explicit and implicit task demands; (b) identifying the important aspects of a message; (c) focusing attention on the major content rather than trivia; (d) monitoring ongoing activities to determine whether comprehension is occurring; (e) engaging in self-questioning to determine whether goals are being achieved, and (f) taking corrective action when failures in comprehension are detected (p. 239).

Thus, in reading, the two key metacognitive factors, *knowledge* and *control*, are concerned respectively with what readers know about their cognitive resources and their regulation. Regulation in reading includes the awareness of and ability to detect contradictions in a text, knowledge of different strategies to use with different text types, and the ability to separate important from unimportant information.

TRAINING READING STRATEGIES - WITH AND WITHOUT METACOGNITION

Given the important role of reading strategies in successful and unsuccessful EFL/ESL reading, a number of questions remain: "How should the relevant reading strategies be taught? What is most effective in the teaching and learning of reading strategies? How important are the metacognitive components of strategy training to effective strategy training? How are these metacognitive components related to the strategies themselves, and can they be teased apart from the strategy training?"

A number of training studies have been conducted, both in L1 reading and in EFL/ESL reading, to teach learners various reading strategies, with or without metacognitive elements in the instruction. Duffy and Roehler (1989) posit "Unlike skill instruction, where the goal is a relatively uncomplicated development of automatized responses, strategy instruction involves the development of metacognitive awareness of strategies *and* the expectation that strategies will eventually be applied automatically" (p. 142).

Traditionally, reading instruction has involved either direct instruction on decoding skills or informal teaching of comprehension. Those who advocate major emphasis on decoding mechanisms in reading tend also toward direct, explicit, deductive instructional approaches, while those who emphasize attention to reading for meaning tend toward learner-directed, informal, inductive instructional approaches. Yet, as Resnick (1979) has argued, there is no reason, in principle, why one cannot have direct instruction in comprehension, or for that matter -- although perhaps more difficult to imagine -- informal instruction in decoding. In the remainder of this section, we discuss relatively direct, explicit instruction in comprehension-fostering reading strategies.

Researchers interested in strategy instruction, appreciating the importance of the learner's active participation, have, therefore, attempted to enlist it through careful and complete explanation of the procedures and values of the particular strategy in question. As Roehler and Duffy point out:

> ..teacher explanations of the processes are designed to be metacognitive, not mechanistic. They make students aware of the purpose of the skill and how successful readers use it to actively monitor, regulate, and make sense out of text, creating in students an awareness and a conscious realization of the function and utility of reading skills and the linkages between these processes and the activities of reading (1984, p. 266).

But, what constitutes a careful and complete explanation of a reading comprehension strategy? Drawing upon the prior work of a number of other instructional researchers, Winograd and Hare (1988) proposed the following five elements as constituting complete teacher explanation:

1)   What the strategy is: Teachers should describe critical, known features of the strategy or provide a definition/description of the strategy (p. 123).

2)   Why a strategy should be learned: Teachers should tell students why they are learning about the strategy. Explaining the purpose of the lesson and its potential benefits seems to be a necessary step for moving from teacher control to student self-control of learning (p. 123).

3)   How to use the strategy: Here, teachers break down the strategy, or re-enact a task analysis for students, explaining each component of the strategy as clearly

and as articulately as possible and showing the logical relationships among the various components. Where implicit processes are not known or are hard to explicate, or where explanatory supplements are desired, assists such as advance organizers, think-alouds, analogies, and other attention clues are valuable and recommended (Roehler & Duffy, 1984, as cited in Winograd & Hare, 1988, p. 123).

4)   When and where the strategy should be used: Teachers should delineate appropriate circumstances under which the strategy may be employed, (e.g., whether the strategy applies in a story or informational reading). Teachers may also describe inappropriate instances for using the strategy (pp. 123-124).

5)   How to evaluate use of the strategy: Teachers should show students how to evaluate their successful/ unsuccessful use of the strategy, including suggestions for fix-up strategies to resolve remaining problems (p. 124).

It will not have escaped our readers that these five elements of complete teacher explanation are related to the three kinds of metacognitive knowledge previously discussed in this chapter: declarative knowledge is addressed through explanations of **what** the strategy is (element 1 above) and **why** it should be learned (element 2 above). Procedural knowledge is addressed through explanations on **how to use** the strategy (element 3 above). Conditional knowledge is addressed through explanations of **where and when** to use the strategy (element 4), and **how to evaluate** its effectiveness (element 5). Figure 1 illustrates the relationship between the three subcomponents of metacognition (declarative, procedural and conditional knowledge) on the part of a reader and various ways of communicating those to a learner through direct teacher explanations.

Figure 1
Metacognitive Knowledge and Elements of Complete Teacher Explanation

Declarative Knowledge	*Procedural Knowledge*	*Conditional Knowledge*
What the strategy is	**How to use** the strategy	**When & Where** to use the strategy
Why the strategy should be learned		**How to evaluate** its effectiveness

Winograd and Hare (1988) have reviewed seven L1 reading strategy training studies which used direct instruction procedures, looking in their review for the presence or absence of the five metacognitive elements.   Each of the studies reported significant gains in the use of the strategy taught (e.g., study skills based on SQ3R, main idea identification, summarizing) and each of the studies reviewed utilized one or more of the five elements.

Adams, Carnine & Gersten (1982) involved the teaching of a study strategy to fifth-grade students with poor study skills but average decoding ability for 30 to 40 minutes daily for four days. Students learned to master a six-step strategy for reading content area texts, with teachers initially modeling the strategy steps and students repeating teachers' models and receiving corrective feedback. The six-step study skills strategy consisted of lessons on (a) previewing headings, (b) reciting subheadings, (c)asking questions for subheadings, (d) reading to find important details, (e) rereading subheadings and reciting important details, and (f) after the whole selection had been read, rehearsing or reading each subheading and reciting important details. Winograd and Hare judged the Adams et al. study as having effectively and completely involved all five elements of metacognition.

Alexander and White (1984) taught fourth grade students of average reading ability an analogical reasoning strategy in two phases, the first intensive training of short duration, and the second intermittent training spread over a longer period of time. The training consisted of lessons on the component processes of encoding, inferring, mapping and applying. In their review of how Alexander and White incorporated complete explanations into the lessons, Winograd and Hare found that they addressed four of the five components of a complete metacognitive explanation -- omitting only the element on **how to evaluate** the effectiveness of the strategy.

Baumann (1984) taught sixth grade high, middle and low reading achievement students a main idea comprehension strategy consisting of lessons on locating explicit and implicit main ideas in paragraphs as well as brief passages, and constructing outlines of main ideas for brief passages. Learners were assigned to one of three groups: strategy, basal, or control. In examining the content of Baumann's five-step instructional procedure, Winograd and Hare determined that Baumann utilized all except one of the five components of complete metacognitive explanation, omitting explanation only of **how to evaluate** the effectiveness of the strategy.

Garner, Hare, Alexander, Haynes and Winograd (1984) trained upper-elementary and middle-grade students to use a text lookback strategy which included lessons on the nature of and proper use of text lookbacks. In the Garner study several components of direct metacognitive explanation were included, but the study omitted the component on **how to evaluate** the strategy's effectiveness.

Hansen and Pearson (1983) taught both good and poor fourth grade readers an inference strategy consisting primarily of prereading questions designed to help students make the connection between known and new information and relating personal experiences to text events and to the prediction of text events. Winograd and Hare found that the report of the Hansen and Pearson study did not mention inclusion of three of the five metacognitive elements: **what** the strategy was, **when and where** the strategy should be used, or **how to evaluate** it.

Hare and Borchardt (1984) taught a summarization strategy based on Day's (1980) work to a group of high school juniors with adequate decoding abilities. The summarization strategy consisted of lessons describing summarization rules and suggestions for rule-checking and a polishing rule. Summary rules included: (a) collapsing lists, (b) using topic sentences, (c) getting rid of unnecessary detail, and (d) collapsing paragraphs. Rule-checking suggestions included: Be sure you understand the text, look back, rethink, and check and double-check. The polishing rule required summary editing. Hare and Borchardt included all five of the metacognitive components, according to Winograd and Hare.

Patching, Kameenui, Carnine, Gersten and Colvin (1983) taught fifth grade students with adequate decoding abilities critical reading strategies on an individual basis. The instruction consisted of lessons on detecting faulty generalizations, false causality and invalid testimonial. In their review of Patching et al., Winograd and Hare note that only one portion of a lesson was available for review. Based upon that lesson they could not determine from the published chapter whether the **why, when and where,** or **how to evaluate** components of metacognitive strategy training were included in the instruction of students.

Based on the Winograd and Hare review, it seems clear that successful L1 reading strategy training may involve some but not necessarily all of the desirable elements of metacognitive strategy training. The components most often included are those involving procedural knowledge (**how to use**), as well as declarative knowledge (**what** and **why**); most often missing tend to be those components involving conditional knowledge (**when and where**, as well as **how to evaluate**).

In second language reading strategy training there have been a number of studies which have also included varying amounts of metacognitive training. Without attempting to be exhaustive, we have selected a small sample of studies for inclusion in this review. Figure 2 below reports the studies in chronological order.

In a text structure strategy training investigation reported in 1985, Carrell provides evidence that all five components of metacognitive training were covered, although the published version of the study does not provide any details as to exactly how each of the five was covered.

Figure 2
Summary of Literature

Study	Declarative What	Why	Procedural How to use	Conditional When & Where	Evaluate
Carrell	yes	yes	yes	yes	yes
Hamp-Lyons	yes	--	--	–	--
Sarig & Folman	yes	yes	possibly	–	--
Carrell Pharis & Liberto	yes	yes	yes	yes	–
Kern	yes	--	yes	–	--
Raymond	yes	yes	yes	yes	yes

The basic objectives of the teaching program were explicitly communicated to the students [**what**] ...We explained to them that sometimes it did not matter how they read...but that at other times, it did. They were told that sometimes, especially as students studying English for academic purposes and headed for the university, they would be called on to read a lot of information and to remember it -- for example, in preparing for exams and class assignments. We explained that the efficiency with which students could read under such circumstances was important, that if they could get the necessary information quickly and effectively, it was likely they would perform well and feel better about the task [**why, when and where**]. We told them that over the training period, we would be teaching them a strategy for reading that should improve their understanding of what they read and their ability to recall it [**why**]. We emphasized that by teaching them a little about the ways in which expository texts are typically organized at the top level [**what**], we hoped to teach them how to use [**how to use**] this knowledge to improve their comprehension of what they read [**why**], as well as to teach them a strategy for using this knowledge to improve their recall of what they read [**why**].

Every day as they left the session, the students were asked to apply what they were learning to all of the reading they did until the next session. This was intended to get the students to use the strategy outside their ESL reading classroom, in other nonteacher-supported reading situations...The study packets included detailed explanations of the benefits of learning the strategy [**why**], along with checklists so students could monitor and regulate their own learning [**how to evaluate**]. (1985, pp. 735-736).

In another 1985 study of what she termed a "text-strategic" approach, Hamp-Lyons appears to have included instruction in the **what** but doesn't indicate anything explicitly about having covered the other metacognitive components.

Sarig and Folman, in a 1987 study, claimed to have included **declarative**, and possibly [their word] **procedural** knowledge relevant to the learning goal -- coherence training (ms., p. 13-14). They are silent on **conditional** knowledge. In a collaborative study published in 1989, Carrell, Pharis and Liberto appear to have covered the **what, why, how to,** and **when and where**, but there is not much indication of the **evaluation** component. Alluding to the **why** of declarative knowledge, and the **when and where** of conditional knowledge, they say:

> ...the students brought up the idea that semantic mapping might be particularly useful for dealing with reading passages that contain a lot of details, but less suitable for passages whose meaning could easily be grasped without such elaboration (p. 656).

In reference to the **what** of declarative knowledge, and the **when and where** of conditional knowledge, Carrell et al. also say " ...and the nature [**what**] and uses [**when and where**] of semantic mapping [were] summarized (p. 658).

In Kern's 1989 description of his training procedures, it appears that he covered both the **what** and possibly also the **how to use** components, but his description gives no indication that he included any focus on the **why, when and where**, or **evaluative** metacognitive components.

Raymond (1993) asserts that all five elements were explicitly included in her study (p. 448), although no indication is given as to how these elements were presented in the training. She says of her training:

> The outside instructor taught the structure strategy by explaining what it was in session one (Step A), why it should be learned in session two (Step B), how to use it in session three (Step C), and when to use it in session four (Step D). Short quizzes were provided to help the subjects evaluate their use of the structure strategy in session five (Step E). These five steps (A-E) have been suggested for the effective, direct instruction of reading comprehension strategies (Winograd & Hare, 1988). (p. 448-449).

In all of these L2 studies, significant positive effects were found for the strategy training when compared with the control or traditional approaches to instruction. Yet, because of the variability in including all five components of metacognition, the research does not show us conclusively which components are essential.

AN EMPIRICAL RESEARCH DESIGN FOR
METACOGNITIVE STRATEGY TRAINING

Despite the growing body of research outlined in this chapter, the following question remains in EFL/ESL reading strategy training: To what extent is direct, explicit instruction in the metacognitive components necessary to achieve success in strategy training? Grabe (1993), in a paper at the TESOL Reading Research Colloquium, pointed out that many EFL/ESL articles stressing metacognitive training are not empirical research studies. To remedy the shortcoming highlighted by Grabe and to answer the question posed above, we are currently engaged in a study testing the hypothesis that EFL/ESL reading strategy training which includes metacognitive strategy training in all three components of metacognition (including conditional knowledge -- **where and when** to use the strategy and **how to evaluate** its effectiveness) contributes significantly more than reading strategy training which includes only metacognitive strategy training in declarative knowledge (**what** the strategy is and **why** the strategy should be learned) and procedural knowledge (**how to use** the strategy).

The following is a brief summary of our study's current status and methodology. Our project is being conducted in an English for Academic Purposes reading program for college-level ESL students at a major southeastern university in the United States. We are using one control group and two experimental groups.

The control group receives the usual curriculum of the EAP advanced reading course. One experimental group receives strategy training in addition to the usual EAP curriculum. The strategy training consists of a number of strategies known to be relevant to EAP college-level reading. These strategies include (1) main idea extraction (Baumann, 1984), (2) text preview and survey methods (SQ3R) (Robinson, 1941), (3) top level rhetorical structure recognition (Meyer, 1977a, 1977b, 1977c), and (4) summarization (Hare & Borchardt, 1984). The strategy training includes information on **what** the strategy is, **why** the strategy should be learned, and **how to use** the strategy.

The second experimental group receives metacognitive strategy training of the same strategies as the first experimental group. This metacognitive strategy training consists of the three elements of the strategy training as given above (**what, why** and **how to use**) plus the following additional metacognitive aspects: added emphasis on **why, when** to engage in utilizing the various strategies in a variety of reading settings and purposes, **when and where** the strategy should be used and not used, whether the strategy is appropriate, and **how to evaluate** one's use of the strategy and its effectiveness.

Control variables include the measurement of the learners' overall second language proficiency (as measured by the TOEFL), the learners' second language reading ability (as measured by the reading section of the TOEFL), and the learners' basic approaches to learning (also referred to as their "learning styles" or their "personalities," as measured by the Myers-Briggs Type Indicator, cf. Myers & McCaulley, 1985).

Our pre- and posttests include a number of measures relevant to the strategies being trained, as well as to the English-for-Academic-Purposes (EAP) curriculum: (a) a test of main idea identification, including both short passages and longer passages, and implicit as well as explicit main ideas; (b) a summary writing task; and © a reading and written recall task for passages with particular top-level rhetorical structures.

We have just completed the data collection phase of this project and are currently undertaking data analysis. As both educators and researchers, we have been struck by the complexities and nuances of metacognitive strategy presentation within the classroom with students of advanced ESL proficiency. We have also been challenged to devise appropriate classroom activities and dependent measures which are sufficiently sensitive to tease apart the effects of each type of training. We hope that our efforts will prove beneficial for researchers, educators, and more importantly, students.

PATRICIA L. CARRELL, LINDA GAJDUSEK, AND TERESA WISE
Georgia State University

REFERENCES

Adams, A., Carnine, D., & Gersten, R. (1982). Instructional strategies for studying content area texts in the intermediate grades. *Reading Research Quarterly, 18*, 27-55.

Alexander, P., & White, C. (1984). Effects of componential approach to analogy training on fourth graders' performance of analogy and comprehension tasks: An exploratory investigation, unpublished manuscript, Texas A&M University, College Station, TX.

Anderson, N. J. (1991). Individual differences in strategy use in second language reading and testing. *Modern Language Journal, 75*, 460-472.

Baker, L., & Brown, A. L. (1984). Metacognitive skills and reading. In P. D. Pearson (Ed.), *Handbook of reading research* (Vol. 1, pp. 353-394). New York: Longman.

Baumann, J. F. (1984). The effectiveness of a direct instruction paradigm for teaching main idea comprehension. *Reading Research Quarterly, 20*, 93-115.

Block, E. (1986). The comprehension strategies of second language readers. *TESOL Quarterly, 20*, 463-494.

Brown, A. L., Bransford, J. D., Ferrara, R. A., & Campione, J. C. (1982). *Learning, remembering and understanding* (Technical Report No. 244). Center for the Study of Reading, Urbana-Champaign,

IL, University of Illinois. Also in J. H. Flavell & E. M. Markman (Eds.), *Carmichael's manual of child psychology* (Vol. 3, pp. 77-166). New York: Wiley, 1983.

Carrell, P. L. (1985). Facilitating ESL reading by teaching text structure. *TESOL Quarterly, 19,* 727-752.

Carrell, P. L. (1987). ESP in applied linguistics: Refining research agenda: Implications and future directions of research on second language reading. *English for Specific Purposes, 6,* 233-244

Carrell, P. L. (1992). Awareness of text structure: Effects on recall. *Language Learning, 42,* 1-20

Carrell, P. L., Pharis, B. G., & Liberto, J. C. (1989). Metacognitive strategy training for ESL reading. *TESOL Quarterly, 23,* 647-678.

Chamot, A. U. (1987). The learning strategies of ESL students. In A. Wenden & J. Rubin (Eds.), *Learner strategies in language learning* (pp. 71-84). London: Prentice-Hall.

Day, J. D. (1980). Training summarization skills: A comparison of teaching methods, unpublished doctoral dissertation, University of Illinois, Champaign, IL.

Devine, J. (1984). ESL readers' internalized models of the reading process. In J. Handscombe, R. Orem & B. P. Taylor (Eds.), *On TESOL '83* (pp. 95-108). Washington, DC: TESOL.

Duffy, G. G., & Roehler, L. R. (1989). Why strategy instruction is so difficult and what we need to do about it. In C. McCormick, G. Miller, & M. Pressley (Eds.), *Cognitive strategy research: From basic research to educational applications* (pp. 133-154). New York: Springer-Verlag.

Flavell, J. H. (1978). Metacognitive development. In J. M. Scandura & C. J. Brainerd (Eds.), *Structural/process theories of complex human behaviour* (pp. 213-245). The Netherlands: Sijthoff and Noordhoff.

Garner, R., Hare, V., Alexander, P., Haynes, J., & Winograd, P. (1984). Inducing use of a text lookback strategy among unsuccessful readers. *American Educational Research Journal, 21,* 789-798.

Grabe, W. (1993). *Rethinking reading strategies: Research and Instruction.* Paper presented at the Reading Research Colloquium, 1993 TESOL Convention, Atlanta, GA.

Hamp-Lyons, L. (1985). Two approaches to teaching reading: A classroom-based study. *Reading in a Foreign Language, 3,* 363-373.

Hansen, J., & Pearson, P. D. (1983). An instructional study: Improving the inferential comprehension of good and poor fourth-grade readers. *Journal of Educational Psychology, 75,* 821-829.

Hare, V. C., & Borchardt, K. M. (1984). Direct instruction in summarization skills. *Reading Research Quarterly, 20,* 62-78.

Hauptman, P. C. (1979). A comparison of first and second language reading strategies among English-speaking university students. *Interlanguage Studies Bulletin, 4,* 173-201.

Hosenfeld, C. (1977). A preliminary investigation of the reading strategies of successful and nonsuccessful second language learners. *System, 5,* 110-123.

Johnston, P., & Byrd, M. (1983). Basal readers and the improvement of reading comprehension ability. In J. A. Niles & L. A. Harris (Eds.), *Searches for meaning in reading/language processing and instruction* (32nd yearbook of the National Reading Conference, pp. 140-47). Rochester, NY: National Reading Conference.

Kern, R. G. (1989). Second language reading strategy instruction: Its effects on comprehension and word inference ability. *Modern Language Journal, 73,* 135-149.

Knight, S. L., Padron, Y. N., & Waxman, H. C. (1985). The cognitive reading strategies of ESL students. *TESOL Quarterly, 19,* 789-792.

Meyer, B. J. F. (1977a). What is remembered from prose: A function of passage structure. In R. O. Freedle (Ed.), *Discourse production and comprehension* (pp. 307-336). Norwood, NJ: Ablex

Meyer, B. J. F. (1977b). Organization of prose and memory: Research with application to reading comprehension. In P. D. Pearson (Ed.), *Reading: Theory, research, and practice* (pp. 214-220). Clemson, SC: National Reading Conference.

Meyer, B. J. F. (1977c). The structure of prose: Effects on learning and memory and implications for educational practice. In R. C. Anderson, R. J. Spiro, & W. E. Montague (Eds.), *Schooling and the acquisition of knowledge* (pp. 179-200). Hillsdale, NJ: Erlbaum.

Myers, I. B., & McCaulley, N. H. (1985). *Manual: A guide to the development and use of the Myers-Briggs Type Indicator.* Palo Alto, CA: Consulting Psychologists Press.

O'Malley, J. M., Chamot, A. U., Stewner-Mazanares, G., Russo, R., & Kupper, L. (1985). Learning strategies applications with students of English as a second language. *TESOL Quarterly, 19*, 285-296.

Paris, S. G., Cross, D. R., & Lipson, M. Y. (1984). Informed strategies for learning: A program to Improve children's reading awareness and comprehension. *Journal of Educational Psychology, 6*, 1239-1252.

Paris, S. G., Lipson, M. Y., & Wixson, K. K. (1983). Becoming a strategic reader. *Contemporary Educational Psychology, 8*, 293-316.

Paris, S. G., Wasik, B. A., & Turner, J. C. (1991). The development of strategic readers. In R. Barr, M. L. Kamil, P. B. Mosenthal, & P. D. Pearson (Eds.), *Handbook of reading research* (Vol. II, pp. 609-640). New York: Longman.

Patching, W., Kameenui, E., Carnine, D., Gersten, R., & Colvin, G. (1983). Direct instruction in critical reading skills. *Reading Research Quarterly, 18*, 406-418.

Pressley, M., Forrest-Pressley, D., & Elliott-Faust, D. (1988). What is strategy instructional enrichment and how to study it: Illustrations from research on children's prose memory and comprehension. In F. Weiner & M. Perlmutter (Eds.), *Memory development: Universal changes and individual differences* (pp. 101-130). Hillsdale, NJ: Erlbaum.

Pressley, M., Snyder, B., & Cariglia-Bull, B. (1987). How can good strategy use be taught to children? Evaluation of six alternative approaches. In S. Cormier & J. Hagman (Eds.), *Transfer of learning: Contemporary research and application* (pp. 81-120). Orlando, FL: Academic Press.

Raymond, P. M. (1993). The effects of structure strategy training on the recall of expository prose for university students reading French as a second language. *Modern Language Journal, 77*, 445-458.

Resnick, L. B. (1979). Theories and prescriptions for early reading instruction. In L. B. Resnick & P. A. Weaver (Eds.), *Theory and practice of early reading* (Vol. 2, pp. 321-338). Hillsdale, NJ: Erlbaum.

Robinson, R. P. (1941). *Effective study*. New York: Harper and Row.

Roehler, L. R., & Duffy, G. G. (1984). Direct explanation of comprehension processes. In G. G. Duffy, L. R. Roehler, & J. Mason (Eds.), *Comprehension instruction: Perspectives and suggestions* (pp. 265-280). New York: Longman.

Sarig, G. (1987). High-level reading in the first and in the foreign language: Some comparative process data. In J. Devine, P. L. Carrell, & D. E. Eskey (Eds.), *Research in reading in English as a second language* (pp. 105-120). Washington, DC: TESOL.

Sarig, G., & Folman, S. (1987). *Metacognitive awareness and theoretical knowledge in coherence production*. Unpublished paper presented at the Communication and Cognition International Congress, Ghent, Belgium.

van Dijk, T. A., & Kintsch. W. (1983). *Strategies of discourse comprehension*. New York : Academic Press.

Vygotsky, L. S. (1978). *Mind in society*. Cambridge, MA: Harvard University Press.

Wellman, H. M. (1988). The early development of memory strategies. In F. Weiner & M. Perlmutter (Eds.), *Memory development: Universal changes and individual differences* (pp. 3-29). Hillsdale, NJ: Erlbaum.

Winograd, P., & Hare, V. C. (1988). Direct instruction of reading comprehension strategies: The nature of teacher explanation. In C. E. Weinstein, E. T. Goetz, & P. A. Alexander (Eds.), *Learning and study strategies: Issues in assessment instruction and evaluation* (pp. 121-139). San Diego: Academic Press.

Zvetina, M. (1987). From research to pedagogy: What do L2 reading studies suggest? *Foreign Language Annals, 20*, 233-238.

PART V: CONCLUSION

This book proudly concludes with a chapter by Robert J. Sternberg, the invited discussant for the special issue of *Instructional Science* on metacognition which included seven of the chapters in this book. This chapter includes an excellent integrative summary of these chapters which pulls together most if not all themes in the book. Sternberg highlights the contributions, areas of convergence across chapters, and thoughtfully critiques each chapter included in that issue. In addition, he presents an insightful case for metacognition as a subset of expertise, with an emphasis on the expert student. He integrates the ideas from this book into his conceptualization of metacognition as to expertise. Sternberg's basic thesis is that metacognition converges with other abilities linked to school success in the construct of developing expertise. Because Sternberg's chapter was written for the journal rather than this book, it preceded the chapter by Ellis and Zimmerman and my three chapters, which is why they are not discussed in Sternberg's chapter.

CHAPTER 12

METACOGNITION, ABILITIES, AND DEVELOPING EXPERTISE: WHAT MAKES AN EXPERT STUDENT?

ROBERT J. STERNBERG

ABSTRACT. The main argument of this chapter is that metacognition is an important part of human abilities, which are in turn forms of developing expertise. To the extent that our goal is to understand the bases of individual differences in student academic success, we need to understand metacognition as representing part of the abilities that lead to student expertise, but only as part.

Anyone who may have had the slightest doubt regarding the importance of metacognition to student success need only read the chapters in this book to remove the doubt. The theory and data of Artzt and Armour-Thomas; Carrell, Gajdusek, and Wise; Everson and Tobias; Gourgey; Mayer; and Wolters and Pintrich make a convincing case. The various researchers use a variety of theoretical frameworks, methodologies, subject-matter areas, and arguments to make a fully persuasive case for the importance of metacognition to school success. One could critique any one study or set of results, but the strength of the symposium is in the converging operations, all of which make the identical case.

THE IMPORTANCE OF METACOGNITION

Because I agree with their fundamental arguments, and believe in the strength of their work, I do not want to fall into the trap of critiquing or arguing about trivia in individual chapters: The authors set out to make a case; they made it. Rather, what I would like to do is discuss the role of metacognition in student expertise.

There are a number of truly interesting ideas and findings in the chapters in this symposium. I have picked one from each chapter that I believe especially merits highlighting.

1. Teachers can be loosely classified into three groups, depending on the extent to which they take students' metacognitive functioning into account. In

247

H.J. Hartman (ed.), Metacognition in Learning and Instruction, 247–260.
© 2001 Kluwer Academic Publishers. Printed in the Netherlands.

essence, the groups represent the teachers' own metacognitive functioning. What Artzt and Armour-Thomas refer to as Group X teachers fully take into account students' patterns of metacognitive functioning; Group Y teachers hardly do so at all; and Group Z teachers show a mixed pattern. The especially attractive feature of Table 1 of the Artzt and Armour-Thomas chapter is that any teacher can read through the table, match his or her own behavior to that of the three groups, and if the teacher wishes, use the table as a basis for conceptual and behavioral change.

As is always true when grouping is involved--whether of students or, as in this case, of teachers, there are dangers of missing fine but potentially important distinctions. With regard to Groups X, Y, and Z, I believe that there are at least three such distinctions that are important.

First, metacognition is diverse. It includes both understanding and control of cognitive processes. Moreover, these constructs are themselves complex. For example, control of cognitive processes includes planning, monitoring, and evaluating activities. A teacher could be high in knowledge of one or several of these aspects, but deficient in others. Assigning an overall group or score might obscure the patterns in the teachers' understandings of students' metacognitive functioning, so that, for example, two teachers who are in Group Y might have very different patterns of understanding.

Second, two issues need to be kept somewhat distinct-understanding of students' metacognition, and knowing how effectively to act upon this understanding. One teacher might understand students' metacognition, but not know how to translate this understanding into effective action. Another teacher might have somewhat less understanding, but a more effective "translation process."

Third, we need, of course, to remember that metacognition interacts with many other aspects of the student--abilities, personality, learning styles, and so on. A teacher's understanding of metacognition will probably be most useful if it is complemented by an understanding of these other aspects of students' functioning, and of how they interact with metacognition.

2. A generalized conclusion that emerges from the Carrell et al. chapter is that what matters is not so much what strategies students use in learning to read in a second language, but rather, their knowing when to use these strategies, how to coordinate between strategies, and having a number of different strategies available. In other words, it is metacognition about strategies, rather than the strategies themselves, that appears to be essential.

I strongly endorse this and other conclusions of the Carrell et al. team. But there is one caveat I would wish to add. Much of language learning is automatic, and occurs at the level of implicit learning rather than explicit learning--one is not even aware that the learning is taking place.

When functioning is automatic, metacognitive activity can actually hamper functioning (Sternberg, 1985). For example, many tennis players have had the experience of finding that when they think too much or too deliberately about what they are doing, the quality of their playing declines. An expert typist who starts thinking about where the keys are will type much more slowly. Thus, although metacognitive activities may be quite useful in many aspects of language learning, they are not necessarily always called for. Students need to learn to automatize, which means, in practice, learning to bypass certain conscious metacognitive activity.

3.   Everson and Tobias have shown in their research that not only is knowledge important to school success, but so is knowledge about one's knowledge: one's estimation of how much one knows. Those who have experience in teaching know how important this higher order knowledge is, because when you don't know you don't know something, you are scarcely motivated to learn it!

I would like to add one caveat to the Everson-Tobias findings. Knowledge monitoring always takes place in a context, and with respect to a particular goal or purpose. Consider one's knowledge of a word, say, "repression." The knowledge one would need in order to be considered "knowledgeable" would differ, say, in an introductory-psychology course versus an advanced graduate seminar. The quantity and quality of knowledge one would need for a multiple-choice test would differ from what one would need for an essay test. Thus, monitoring of knowledge must always take into account the context of learning or testing, and the purpose to which the knowledge will be put. The student who successfully monitors what he or she needs to know to get an A on a test in college may or may not be the person who successfully monitors as a professional in a given field. The relationship between the somewhat superficial monitoring that is needed and the deeper monitoring needed by a professional remains to be examined. In general, many successful students become less than successful professionals, and vice versa, so the relationship is probably worth studying at some future time.

4. Gourgey shows that students should not be expected wildly to welcome instruction on metacognitive skills. On the contrary, they may actively resist it, an experience I have had with my own students. When students have become used to and have been rewarded over the years for passive and rather mindless learning, they will not jump at the chance to take a more thoughtful or mindful approach to

what they are doing. Often the teacher's greatest challenge is to interest the students in the first place in metacognitive procedures.

The fact that students often do not welcome metacognitive training shows, in my opinion, a failure in our schooling. Students acquire the notion that knowledge is command of a large body of factual data. Metacognitive procedures, in this context, may seem largely irrelevant. Yet what is truly important in life is knowledge for use, not static knowledge that goes not further than demonstration on a rote-recall test. Students need to learn that metacognitive procedures for learning and using information are at least as important as is knowledge of the information to which these procedures are applied.

5. Mayer shows across a variety of problem-solving domains the importance of metaskill, of the ability to control and monitor cognitive processes. Part of developing metaskill in students is the students' developing the individual interest, and the teacher's developing the situational interest, that will motivate the students to think about their problem-solving practices.

Schools insufficiently emphasize metaskills, and I believe that one reason is that teachers are themselves uncertain as to just what the metaskills are, or if they are aware of them, of how they should teach them. We need to train teachers explicitly about what the skills are, and how they can be taught.

6. Wolters and Pintrich show that whereas students report differences in levels of motivational and cognitive components of self-regulated learning in different academic contexts, the relations among these components are similar across the various contexts. In other words, the pattern of relation between motivation and cognition is similar across domains. These results suggest that understanding of cognition is neither domain-specific nor domain-general, but domain-specific in some aspects and domain-general in others.

This finding may apply in the domains and with the materials that Wolters and Pintrich studied, but it is probably not as general finding as it may seem. Generally, students will be motivated to pursue areas where they excel, and will excel in areas where they are motivated, yielding a correlational relation between motivation and cognition. But there are certainly dissociations, as we discover when students are motivated to do some kinds of things in which they do not excel (e.g., the child who wants to be a doctor who can barely get through science courses, or the child who wants to be a lawyer who does not reason well analytically). At the same time, a student may have the ability to do, say, math or science well, but not be interested in it. In these cases, the relation breaks down. The teacher may choose to help try to restore the relation, either by helping the student increase abilities for pursuing a particular field, or by helping a student become more motivated in an area in which he or she excels, but has not been previously motivated.

7. Schraw makes the important distinction between knowledge and regulation of cognition described above, and argues that metacognitive knowledge is multidimensional, domain-general in nature, and teachable. This point of view is optimistic, although perhaps just a bit too optimistic. At one level, it is probably correct. For example, the need to formulate strategies, or to represent information, is domain-general. But the person who is well able to formulate a strategy or represent information in solving physical-science problems may not be the person who is well able to do the same things in the domain of writing a literary composition, and vice versa.

In our own research (Sternberg, 1985), we have found that content effects can be as large as or larger than process effects on individual differences. Thus, we should not assume that because a given metacognitive or other process has the same name or description across domains, it is equally easy for a given individual to implement across domains, or that patterns of individual differences will be comparable. The best physicists and literary critics, for example, may all be excellent metacognitively, but they might not be in each others' domains, despite the names of the processes (such as strategy formulation) being the same.

What exactly is the role of metacognition, then, in student expertise? And why do we need to discuss the role of metacognition in student expertise? What does it even mean to discuss its "role"? Here's the problem. In the abilities domain, as noted by Spearman (1904) and pretty much everyone since who has studied the problem, everything correlates with everything. The result has been a large, and at times overwhelming, documentation of the role of many things in abilities or in student success (see, e.g., Sternberg, 1994, for discussions of many of these factors). Researchers have found, for example, that abilities can be understood in terms of nerve conduction velocity (Vernon & Mori, 1990, 1992), choice reaction time (Jensen, 1993), inspection time (Nettelbeck, 1987), speed of components of inductive reasoning (Sternberg & Gardner, 1983), lexical-decision time (Hunt, 1978, 1987), scores on psychometric factors of abilities (Carroll, 1993), knowledge base and its organization (Chi, Glaser, & Rees, 1982), metacognition (Mayer, 1992, and all the chapters in this symposium); and many other things. This list only scratches the surface.

The problem is that when there is a positive manifold, almost everything correlates with everything else, and it is easy to slip into causal inferences from these correlations, despite admonitions to the contrary from elementary statistics teachers. Thus, in all of the above cases, arguments have been made not only that these attributes are correlated with abilities or with school success, but that they are somehow causal, necessary, or at least, highly desirable. The last claim is probably the best supported one. I will argue in this chapter that metacognition converges with other attributes that have been linked to the abilities necessary for school success in a construct of developing expertise.

SCHOOL-RELEVANT ABILITIES AS FORMS OF DEVELOPING EXPERTISE

The Abilities as Developing Expertise View

How might we best view the abilities necessary for success in school? I would like to argue that these abilities should be viewed in a way that is somewhat distinct from the typical way in which abilities are viewed.

The best available answer to the nature of school-relevant abilities is quite different from the one that is conventionally offered. The argument here is that the scores and the difference between them reflect not some largely inborn, relatively fixed "ability" construct, but rather a construct of developing expertise. I refer to the expertise that all these assessments measure as "developing" rather than as "developed" because expertise is typically not at an end state, but in a process of continued development.

In a sense, the point of view represented in this chapter represents only a minor departure from some modern points of view regarding abilities. Abilities are broadly conceived, and are seen as important to various kinds of success. They are seen as modifiable, and as capable of being flexibly implemented. What is perhaps somewhat new here is the attempt to integrate two literatures--the literature on abilities with that on expertise, and to argue that the two literatures may be talking, at some level, about the same thing. Furthermore, metacognition is viewed as part of the concept of developing expertise.

Traditionally, abilities are typically seen either as precursors to expertise (see essays in Chi, Glaser, & Farr, 1988) or as opposed to expertise (Fiedler & Link, 1994) as causes of behavior. Sometimes, abilities are held up in contrast to deliberate practice as causes of expertise (Ericsson, Krampe, & Tesch-Romer, 1993). Here, abilities are seen as themselves a form of developing expertise. When we test for them, we are as much testing a form of expertise as we are when we test for accomplishments of various kinds, whether academic achievement, in playing chess, skill in solving physics problems, or whatever. What differs is the kind of expertise we measure, and more importantly, our conceptualization what we measure. The difference in conceptualization comes about in part because of we happen to view one kind of accomplishment (ability-test scores) as predicting another kind (achievement test scores, grades in school, or other indices of accomplishment). But according to the present view, this conceptualization is one of practical convenience, not of psychological reality.

According to this view, although ability tests may have temporal priority relative to various criteria in their administration, they have no psychological priority. All of the various kinds of assessments are of a kind. What distinguishes ability tests from the other kinds of assessments is how the ability tests are used, rather than what they measure. There is no qualitative distinction among the various kinds of assessments.

One comes to be an expert in taking ability tests in much the same ways one becomes an expert in anything else--through a combination of genetic endowment and experience.

Characteristics of Expertise

The characteristics of experts as reflected in performance on ability tests are similar to the characteristics of experts of any kind (see Chi, Glaser, & Farr, 1988; Sternberg, 1996; p. 374). For example, operationally, by *expertise*, I refer, in a given domain, to people's: (a) having large, rich schemes containing a great deal of declarative knowledge about a given domain, in the present case, the domains sampled by ability tests; (b) having well-organized, highly interconnected units of knowledge about test content stored in schemes; (c) spending proportionately more time determining how to represent test problems than they do in search for and in executing a problem strategy; (d) developing sophisticated representations of test problems, based on structural similarities among problems; (e) working forward from given information to implement strategies for finding unknowns in the test problems; (f) generally choosing a strategy based on elaborate schemes for problem strategies; (g) having schemes containing a great deal of procedural knowledge about problem strategies relevant in the test-taking domain; (h) having automatized many sequences of steps within problem strategies; (i) showing highly efficient problem solving; when time constraints are imposed, they solve problems more quickly than do novices; (j) accurately predicting the difficulty of solving particular test problems; (k) carefully monitoring their own problem-solving strategies and processes; and (l) showing high accuracy in reaching appropriate solutions to test problems.

Ability tests, achievement tests, school grades, and measures of job performance all reflect overlapping kinds of expertise in these kinds of skills. To do well in school or on the job requires a kind of expertise; but to do well on a test also requires a kind of expertise. Of course, part of this expertise is the kind of test-wiseness that has been studied by Millman, Bishop, and Ebel (1965) and others (see Bond & Harman, 1994); but there is much more to test-taking expertise than test wiseness.

Most importantly from the present point of view, many of the aspects of expertise directly involve metacognition (or what I have called metacomponential functioning [Sternberg, 1985]). For example, in terms of the above list of characteristics of expertise, time allocation (c), development of representations (d), selection of strategies (f), prediction of difficulty (j), and monitoring (k) are all aspects of metacognitive functioning. Thus, metacognition represents an extremely important part of developing expertise, but not the only part, of course. Similarly, aspects of functioning studied by other investigators, such as speed of thinking or organization of knowledge base, also form part of developing expertise in students.

People who are more expert in taking IQ-related tests have a set of skills that is valuable not only in taking these tests, but in other aspects of Western life as well. Taking such a test typically requires metacognitive and other skills such as (a) figuring out what someone else (here, a test constructor) wants, (b) command of English vocabulary, (c) reading comprehension, (d) allocating limited time, (e) sustained concentration, (f) abstract reasoning, (g) quick thinking, (h) symbol manipulation, and (i) suppression of anxiety and other emotions that can interfere with test performance, and so on. These skills are also part of what is required for successful performance in school and many kinds of job performance. Thus, an expert test taker is likely also to have skills that will be involved in other kinds of expertise as well, such as expertise in getting high grades in school.

It is, in my opinion, not correct to argue that the tests measure little or nothing of interest. At the same time, there are many important kinds of expertise that the tests do not measure, for example, what Gardner (1983, 1993) would call musical, bodily-kinesthetic, interpersonal, and intrapersonal intelligences, and what I would call creative and practical intelligence (Sternberg, 1985, 1988).

To the extent that the expertise required for one kind of performance overlaps with the expertise required for another kind of performance, there will be a correlation between performances. The construct measured by the ability tests is not a "cause" of school or job expertise; it is itself an expertise that overlaps with school or job expertise. On the overlapping-expertise view, the traditional notion of test scores as somehow causal is based upon a confounding of correlation with causation. Differences in test scores, academic performance, and job performance are all effects--of differential levels of expertise.

Acquisition of Expertise

Individuals gain the expertise to do well on ability tests in much the same way they gain any other kind of expertise-through the interaction of whatever genetic dispositions they bring to bear with experience via the environment. I refer to as measuring *developing* expertise because the experiential processes are ongoing. In particular, individuals (a) receive direct instruction in how to solve test-like problems, usually through schooling; (b) engage in actual solving of such problems, usually in academic contexts; (c) engage in role modeling (watching others, such as teachers or other students, solve test like problems); (d) think about such problems, sometimes mentally simulating what they might do when confronting such problems; and (e) receive rewards for successful solution of such problems, thereby reinforcing such behavior. Individual Differences in Expertise

Individual Differences In Expertise

None of these arguments should be taken to imply that individual differences in underlying capacities do not exist. The problem, as recognized by Vygotsky (1978), as well as many others, is that we do not know how directly to measure these capacities. Measures of the zone of proximal development (e.g., Brown & Ferrara, 1985; Brown & Frensch, 1979; Feuerstein, 1979) seem to assess something other than conventional psychometric ~, but it has yet to be shown that what it is they do measure is the difference between developing ability and latent capacity.

Individual differences in developing expertise result in much the same way they result in most kinds of learning--from (a) rate of learning (which can be caused by amount of direct instruction received, amount of problem solving done, about of time and effort spent in thinking about problems, and so on), and from (b) asymptote of learning (which can be caused by differences in numbers of schemes, organization of schemes, efficiency in using schemes, and so on). Ultimately, such differences will represent a distinct genetic-environmental interaction for each individual.

There is no evidence, to my knowledge, that individual differences can be wiped out by the kind of "deliberate practice" studied by Ericsson and his colleagues (e.g., Ericsson & Charness, 1994; Ericsson, Krampe, & Tesch-Romer, 1993; Ericsson & Smith, 1991). Ericsson's work shows a correlation between focused practice and expertise; it does not show a causal relation, any more than the traditional work on abilities shows causal relations between measured abilities and expertise. A correlational demonstration is an important one; it is not the same as a causal one.

For example, the fact that experts have tended to show more deliberate practice than novices may itself reflect an ability difference (Sternberg, 1996b) . Meeting with success, those with more ability practice may more; meeting with lesser success, those with lesser ability may give up. Or both focused practice and ability may themselves be reflective of some other factor, such as parental encouragement, which could lead both to the nurturing of an ability and to practice. Indeed, deliberate practice and expertise may interact bidirectionally, so that deliberate practice leads to expertise, and the satisfaction of expertise leads to more deliberate practice. The point is that a variety of mechanisms might underlie a correlational relationship. It seems unquestionable that deliberate practice plays a role in the development of expertise. But it also seems extremely likely that its role is as a necessary rather than sufficient condition.

Deliberate practice may play a somewhat lesser role in creative performance than in other kinds of performance (Sternberg, 1996a). We might argue over whether someone who practices memorization techniques can become a mnemonist. Probably, they can become a mnemonist at least within certain content domains (Ericsson, Chase, & Faloon, 1980). It seems less plausible that someone who practices composing will become a Mozart. Other factors seem far more important in the development of creative expertise, such as pursuing paths of inquiry that others ignore or dread, taking intellectual risks, persevering in the face of obstacles, and so on (Sternberg & Lubart, 1995, 1996).

Relations Among Various Kinds of Expertise

Although all of the various assessments considered here overlap, the overlap is far from complete. Indeed, a major problem with both ability tests and school achievement tests is that the kinds of skills measured in many respects depart from the skills that are needed for job success (see, e.g., Sternberg, Ferrari, Clinkenbeard, & Grigorenko, 1996; Sternberg, Wagner, Williams, & Horvath, 1995).

An individual can be extremely competent in test and school performance, but flag on the job because of the differences in the kinds of expertise required. For example, success in memorizing a textbook may lead to a top grade in a psychology or education course, but may not predict particularly well whether someone will be an expert researcher or an expert teacher. The creative and practical skills needed for these kinds of job success may be only minimally or not at all tapped in the ability-testing and school-assessment situations. Thus, it is not particularly surprising that although test scores and school grades correlate with job performance, the correlations are far from perfect.

There are various measures that correlate with IQ that do not, on their face, appear to be measures of achievement. But they are measures of forms of developing expertise. For example, the inspection-time task of Nettelbeck (1987; Nettelbeck & Lally, 1976) or the choice reaction-time task of Jensen (1982) both correlate with psychometric g. However, performances on both tasks reflect a form of developing expertise, in one case, of perceptual discriminations, in the other case, of quick response to flashing lights or other stimuli.

Temporal Priority Is Not Psychological Priority

The argument here is that ability tests are typically temporally prior in their measurement to measurements of various kinds of achievements, but what they measure is not psychologically prior. The so-called achievement tests might just as well be used to predict scores on ability tests, and sometimes are, as when school officials attempt to guess college admissions test scores on the basis of school achievement. In viewing the tests of abilities as psychologically prior, we are confounding our own typical temporal ordering of measurement with some kind of psychological ordering. But in fact, our temporal ordering implies no psychological ordering at all. The relabeling of the *SAT* as the *Scholastic Assessment Test*, rather than *Scholastic Aptitude Test*, reflects this kind of thinking. Nevertheless, the *SAT* is still widely used as an ability test, and the *SAT-II*, which measures subject-matter knowledge, as a set of achievement tests.

An examination of the content of tests of intelligence and related abilities reveals that IQ-like tests measure achievement that individuals should have accomplished several years back. Tests such as vocabulary, reading comprehension, verbal analogies, arithmetic problem solving, and the like are all unequivocally tests of achievement. Even abstract-reasoning tests measure achievement in dealing with geometric symbols, skills taught in Western schools. One might as well use academic performance to predict ability-test scores. The problem with regard to the traditional model is not in its statement of a correlation between ability tests and other forms of achievement, but in its proposal of a causal relation whereby the tests reflect a construct that is somehow causal of, rather than merely antecedent to, later success.

Even psychobiological measures (see, e.g., Vernon, 1990) are in no sense "pure" ability measures, because we know that just as biological processes affect cognitive processes, so do cognitive processes affect biological ones. Learning, for example, leads to synaptic growth (Kandel, 1991; Thompson, 1985). Thus, biological changes may themselves reflect developing expertise. In sum, if we viewed tested abilities as forms of what is represented by the term *developing expertise*, then I would have no argument with the use of the term *abilities*. The problem is that this term is usually used in another way--to express a construct that is psychologically prior to other forms of expertise. Such abilities may well exist, but we can assess them only through tests that measure developing forms of expertise expressed in a cultural context. All abilities, including metacognitive ones, are not fixed, but rather forms of developing expertise. Rather than correlating individual aspects of abilities or achievement--such as metacognitive functioning or reaction time or whatever to scores on tests of abilities or achievement--we need to understand all these aspects not as precursors, but as integral elements in the development of varied forms of expert performance, including those required to achieve high scores on tests.

ROBERT J. STERNBERG
Department of Psychology
Yale University

Author Notes

Preparation of this chapter was supported under the Javits Act program (Grant #R206R50001) as administered by the Office of Educational Research and Improvement, U.S. Department of Education. The opinions expressed in this report do not reflect the positions or policies of the Office of Educational Research and Improvement or the U.S. Department of Education. I am especially grateful to Michel Ferrari, Elena Grigorenko, Joseph Horvath, Todd Lubart, Richard Wagner, and Wendy Williams for collaborations that have led to the development of many of the ideas expressed in this chapter. Requests for reprints should be sent to Robert J. Sternberg, Department of Psychology, Yale University, Box 208205, New Haven, CT 06520-8205.

REFERENCES

Bond, L., & Harman, A. E. (1994). Test-taking strategies. In R. J. Sternberg (Ed.), *Encyclopedia of human intelligence* (Vol. 2, pp. 1073-1077). New York: Macmillan

Brown, A. L., & Ferrara, R. A. (1985). Diagnosing zones of proximal development. In J. V. Wertsch (Ed.), *Culture. communication, and cognition: Vygotskian perspectives.* New York: Cambridge University Press.

Brown, A. L., & Frensch, L. A. (1979). The zone of potential development: Implications for intelligence testing in the year 2000. *Intelligence, 3,* 255-277.

Carroll, J. B. (1993). *Human cognitive abilities: A survey of factor-analytic studies.* New York: Cambridge University Press.

Chi, M. T. H., Glaser, R., & Farr, M. (Eds.) (1988). *The nature of expertise.* Hillsdale, NJ: Erlbaum.

Chi, M. T. H., Glaser, R., & Rees, E. (1982). Expertise in problem solving. In R. J. Sternberg (Ed.), *Advances in the psychology of human intelligence.* Vol. 1, pp. 7-75. Hillsdale, NJ: Erlbaum.

Ericsson, K. A., & Charness, N. (1994). Expert performance: Its structure and acquisition. *American Psychologist . 49,* 725747.

Ericsson, K. A., Chase, W. G., & Faloon, S. (1980). Acquisition of a memory skill. *Science. 208* 1181-1182.

Ericsson, K. A., Krampe, R. T., & Tesch-Romer, C. (1993). The role of deliberate practice in the acquisition of expert performance. *Psychological Review,* 100, 363-406.

Ericsson, K. A., & Smith, J. (Eds.) (1991). *Toward a general theory of expertise: Prospects and limits* New York: Cambridge University Press.

Feuerstein, R. (1979). *The learning potential assessment device.* Baltimore, MD: University Park Press.

Fiedler, F. E., & Link, T. G. (1994). Leader intelligence, interpersonal stress, and task performance. In R . J. Sternberg & R. K. Wagner (Eds.), *Mind in context* (pp. 152-167). New York: Cambridge University Press.

Gardner, H. (1983). *Frames of mind.* New York: Free Press.

Gardner, H. (1993). *Multiple intelligences: The theory in practice.* New York: Basic Books.

Hunt, E. B. (1978). The mechanics of verbal ability. *Psychological Review,* 85.

Hunt, E. B. (1987). The next word on verbal ability. In P. A. Vernon (Ed.), *Speed of information processing. and intelligence processing* (pp. 347-392). Norwood, NJ: Ablex.

Jensen, A. R. (1982). The chronometry of intelligence. In R. J. Sternberg (Ed.), *Advances in the psychology of human intelligence* (Vol. 1, pp. 255-310). Hillsdale, NJ: Erlbaum.

Jensen, A. R. (1993). Test validity: g versus "tacit knowledge," *Current Directions in Psychological Science,* 1, 9-10.

Kandel, E.(1991). Cellular mechanisms of learning and the biological basis of individuality. In E. R. Kandel, J. H. Schwartz, & T. M. Jessell (Eds.), *Principles of neural science* (3rd ed.). New York: Elsevier

Mayer, R. E. (1992). *Thinking. Problem solving cognition* (2nd ed.). New York: W. H. Freeman.

Millman, J., Bishop, H., & Ebel, R. (1965). An analysis of test-wiseness. *Educational and Psychological Measurement.* 25, 707-726.

Nettelbeck, T. (1987). Inspection time and intelligence. In P. A. Vernon (Ed.), *Speed of information processing and intelligence. Norwood, NJ: Ablex.*

Nettelbeck, T., & Lally, M. (1976). Inspection time and measured intelligence. *British Journal of Psychology,* 67, 17-22.

Spearman, C. E. (1904). 'General intelligence' objectively determined and measured. *American Journal of Psychology,* 15, 201-293.

Sternberg, R. J. (Ed.) (1982). *Handbook of human intelligence.* New York: Cambridge University Press

Sternberg, R. J. (1985). *Beyond IQ: A triarchic theory of human intelligence.* New York: Cambridge University Press.

Sternberg, R. J. (1986). *Intelligence applied.* Orlando, FL: Harcourt Brace College Publishers.

Sternberg, R. J. (1988). *The triarchic mind: A new theory of human intelligence.* New York: Viking-Penguin

Sternberg, R. J. (1990). *Metaphors of mind: Conceptions of the nature of intelligence.*

Sternberg, R. J. (Ed.) (1994). *Encyclopedia of human intelligence* (2 vols.). New York: Macmillan.

Sternberg, R. J. (1995). For whom the bell curve tolls: A review of The Bell Curve. Psychological Science 6(5), 257-261.

Sternberg, R. J. (1996a). *Cognitive psychology.* Orlando: Harcourt Brace College Publishers.

Sternberg, R. J. (1996-b). Costs of expertise. In K. A. Ericsson (Ed.), *The Road to Excellence.* (pp 347-354.) Mahwah, NJ:Lawrence Erlbaum Associates

Sternberg, R. J., Conway, B. E., Ketron, J. L., & Bernstein, M. (1981). People's conceptions of intelligence. *Journal of Personality and Social Psychology* 41, 37-55.

Sternberg, R. J., Ferrari, M., Clinkenbeard, P., & Grigorenko, E. L. (1996). Identification, instruction, and assessment of gifted children: A construct validation of a triarchic model. *Gifted Child Quarterly,* 40, 129-137.

Sternberg, R. J., & Gardner, M. K. (1983). Unities in inductive reasoning. *Journal of Experimental Psychology* : General, 112, 80-116.

Sternberg, R. J., & Horvath, J. A. (1995). A prototype view of expert teaching. *Educational Researcher.* 24 (6), 9-17.

Sternberg, R. J., & Lubart, T. I. (1995). *Defying the crowd: Cultivating creativity in a culture of conformity* . New York: Free Press.

Sternberg, R. J., & Lubart, T. I. (1996). Investing in creativity. *American Psychologist, 51,* 677-688

Sternberg, R. J., & Spear-Swerling, L. (1996). *Teaching for thinking.* Washington, DC: APA Books

Sternberg, R. J., Wagner, R. K., Williams, W. M., & Horvath, J. (1995). Testing common sense. *American Psychologist*, 50(11), 912-927.

Thompson, R. F. (1985). *The brain: An introduction to neuroscience*. New York: Freeman.

Vernon, P. A. (1990). The use of biological measures to estimate behavioral intelligence. *Educational Psychologist*. 25, 293-304.

Vernon, P. E. (1971). *The structure of human abilities*. London: Methuen.

Vernon, P. A., & Mori, M. (1990). Physiological approaches to the assessment of intelligence. In C. R. Reynolds & R. W. Kamphaus (Eds.), *Handbook of psychological and educational assessment of children: Intelligence and achievement*. New York: Guilford Press

Vernon, P. A., & Mori, M. (1992). Intelligence, reaction times, and peripheral nerve conduction velocity. *Intelligence, 8*, 273-288.

Vygotsky, L. S. (1978). *Mind in society: The development of higher psychological processes*. Cambridge, MA: Harvard University Press.

AUTHOR INDEX

266

272

SUBJECT INDEX

F

G

H

282

NEUROPSYCHOLOGY AND COGNITION

The purpose of the Neuropsychology and Cognition series is to bring out volumes that promote understanding in topics relating brain and behavior. It is intended for use by both clinicians and research scientists in the fields of neuropsychology, cognitive psychology, psycholinguistics, speech and hearing, as well as education. Examples of topics to be covered in the series would relate to memory, language acquisition and breakdown, reading, attention, developing and aging brain. By addressing the theoretical, empirical, and applied aspects of brain-behavior relationships, this series will try to present the information in the fields of neuropsychology and cognition in a coherent manner.

NEUROPSYCHOLOGY AND COGNITION

16. I. Lundberg, F.E. Tønnessen and I. Austad (eds.): *Dyslexia: Advances in Theory and Practice*. 1999   ISBN 0-7923-5837-6
17. T. Nunes (ed.), *Learning to Read: An Integrated View from Research and Practice*. 1999   ISBN 0-7923-5513-X
18. T. Høien and J. Lundberg: *Dyslexia: from Theory to Intervention*. 2000
                     ISBN 0-7923-6309-4
19. H.J. Hartman (ed.): *Metacognition in Learning and Instruction*. Theory, Research and Practice. 2001   ISBN 0-7923-6838-X

KLUWER ACADEMIC PUBLISHERS – DORDRECHT / BOSTON / LONDON